# LOVE IS IN THE EARTH -

## KALEIDOSCOPIC PICTORIAL SUPPLEMENT A

Published by
**EARTH-LOVE PUBLISHING HOUSE**
3440 Youngfield Street, Suite 353
Wheat Ridge, Colorado 80033 USA

First Printing 1997
Second Printing 1999



This book is a reference work based upon research by the author and by those who are mentioned in the acknowledgements as providing information. The opinions expressed herein are not necessarily those of, or endorsed by, the Publisher. The information as stated in this book is in no way to be considered as a substitute for consultation with a duly licensed holistic physician.

**Library of Congress Catalogue Card Number: 96-086276**

**ISBN: 0-9628190-7-7**

Printed in Hong Kong

# LOVE IS IN THE EARTH -

## KALEIDOSCOPIC PICTORIAL SUPPLEMENT A

**By: ♪ ♬ ♪ MELODY ♬ ♪ ♬**

**Primary Photography by Jim Hughes**
**Assisted by ♪ Melody ♬**
**Additional Photography by Dave Shrum, Colorado Camera**

***Illustrated by Julianne Guilbault***

EARTH-LOVE PUBLISHING HOUSE

3440 Youngfield Street, Suite 353
Wheat Ridge, CO. 80033

Illustrations created by Julianne Guilbault - I would like to thank Julianne Guilbault for creating the illustrations shown within this "**Love Is In The Earth - Kaleidoscopic Pictorial Supplement A**". Julianne and I have been friends through many lifetimes and have worked together toward the furtherance of the "brotherhood" of "All That Is". She has been active in crystal awareness for years and is truly the personification of creativity, both living and being the essence of originality and ingenuity. She has been involved in graphics design and illustrating for over twenty years, utilizing the mediums of watercolour, pastels, charcoal, pen and ink, and acrylic. She has sculpted fantasy art deco crystal/crystal ball holders; previous sculptures, including flower faeries and crystal holders, are in private collections throughout the world. She is also continuing work in completing her first fiction/fantasy novel. I thank her also for her encouragement and support in both the preparation of this Supplement and in the compilation and illustration of all "Love Is In The Earth" books. Julianne may be contacted c/o Earth-Love Publishing House LTD.

Cover Art created by Charley Berryhill - I would like to thank Charley Berryhill for his aesthetic creation of the cover art, entitled "Alice In Crystal Land" or "Aja's Melody", which he created for this "**Love Is In the Earth - Kaleidoscopic Pictorial Supplement A**". Charley and I have been friends for many lifetimes - he is a Native American who truly understands the peace of the universal "brotherhood" and has actualized the creative talents of his inherent precision. His art is in collections throughout the world and is available through his studio, "The Wildlife Art Studio" in Cheney, Washington, USA. With his sensitivity to, and practical application of, the many mediums available, Charley conceives, creates, and originates the captivating and enchanting. Charley may also be contacted c/o Earth-Love Publishing House LTD.

I would like to thank Jim Hughes for the quality time we shared during the photographing of the minerals in this book. Jim and I are becoming "old" friends, and the rapport between us has grown; we both truly enjoyed the photography sessions. He always has a smile and a refreshing, gracious, and relaxing attitude. Jim's photography techniques bring the soul of beauty and the ever present essence of each subject to allow the panorama of energies to be shown. Jim's studio, "Footprints Fine Photography", is located in Colorado, USA.

I am especially grateful and give my warmest thanks to Lynn Fielding, our attorney, through whom this book and the the prior books in the "Love Is In The Earth..." series have become a reality. Lynn and I are very good friends and I sincerely appreciate his help, his guidance, his love, and his encouragement in pursuing my path. His expertise and his expediency has enabled us to continue to make this series of books available to you, my friends.

Cover Colour Separations by Pacific Scanning.

The author may be contacted c/o Earth-Love Publishing House LTD.

# DEDICATION

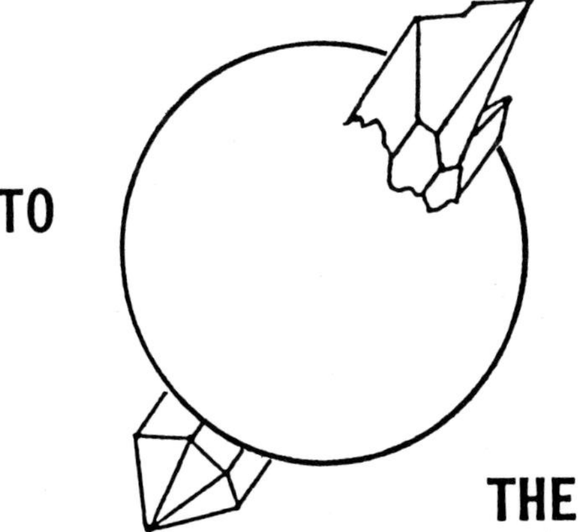

TO

THE

EARTH

## ACKNOWLEDGEMENTS

I truly thank the following people for their assistance in helping to make this book a reality.

Jose Orizon, MariInez, Ricardo, and Daniel de Almeida - for their true friendship and true hospitality during the times we have shared, for their delightful ways, for their many gifts of minerals and time, and for their love.

Charley Berryhill - for his love and encouragement, for his spiritual artwork created for the cover of this book, and for taking time to teach me more about the Native American ways.

Bob Beck - for his being, for his smile, and for his love.

Bob & Micki Bleily - for their loving nature, their love and encouragement, their love and respect of the mineral kingdom, and their lovely fabrication of exotic cabochons.

Jose Roberto Bortoluzzi - and his family, for their love and their hospitality, for their smiles and good tidings, and for their love of the mineral kingdom.

Mike Brown - for his love and encouragement, for his sensitivity to the sanctity of the Native American ways, and for his awareness and practice within crystal-consciousness.

Pai Carumbe - for his being and for our connection of understanding and love between Brasil and America.

John Crowley - for his love, encouragement, his light which shines through his presence.

Edward Salisbury Dana - for teaching me, via his textbooks of mineralogy, about the multitude of crystalline structures which exist today.

Howard Dolph - for his love, for his being, and for the eternal light which glows from his being and shines through his eyes.

Lynn Fielding - for his assistance in making the "Love Is In The Earth" series a reality and for his continuing friendship and expertise applied to my life.

Betty & Wayne Green - for lovely smiles and unconditional love.

Julio and Solange Gros - for their continued love and encouragement, their delightful presence, and their wonderful hospitality.

Lucy Gross [Mama] - for her being, her inner and outer radiance, her love, encouragement, understanding, assurance, motivation, patience, and support in all I attempt and all that I am, for stimulating my interest in all of the kingdoms of the Earth, and for further helping me to both recognize and understand my heritage.

♬

W. R. Horning - for his love and encouragement, and for continually stimulating my interest in the mineral kingdom.

Robert Jackson - for his love and encouragement in my life, for his patience, for his assistance in providing information for this book, for making available [via Earth-Love Minerals, 3440 Youngfield Street, Suite 353, Wheat Ridge, CO 80033 USA, and via Earth-Love Gallery, 3266 Youngfield Street, Wheat Ridge, CO 80033 USA] the wonderful minerals of the world, for his creations as a silver/goldsmith, and for sharing in the adventure that is my life and my road.

Herbert Kiesler - for his continuing progression toward the understanding of the unknown.

Jose Maria - for his being, for his love of the beautiful minerals of Brasil, for his radiant smile, and for his hospitality.

Marguerite Martin - in memory and for stimulating my interest in the greater realm of minerals and for her love and encouragement toward continuing interest in the mineral kingdom.

Mano - for his love, for his appreciation of the mineral kingdom, and for his hospitality.

Julie Murphy - for her unconditional love, confidence, reassurance, and for her "knowing".

Elenita, Natalino, Rackel, Gustavo, and Mariana Oliveira - for their true hospitality during the times we have shared, for their gifts of lovely mineral specimens, and for their love and our many good times.

Osho - for his being and for initiating consciousness.

Chris Pittario - for her love and encouragement and her delight in life.

Antar Pushkara & Jude Painton - for their love and encouragement in my life, for being my kinsmen, and for sharing their radiance and manifestation of inner calm, peace, and understanding with all who touch their lives.

Gregory Sluszka - for his love and encouragement and never-ending and astute insights into all worlds and all realms.

Rob Smith - for his love and encouragement, for his friendship and his ever-present smile, and for his love of the mineral kingdom.

Milt Szulinski - in his memory, for his being, for his love, and for his encouragement.

Layton Talbott - for his love and encouragement and for his sweetness and light.

Angel Torrecillas - for his love, encouragement, absolute honesty, sharing celebrations, and his lovely smile, lasting friendship, and radiant glow.

Don Toth - for his love, encouragement, for the united elixir recipes shown within this book.

Richard Two-Bears and Martine - for their love and encouragement, and for making the ultimate spiritual drums and rattles available for those on the path.

Josef Vajdak - for his love and encouragement and for his love of the mineral kingdom.

Liza Van De Linde - for her love and encouragement, for her openness and care, and for her friendship.

Antonio Viana - for his being, for his love of the beautiful minerals of Brasil, and for his hospitality.

I sincerely thank those people who both introduced and gifted me with "new" minerals: Michael Alexander (Delafossite); Jose Orizon de Almeida (Zoned Smokey/Clear and Smokey/Citrine Quartz); Joe Ardito (Massive Electrified Translucent Halite); Bob & Micki Bleily (Lemon Opal); LizBeth Christensen & Peter Bane - (Pyrargyrite); John Crowley (Horn Coral); Jean Jacques Eclancher (Porphyry - Imperial and "Isis and Osiris"); Si Frazier (Growth Interference Crystals); Peter Giangrande (Binghamite); Jeff Grundmann & Barbara Billings (Engraved Smokey Quartz); Maria Grundner (Gaspeite); W.E. Hagestein (Mookaite Jasper); W. R. Horning (Bi-Colour Sunstone); Bob Isaacs (Candle Quartz); Bob Jackson (Banded Rosasite, Cat's Eye Opal, Green Smithsonite, "Super Seven", and Skeletal Smokey Quartz with Lepidocrocite and Hematite); Margaret Julian (Rhodizite); Jeri Justice (Brasilian Tube Agate); Judy Lacavera & Ray St. Marie (Rhonite and Rose Quartz Buttons); Bob Lewis (Man-Made Silicon); Bonni MacKintosh (Cumengéite); Natalino Oliveira (Perforated Onyx); Robert Poley (White Elestiated Calcite); Tony Swerus (Prasiolite); Gil Nelson (Purple Sage Agate); Peter & Sylvia Simpson (Blue John Fluorite); Marcia & Doug Theiner ("Aurora Borealis Stone"); Frank Timms (Flame Aura); Angel Torrecillas (Oaxaccamers (Amethyst Herkimers), "Red Malachite", and Pyrargyrite); Roger Trontz (Velvet Pyrolucite); Richard Two-Bears and Martine (Kauri Gum); Jesse Williams (Golden Aura and Silver Aura Garnet).

In addition, I want to thank the following people who provided information about properties of specific minerals: Peshotan Mehta, PhD. (Tibetan Quartz); George Mikesell (Epidote); J. Mark Tillotson, M.D. (Sheen Obsidian); Rev. David R. Bingell (Green-Phantom Quartz); Clara Utter (Various); Don Toth (Various).

I also want to recognize the delightful "words of wisdom", shown and credited throughout this book, which were provided by the loving and astute minds of others: Bob Jackson, John Crowley, Rob Dubois, Judge Felix Frankfuter, Julianne Guilbault, Julie Murphy, Mulla Nasruddin, Kimi "Fire Within" Nichols, Osho, Jude Painton, Antar Pushkara, Don Toth, and Gary "Horsefeathers" Wallace.

I also thank Jose Eduardo, Salim, Villani, and Jose Estrada, for their assistance and their kindnesses. I truly am thankful to all of those people who have touched my life and have assisted in the furtherance of my being. Thanks to my many friends on this wonderful Earth.

**"IT'S ESSENTIAL TO BELIEVE IN MAGIC AS LONG AS YOU DO NOT RELY UPON IT"**

Bob Jackson
Earth-Love Gallery
Colorado, USA

# TABLE OF CONTENTS

EARTH NOTES

# INTRODUCTION

**"Sleeping God"**

**"The Creator Sleeps but as the
Great God Slumbers - He Dreams ...
And Infinitesimal ...
We are the Dreams of the Diety."**

Don Toth
Ohio, USA

# TO THE READER

This first Supplement to "Love Is In The Earth - A Kaleidoscope Of Crystals Update" and "Love Is In The Earth - Mineralogical Pictorial" has been prepared to serve as a companion for these two books. In addition to the Table of Contents, the Acknowledgements, the Introduction, and the Index, the following information can be found within:

1) Descriptions of the properties of over 100 "new" minerals;
2) Photographs of typical specimens of these "new" minerals;
3) Descriptions and Photographs of two Laboratory-Produced minerals;
4) Descriptions of the properties of minerals and configurations which were reported in "Love Is In The Earth - A Kaleidoscope Of Crystals Update", and for which information from further research has become available;
5) Descriptions of minerals and configurations which were not in "Love Is In The Earth - A Kaleidoscope Of Crystals Update", but were shown in "Love Is In The Earth - Mineralogical Pictorial";
6) Photographs of typical specimens of minerals which were not in "Love Is In The Earth - Mineralogical Pictorial", but which were reported in "Love Is In The Earth - A Kaleidoscope Of Crystals Update";
7) A Cross-Reference Index relating the Zodiacal Designations and the Mineralogical Associations; and,
8) A Cross-Reference Index relating the Numerical Vibrations with the Mineralogical Associations.
9) Illustrations of Quartz Structures and Configurations to assist the reader in identification of the varied formations.

The mineralogical information accompanying the photographs and the description of the properties have been obtained from "Dana's Textbook Of Mineralogy", Nickel & Nichols "Mineral Reference Manual", "Hey's Mineral Index - Third Edition", "Glossary of Geology - Third Edition", and from mineralogists throughout the world. Where there was disagreement between the references, either both sets of information were given or the most recent set of information was given.

This supplement provides a continuation of the path such that the reader may travel further into the subtle realms of crystal energy, providing for additional adventures into the avantgarde and assisting one in maintaining a loving affinity with crystals. Information has been derived from "hands-on" experience, geological research, experimentation, and channeled information; prior to inclusion herein, all channeled information and experiences have been validated via further experimentation and in a controlled environment. The information presented is based upon the combination of the physical principles of interaction and the scientific principles of molecular bonding.

Although each of us has the infinite power of the universe within the self, we tend to find it easier and are predisposed to accept support from that which is from outside of the self. Each crystalline structure/form has its own individual energy and its own "personality". Mineralogical structures which contain more than one mineral possess a melding of the energies of the minerals contained. Each can be used in unique ways to assist one in understanding the multi-faceted nature of existence on the Earth plane. The consciousness of the planet is leading humanity to the re-discovery of an ancient and forgotten healing art in which the utilization of crystals is prominent. Dis-ease or disorder in ones life usually entails lessons which will allow one to release the burdens of unconsciousness. Although one must ultimately heal oneself, the healing process may be facilitated by the catalytic presence of many things. To experience dis-ease is to experience a total or partial disconnection from wholeness, a loss of awareness of the innate and universal source of perfection. The members of the mineralogical kingdom have been used for centuries to act as catalysts and to assist one in becoming re-united with that source. Right intention during use of the mineral further stimulates the melding of ones personal energy with that of the mineral kingdom, furthering the propagation of the light, the love, and "the good of all".

May you continue to your state of fulfillment, always knowing that you are the wonder of the world. I wish you peace within yourself, love to guide you, and the understanding leading to bliss. May you know and experience love - from within, from upon, and from surrounding the Earth ♥ The Reader is encouraged to <u>read</u> the remainder of this section prior to continuing to the information given within the text.

## MINERALS WHICH NEVER NEED CLEANSING

After many requests by readers, of the "....Kaleidoscope...", who had been searching for the names of the minerals which never need cleansing, the ensuing list was prepared. The following minerals never need cleansing and never hold negativity: Kyanite, Citrine, Yoderite, Citrine/Smokey Combination, Phillipine Tektite, Rhodizite, "Super Seven", Guangdong Tektite, and Electrified Translucent Massive Halite.

Please note that, due to the discovery of the properties of "new" minerals, there are now more than the four original minerals which were previously reported.

## ASTROLOGICAL SIGNS

This paragraph is meant to clarify the utilization of the Astrological Signs which are related to each mineral.

If one selects a mineral with a specific Astrological Sign, that means that attributes of that sign are reflected by that mineral. Hence, if one is a Virgo by birth sign, and if one were to select a mineral with respect to the qualities of an Astrological Sign, one would most likely choose a sign different from ones birth sign in order to bring in other attributes which one does not currently have.

Where the Astrological Sign designation is "All", the positive attributes of each sign, dependent upon intent, are brought to play.

## ELIXIRS - FURTHER INFORMATION

### CONSERVATISM

The sections within this book which provide information with respect to the properties of the "new" minerals, provide also for more conservatism with respect to recommendations for the preparation of elixirs via the "normal" and "non-normal" methods. This will be an continuing practice.

These varying methods are discussed in "Love Is In The Earth - A Kaleidoscope Of Crystals Update". If there is a question concerning the toxic nature of a mineral, always research the chemical composition prior to utilization of that mineral.

## PREPARATION

The preparation of an elixir is based upon the concept of energy transfer. Our world is comprised of atoms; atoms are the smallest unitary constituent of any chemical element and are comprised of a complex aggregate of protons, neutrons, and electrons.

The number and arrangement of the protons, neutrons, and electrons determine the element. When an element is stimulated (e.g., via heat or pressure), electrons are emitted. In our world today, virtually nothing exists in a vacuum; hence, there is a somewhat constant, if erratic, stimulation occurring continuously, and a subsequent egress and ingress of the electrons from the minerals.

When a mineral is placed into water, for example, for the preparation of an elixir, the electrons of that element are stimulated and tend to mix with the water; hence, bringing the essence of the mineral to the water. Although the change is not seen by the physical eye, it has been felt over and over again by those experiencing the essence of elixirs.

For the alternate methods of elixir preparation, there remains the emergence of the electrons and the permeation of the water by the electrons.

## EXAMPLES OF UNITED ELIXIRS (See Acknowledgement Section)

The following elixirs provide further examples of elixirs created with more than one mineral; these elixirs were designed to treat the non-physical aspects of dis-ease as well as the physical aspects.

All of the stones listed may be used to prepare the elixir via gridding and/or a portion in gridding with a portion in the water. Note that anytime the Milky Quartz appears in the elixir recipe, it is intended as an amplifier.

## Elixir Of The Spirit - To Enhance and Balance

Alexandrite
Ametrine
Aquamarine
Azurite (Vibrational Grid)
Blue Calcite
Emerald
Enstatite
Gold (or Gold in/on Quartz)
Halite
Jade (Green & Lavender)
Lapis Lazuli
Lazulite
Magnetite
Peridot
Sphene (or Titanite)
Milky Quartz

## The People's Elixir

Developed and formulated to apply the energies of continuity to proceed from where the Elixir of the Spirit concludes.

Amber
Apatite
Beryl
Bloodstone
Boji Stones (pair/grid)
Copper (grid)
Coral
Cuprite (grid)
Diamond
Diopside or Enstatite
Eilat Stone (grid)
Fluorite
Gold (or Gold in Quartz)
Halite (grid)
Herderite (grid)
Jade
Kunzite
Lapis Lazuli (grid)
Lepidolite/Rubellite
Malachite (grid)
Moonstone
Mother of Pearl
Moss Agate
Onyx
Opal
Peridot
Pyrite (grid)
Rhodochrosite
Ruby
Sapphire
Star Sapphire
Scarab
Shattuckite (grid)
Silver
Smithsonite (grid)
Sodalite
Spinel
Sugilite
Green Tourmaline
Turquoise (grid)
Petrified Wood
Herkimer Diamond
Ametrine
Aventurine (green)
Rose Quartz & Milky Quartz
Rutilated Quartz

# BE MAGNIFICENTLY HUMBLE AND BECOME HUMBLY MAGNIFICENT

W.E. Hagestein
Cambridge, New Zealand

# "NEW MINERALS"

**♪ YOU ARE THE ONLY GATE**
**YOU ARE THE GATELESS GATE ♫**

## AGATE - BRASILIAN TUBE

[Astrological Signs of Gemini, Taurus, & Aries]

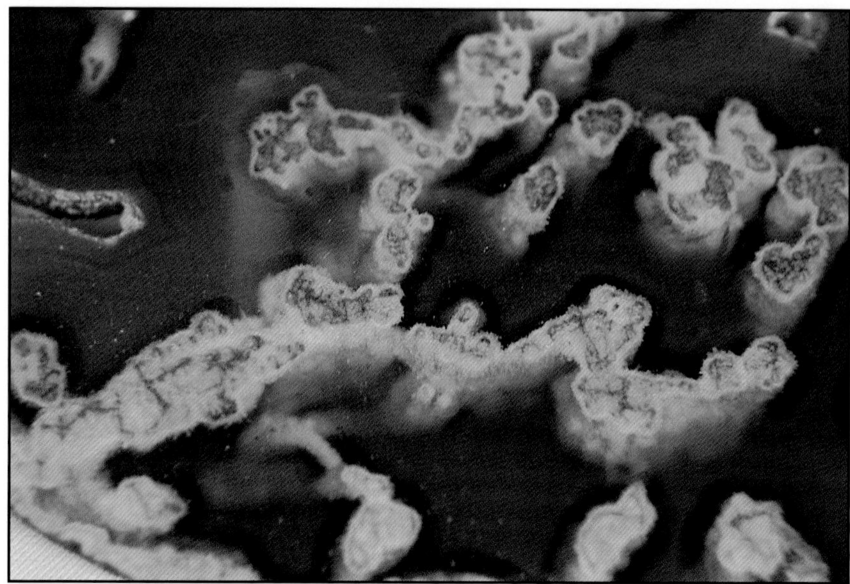

***AGATE - BRASILIAN TUBE*** - $SiO_2$ with other polymorphs of silica and tubular inclusions of Quartz/Agate; Hardness 7; Locality: Rio Grande do Sul, Brasil; Photography by Jim Hughes, Assisted by ♪ Melody ♫; Collection of ♪ Melody ♫, Applewood, CO, USA. Gift of Jeri Justice, Illinois, USA.

Brasilian Tube Agate is a variegated class of chalcedony, usually exhibiting coloured bands or other markings, with tubular inclusions which, sometimes, are in a winding or curved configuration. Agate was first described by Pliny in 77 A.D. and was named for the River Achates in Sicily, a location where it is found.

The following properties are in addition to those listed in the AGATE and CHALCEDONY sections of "Love Is In The Earth - A Kaleidoscope Of Crystals Update".

This mineral has been used to eliminate ones focus upon the lack of employment and/or the aversion to ones current employment, assisting in the concentration of energy toward the type of employment which is desired and which will, in turn, bring the greatest "reward". It removes the "dwelling" on "lack" or "discontent", allowing for one to concentrate on that which is preferable and/or an improvement; hence, eliminating the negative concentration and promoting the positive. It further assists one in "letting go" and in trusting the instinctive choices so that ones chances both in employment and in finances are greatly improved. It promotes the dependence upon the self and supports one in decreasing the times when one "follows" and/or has courses and events dictated.

It assists one in the ability to celebrate the forging of friendships which are as effortless and as spontaneous as that of two children, and which bring concomitant stimulus and emotions rarely felt by adults.

Brasilian Tube Agate can be used to "redirect the pathway around the pitted road", eliminating snares and traps which can cause delays and bringing uninterrupted and forthright progress toward ones goal or toward ones intent and purpose.

It is a "stone of nurturing", promoting the promulgation of new perfect forms and new perfect life in our world. It brings the energy of creation and new beginnings in such a way that there are no errors and no wishes to "start at the beginning and change that which one can control". The mineral has been used to release demoralizing apprehension and panic which is produced during times of stress and tension; it further repels the need for frantic action and assists one in remaining centered.

Brasilian Tube Agate provides the key to the fundamental principle of "right views" and promotes the facilitation of same within the mind and the emotional systems. It increases ones awareness of the "view from the top", promoting recognition of correctness in attainment and in action upon gaining that position.

Advancing ones progress through tunnels of light during the meditative state, it can also be used to expedite telepathic transfer and channeling with awareness.

It has been used in the treatment of disorders of the bronchial system, the veins, and the intestines. It can also assist in the healing of wounds and in the elimination of parasites from the body.

Vibrates to the number 5.

## AGRELLITE

[Astrological Sign of Aquarius]

***AGRELLITE*** **-** $NaCa_2Si_4O_{10}F$; Hardness 5.5; Locality: Kipawa River, Quebec, Canada; Photography by Jim Hughes, Assisted by ♪ Melody ♫; Collection of ♪ Melody ♫, Applewood, CO, USA.

Agrellite crystallizes as fibrous masses in the colour range of pearly white to light grey-green. The mineral was first described by J. Gittins, M.G. Brown, and D.Sturman in 1976 and was named for S.O. Agrell.

This mineral promotes "control" - the increase of control with respect to ones reality and the release of controlling others; it actually supports one who has been controlling and assists the person in allowing another to have independence <u>and</u> supports the other in the acceptance and understanding of consequences which can occur due to decision-making without outside control.

Agrellite can promote unexpected developments which can assist the user in realizing the importance of individuals which have been ignored or neglected. It is an energy to further ones depth of self, to bring recognition to beneficial energies, and to expose any domestic or personal matters which have been buried and which need attention in order for one to grow and to progress with peace. The energy does not permit the continuance of stifling of emotions; it acts to bring these emotions, and the foundation supporting them, to the consciousness so that the negative can be released and loyalty to the self is strengthened. The energy allows for this confrontation with the self or with external forces to be accomplished without the normal trauma.

Agrellite relieves harshness and severity in temper and expression. It is a lovely mineral to give to the proverbial sullen and surly acquaintance.

It also stimulates precision in thought and heightens the stabilization of the frequency of brain wave transmissions. It can provide for a connection to the psychic self, awakening the energy of the third-eye and expediting the verbalization of experiences.

It can be used to locate energy blockages within the body; placing the mineral upon the different areas of the body, one can usually feel a slight resonance at the location of the obstruction.

It has used extensively in dynamic healing and to provide receptivity to radionic treatment. In addition, it provides for amplification of the entire energy field of the body and has also been used by healers in Canada for both diagnostic healing and for communicating with the spirits for diagnostic communications.

It is an interesting exercise when one uses this mineral as a control energy when determining ones intuitive capabilities and ones awareness level with respect to the stimulation which is actually received during healing situations.

It further encourages one to act on the impulses which are instinctual (e.g., moving minerals and transferring energies).

Agrellite has been used in the treatment of cellular swelling and infections, disorders of the immune system, bruising, to provide purification within the body, to alleviate the effects of chemotherapy, and to balance the alkalinity of the body.

Vibrates to the master number 44.

## ALGODONITE

[Astrological Sign of Sagittarius]

***ALGODONITE*** - $Cu_6As$; Hardness 4; Locality: Mohawk Mine, Keweenaw Co., MI, USA; Photography by Jim Hughes, Assisted by ♪ Melody ♫; Collection of ♪ Melody ♫, Applewood, CO, USA.

Algodonite crystallizes in the form of masses. The colour ranges through the metallic grey to white realm. The mineral was first described by F. Field in 1857 and was named for the Algodones Silver Mine in Chile, a locality where it is found.

This mineral is prime sacred geometry, representing the internal energies of the platonic bodies which provide the concept of impermanent representations of unchanging ideas and ideals which, as abstractions and thoughts, give true knowledge as they are known by the mind. The energy of the mineral truly stimulates the recognition of "truth".

Algodonite provides the vehicle for measurement of truth in the intellectual, emotional, and spiritual realms. It can promote "knowing" with respect to when others are being truthful or deceitful and can support one in the determination of when another is manifesting loquacious communication or quiet verity. It has also been known as the "coping stone", bringing the crown or the completion to knowledge with respect to surviving and surrendering, and furthering ones stability in management of all situations.

This mineral can be used to both support and to "preserve" one during changes, helping to fortify and to strengthen one for transformation, and allowing for the temperate understanding of the obscured stratum of "bases" which intensify the conditions of distress and dis-ease. It further serves one in separating from the basis and lessens and diminishes the consequence.

In addition, it serves to rejuvenate, to reconstruct, and to revitalize, while actually provoking dominant cycles of change, and assisting one to direct the beginnings and endings of all phases of ones life. It conveys an energy to deliver the capability for one to make a unique and favourable new "start" in unfavourable circumstances.

Algodonite has been used to grid areas subject to tidal waves, volcanic action and earthquakes, and to secure and to balance the energies associated with same.

It is a mineral to provide a connection to the elders who "remember" and has been used to accentuate the power of ceremony in the advancement of a pursuit. Used with Catlinite, it has assisted one in maintaining the lessons of the vision quest for many years after the venture is completed.

It also brings the energy of perception such that one may search the eyes of another and know whether the message came from the heart.

Algodonite has been used in the treatment of disorders of the tarsal bones, the lattice of the veins, and sciatica, to alleviate nightmares, to provide energies to rectify the deformation of the skeletal structure, and to augment the creative and regenerative forces of the body.

The slight arsenide content of this mineral precludes its use in the normal method of preparation of an elixir.

Vibrates to the number 3.

## AMETHYST - ELESTIAL

[Astrological Signs of Gemini, Scorpio, & Aquarius]

***AMETHYST - ELESTIAL*** - $SiO_2$ with ferric iron; Hardness 7; Locality: Amazona, Brasil; Photography by Jim Hughes, Assisted by ♪ Melody ♫; Collection of ♪ Melody ♫, Applewood, CO, USA.

Amethyst has been described as early as 315 B.C. (by Theophrastus) and was named for the Greek word "not drunken", since it was thought to prevent intoxication. The word "Elestial" has been coined within the last 15 years by the lapidary industry to represent a condition of overgrowth of terminations upon a crystal structure. The following properties are in addition to those listed in the AMETHYST and ELESTIAL sections of "Love Is In The Earth - A Kaleidoscope Of Crystals Update".

This mineral has been known as the "stone of elestial landings", assisting in the descent to the Earth from the other planetary constellations. It has been used to assist one in heuristic discovery and investigation such that ones knowledge of the other-worldly beings is enhanced and one is protected from any negativity which could possibly ensue.

The energy has also been used to teach one the lessons of "opportunity costs", promoting decision-making based upon the acknowledgement of existing constraints, alternatives, and action versus inaction; it promotes the knowledge of the method and the procedure for evaluating what each decision will bring.

The Amethyst Elestial facilitates change on a spiritual level, assists one in transitions, and helps to elevate changes in metaphysical growth. It further banishes restlessness and conflict, and facilitates the completion of "unfinished business".

The energy has been likened to the protective forces of Hesperides, who guarded the golden apples. The focus is direct and mindful, and the security and safety is magnanimous.

It can inspire the boundless energies of the macrocosm to activate the preserving energies of the body, assisting one in the achievement of the foremost state of physical excellence. It allows one to recognize the consistency of the universe and to understand that each portion of the universe preserves an intrinsic perfection which is accessible to all.

The Amethyst Elestial has also been used to eliminate psychic attack and to assist earth-bound spirits to leave an area. Gridding with the mineral can protect one and ones environment from the return of negative energies.

It is helpful for time travel, assisting one to, via inner sight, progress or ascend to the specific time periods desired; it also assists one in remembering that which is experienced, seen, or learned.

It can further the conduction of charged energies and can magnify the energy transfer, from the healer or from minerals, to the subject of the healing. When two pieces are used, it can balance the energies of the body and can maintain stability and wellness within the chemistry of the blood and cellular structures. It has been used to assist in acupressure/acupuncture treatments to induce the movement of the Chi, to treat disorders of the brain, to relieve the pressure of tumors and growths and to constrict same, and to assist in the natural composition and formation of the cells.

Vibrates to the number 5.

## AMETHYST - FLOWER [Astrological Signs of Virgo & Libra]

***AMETHYST - FLOWER*** - $SiO_2$ with ferric iron; Hardness 7; Locality: Rio Grande do Sul, Brasil, South America; Photography by Jim Hughes, Assisted by ♪ Melody ♫; Collection of ♪ Melody ♫, Applewood, CO, USA.

The Amethyst Flower is a plate-like structure with softly ruffled lacy and garden-like projections. The colour range for the formation includes purple, green, yellow, and white to colourless. The Quartz Flower (mostly clear to milky quartz) also has equitable properties. Amethyst has been described as early as 315 B.C. (by Theophrastus) and was named for the Greek word "not drunken", since it was thought to prevent intoxication. The word "Flower" has been coined within the last 5 years to represent the structure looking like an impressionistic floral garden. The following properties are in addition to those listed in the AMETHYST section of "Love Is In The Earth - A Kaleidoscope Of Crystals Update".

Amethyst Flowers provide for the melding and cohesiveness of the two forces of yin/yang, bringing all the remaining details and circumstances to a comfortable and integrated bonding. Reminiscent of the lotus blossom and tending to capture the energies of the eternal meditation, they bring a selectiveness to the choices in ones path. The configuration further allows one to recognize that the study of what is beautiful can never be wasted, especially if one is seeking to understand and preserve it. The energies produce a dazzling splendor, illuminating far beyond what one can normally see, providing for balance of an equalizing nature.

The Amethyst Flower is "a stone of love", "a stone of healing", and "a stone of blessings". It provides a for connection between the crown chakra and the heart chakra, being quite effective at the heart chakra, stimulating a resonant love which can be felt by others and which is totally "in-tune" with the vibratory energies of the perfect state of the universe (crown chakra correlation).

It can assist in reminding one of the reasons for being in the physical body and for living on the Earth plane. It helps one to forgive oneself and others, enhancing ones understanding of the lessons which have been chosen for this visit to the physical realm. It is useful in facilitating memory to answer the question "why am I here?"; it can further help one to determine methods for bringing ones gifts to this world.

It is a stone for the "Indigo Children" of today and tomorrow. Allowing for the presence of the angelic realm to manifest with clarity, protection, and love. It further assists in providing for clarity of communication between the worlds, enhancing messages with clarity, simplicity, and precision, and allowing for a re-charging effect for all. An Amethyst Flower elixir is excellent for activating contact and bridging the interval of frequency and the distance.

For discouragement or despair, placing the Amethyst Flower in ones environment, provides for the flow of gentle, loving information from the spiritual world to the mental plane, bringing peace and relaxation to the user. It has been used to dispel all types of discomforts and feelings of disorder; one may hold the stone and allow the negative energy of the discomfort to be released into the angelic ruffles. It can also be used to clear fluids in the cells of the body and to promote the release of impurities. It has been used to enable the opening of the heart center, allowing for the dissolution of stress and tension.

Vibrates to the number 1.

## AMETHYST - PINK SNOWBALL

[Astrological Signs of Libra & Cancer]

***AMETHYST - Pink Snowball*** - $SiO_2$ with ferric iron and inclusions (snowball-like formations) of the combination of hematite and kaolinite; Hardness 7; Locality: Minas Gerais, Brasil; Photography by Jim Hughes, Assisted by ♪ Melody ♫; Collection of ♪ Melody ♫, Applewood, CO, USA.

Amethyst has been described as early as 315 B.C. (by Theophrastus) and was named for the Greek word "not drunken", since it was thought to prevent intoxication. The addition of "Pink Snowballs" to the name is due to the exhibition of the pink-snowball-like inclusions within the mineral. The following properties are in addition to those listed in the AMETHYST section of "Love Is In The Earth - A Kaleidoscope Of Crystals Update".

Amethyst with Pink Snowballs assists one to focus on global spirituality, bringing positivity in all areas, and promoting advanced healing in our world. The energy furthers the sending of love, even during experiences which one considers to be negative; it furthers the centering of the self with kindness and the projection of positivity to those who need it most. It always seems easy to send love and blessings to those who are of our same mind - the true test comes when we can send the same to those who are dissimilar to us and who may also project negativity. The energy conveys the energy to send blessings, to promote the realization to correcting ones dissenting thoughts/ways, and to advance ones spirituality. The lesson this mineral brings is to be aware as we travel the highway toward the furtherance of our own spirituality, always remembering that each one of us can make a difference and that each lesson brings us more knowledge that we need - sometimes difficult, sometimes easy. As long as we are learning and growing, we are fulfilling our purposes.

This mineral has been used to stimulate the heart chakra and the crown chakra, providing a direct connection between one and another on the emotional and spiritual planes. It can be used to eliminate the feeling of abandonment and restraint, and to assist one in continuing toward ones goals without confinement.

At the heart chakra, it seems to clean the area and to promote protection and love concurrently. It assists one in seeing and in understanding the stages of ones life and acts to provide insight to changes required to promote peace and happiness within ones life.

It can be used to stimulate the energy of the crown and the throat, concurrently, and provides an excellent energy to supplement the process of "toning".

It is a "stone of conditioning", assisting one to both overcome and to progress toward excellence. It elevates ones sense of self-preservation and helps one to understand and to actualize the intrinsic states of rejuvenation which are available.

It can help one to become attuned to the Earth and can provide direction to assist one in increasing the ionization of the atmosphere. It can also assist one in communication with the spiritual forces of the Earth and can help one to understand that which is required in order that the Earth may heal itself.

It has been used in the treatment of disorders of the lungs, the breasts, and the kidneys.

Vibrates to the number 7.

## ANDERSONITE

[Astrological Signs of Leo & Cancer]

***ANDERSONITE*** - $Na_2Ca(UO_2)(CO_3)_3$♥$6H_2O$; Hardness = ?; Locality: Kane Creek Canyon, San Juan Co., UT, USA; Photography by Jim Hughes, Assisted by ♪ Melody ♫; Collection of ♪ Melody ♫, Applewood, CO, USA.

Andersonite crystallizes as a secondary mineral (i.e., a mineral formed subsequent to the formation of the rock enclosing it, and as a result of weathering, metamorphism, or introduction of solution) in the colour range from yellow to pale green. It is very fluorescent, even without UV light. The mineral was first described by J Axelrod, F. Grimaldi, C. Milton, and K.J. Murata, in 1948, and was named C.A. Anderson.

This mineral promotes analytical pursuits and is excellent for stimulating the thinking of the left brain while enhancing the pursuits of the right brain. It produces a melding of the two and encourages action from both avenues.

It is the "stone of right aspirations", bringing correctness to ones ambitions and endeavors. It provides the energy for authentification of ones goals, leading one toward the most fruitful path.

It has been used to access the verity and the genuine-ness of the apocrypha, bringing communication with the definite authors and assisting in translation of meaning of same. It tends to hold the information within the structure and to provide all or parts of sections in one session.

It has acted as an annunciator for the application of stimulus to ones energy fields, promoting the recognition of increased energy and positive forcefields which act to strengthen the chakras and to enhance the auric field.

Andersonite provides clarity of vision and reduction of distortion in all endeavors of telepathy, journeying, and intuitive reckoning. It further dispenses the energy and procedure for resolving variances in ones life, especially when the variances are associated with diverse factors.

This mineral has been used to activate the process of re-birthing, to assist in hands-on healing, and to facilitate muscle testing. The muscle testing tends to be enhanced when one holds the Andersonite in the hand which is not the "hand of preference" or places it at the area of the feet.

It can also be used to deflect (and transform), and to protect against, negativity. It acts to preserve one from being victimized by the dissenting energy of another. It has also been used as an energy diverter, being an excellent stone for those with potential for exposure to excessive amounts of radiation or toxic chemical waste.

It provides for an increase in ones physical endurance, emotional equilibrium, and intellectual discrimination, and can maintain ones vigor for life.

Andersonite is also a mineral of activation, mobilizing the energies of other minerals for use in healing. It has been used to facilitate ease in birthing, in the treatment of disorientation, for balancing the adrenal glands, to draw-out infection, and as an emetic.

This delicacy of this mineral precludes its use in the normal method of preparation of an elixir.

Vibrates to the number 7.

## ANKERITE [Astrological Signs of Aries & Capricorn]

***ANKERITE*** - $Ca(Fe,Mg,Mn)(CO_3)_2$; Hardness 3.5-4; Locality: Washburn Vin., Boulder, CO, USA; Photography by Jim Hughes, Assisted by ♪ Melody ♫; Collection of ♪ Melody ♫, Applewood, CO, USA.

Ankerite crystallizes in the form of rhombohedral crystals, masses, nodules, and grains. The colour ranges from white to grey and yellow to red-brown. The mineral was first described by W. Haidinger in 1825 and was named for M.J. Anker.

This mineral can be used to act as a manual to past-lives and to further access to the ancient wisdom concerning the principles of human-potential, allowing one to create the reality desired.

It acts as an energy vortex center, enhancing all psychic abilities and producing [when directed] experiences which include the direct contact with those of the spirit world, visions, and healings to unusual manifestations.

It further assists one in understanding the cause, effect, and karmic lessons which one has/is experiencing, while stimulating awareness of the methods which can be effectively utilized to transcend undesirable circumstances.

Ankerite encourages charitable actions and relieves sorrow in such a way as to assist one to recognize that there are actually no reasons to be sorrowful [i.e., "everything happens for a reason"]. It encourages energetic and impulsive original thinking and manifestation. It also assists in producing stamina when one is dealing with hyper-active individuals.

It can assist one in projecting the mind, to allow for visitation to other realms on this plane and in other dimensions.

It can be used to enable one to attain an altered state of consciousness and to encourage the Higher Self to act as a guide to access the ancient teachings of the universe. At this level of awareness, one can act to reveal the mysteries via automatic writing and/or mystic communication. Placement of a piece of the mineral upon written material which is difficult for one to understand, can increase discernment of the knowledge and perception into the diverse, and sometimes contradictory, range of information.

It has been used to induce deep relaxation and to generate ideas and solutions. It can facilitate the attainment of awareness and can allow one to open to unconscious impressions. It tends to release images from the unconscious mind and to assist one in achieving the Theta state. It is an excellent stone for meditation.

It can be worn, carried, and used as an elixir. It is quite useful for energy alignment, balancing, and blockage removal. It can also be used to arrest leakages of energy from the chakras.

It can be used in the treatment of conditions which are considered age-related disorders. It has also been used to inhibit the degeneration of cellular structures and to balance the RNA/DNA structures to facilitate healthy cellular development and maintenance. The energy has also tended to assist one in the assimilation of iron.

Vibrates to the number 2.

## APATITE - Blue/Green

[Astrological Sign of Gemini]

***APATITE - Blue/Green crystalline*** - $Ca_5(PO_4)_3(F,OH,Cl)$ - Vitreous; Hardness 5; Locality: Madagascar; Photography by Jim Hughes, Assisted by ♪ Melody ♫; Collection of ♪ Melody ♫, Applewood, CO, USA.

Blue/Green Apatite occurs in very small crystalline formations. Apatite was first described by A.G. Werner in 1786 and was named from the Greek word "to deceive", since it had been previously mistaken for several other minerals. The addition of "Blue/Green" to the name was due to exhibition of the luscious wholesome blue/green colour. The following properties are in addition to those listed in the APATITE section of "Love Is In The Earth - A Kaleidoscope Of Crystals Update".

This mineral has been used to assist one in defining ones life-journey and ones life-image, providing the insight that immersed within one there exists a total uniqueness which one has selected to effect during this lifetime. It further assists one in recognizing that specific uniqueness, in aligning the self with the essential purpose, and in guiding one such that ones life-path follows an expanded sense of meaning. Hence, the energy actually provides for a guiding hand and for the release of difficulties, stress, and the feelings of non-achievement.

It is an energy which promotes the awareness that the issues and programs one needs to remember (to fulfill ones life purpose), one does not realize one had forgotten. An excellent energy for assistance in directing one to, and on, the path, it provides an extremely strong catalyst for transformational energy and shifts.

Providing a connected-ness with the astral plane, it further facilitates the perusal of ones personal Akashic records.

It has been used in the art of Feng Shui for gridding areas to assure "right placement" and "right energy". Blue/Green Apatite actually assists in the relocation of discordant energies such that the sweeping of flowing energies of movement are facilitated.

It assists one in acquiring courage to express ones full potential and can be used to eliminate hostility, prejudice, alienation, uncharitable actions, jealousy, vengefulness, and other opposing attributes.

The mineral also assists one, in times of tragedy, to remember the smallest kindnesses, and to revere and to honour them amid the confusion and despair of events. It assists one in advancing from despair to hope and from fear to courage.

It further provides a luminescence of the aura and a brilliant glow which permeates one being. The strength of the energy produces an awareness in others of this new radiance and tends to facilitate a higher level of respect and consideration for the "radiant one".

Blue/Green Apatite is a mineral to teach "right speech", providing for speech after thought, action and not reaction, and centering within both the being and the intellect prior to communication of issues and ideas.

This mineral has been used in the treatment of panic disorder and personality disorders. It has been successful in holistic healing and in bringing stability to environments for massage and chiropractic adjustments. The combination of Blue/Green Apatite with Ayurvedic medicine has been quite successful.

Vibrates to the number 8.

## ASPHALTUM

[Astrological Signs of Taurus & Cancer]

***ASPHALTUM*** **-** Mineral Pitch; Hardness 2-2.5; Locality: Francois Lake, British Columbia, Canada; Photography by Jim Hughes, Assisted by ♪ Melody ♫; Collection of ♪ Melody ♫, Applewood, CO, USA.

Asphaltum is a mineral pitch containing a mixture of both oxygenated and non-oxygenated hydrocarbons. The colour ranges from a lustrous bright black to brown-black. The mineral was first described by J.D. Dana in 1837 and was named from the Greek word "mineral pitch".

This mineral brings solidity to ones central and dominant essence, facilitating an "out-reach" of energy to "touch" that which provides concentration. It furthers ones actions in all endeavors, bringing stability and constructive modification to ones behavioral qualities, as required for expedition of the process.

It is an energy to assist one in "not missing the point" of any incidents related to affairs of the heart, furthering ones learning process and the opportunities to recharge ones energies of astuteness. It serves to remind one of the times which are appropriate for guidance via intuition and for guidance via the intellect.

Asphaltum has been known as the "stone of the gypsy", bringing warnings when necessary, bringing insight when required, and inducing the recognition of the difference. It has been used to protect and to shield one from psychic assaults on the physical form, and to reverse the effect such that the consequence to the sender is only the realization of infringement and intrusion upon another; hence, producing a loving message, a karma-free retaliation.

The mineral assists one in achievement of aspirations in career and in personal gratification. It is an energy which promotes the recognition of the remaining self-limiting programs which one values for some reason, helping one to delve deep into the basis for the programs and to either release these hidden agendas or to understand the justification for retaining same.

It is a stone for accessing the mass consciousness and for focusing energy on that which one wishes to remove from same. Holding the mineral or placing the mineral at the third-eye, one can transit the planes of existence and can approach the "beliefs" which are located in the mass consciousness; subsequent removal of the selected "belief" is facilitated and the action of the precept relative to the basis of the "belief" within ones life is also eliminated.

It is also one of the minerals which has been used for the process of Tibetan pulsing with laying-on-of-hands with laying-on-of-stones; it serves to support the energy transfer and to bring centering to the practitioner. For this utilization, it is usually placed at the area of the crown chakra of the practitioner.

Asphaltum has been used during meditation to access the ancient writings of the Dead Sea Scrolls.

It has been used to enhance the assimilation of minerals and amino-acids, in the treatment of poor circulation in the extremities, hot "flashes", mobility of the arms and hands, and in maintaining a balanced body temperature, and for disorders related to rashes and hives, nausea and influenza, and muscle sprains and connective tissue.

Vibrates to the number 3.

## "AURORA BOREALIS STONE"

[Astrological Signs of Pisces & Sagittarius]

***AURORA BOREALIS STONE*** **-** A type of Marble - $CaCo_3$ with impurities; Hardness Variable; Locality: Old Thorp Mine, Talkeetna Mtns., South Central Alaska, USA; Photography by Dave Shrum, Colorado Camera; Collection of ♪ Melody ♫, Applewood, CO, USA. Gift of Doug & Marcia Theiner, Alaska, USA.

The Aurora Borealis Stone is a type of gold-bearing marble, occurring in masses, in the colour range displayed. The origin of the name is unknown to the author. The following properties are in addition to those listed in the MARBLE and GOLD sections of "Love Is In The Earth - A Kaleidoscope Of Crystals Update".

It should be noted that pieces of the mineral may not exhibit the gold, and that due to the molecular structure the energy of the stone remains the same, with or without the inclusion of gold.

This mineral is a "stone of the night", bringing phenomenal and prophetic lucid dreams, visions, and revelations.

It has also been used for polarity balancing of the body, for equalizing the yin/yang attributes, and for equilibrating the thought processes of the brain. It has facilitated clarity in communication and acts as a non-aphasic facilitator, bringing precision in understanding that which is communicated in the physical, emotional, and other-worldly realms.

It promotes a connection with both the aurora borealis and the aurora australis of the hemispheres, assisting in the retrieval of information from both and in a connected-ness with the ethereal forms of life; therein lies the answers to many questions of being and existence. It further assists one in the alignment with the higher realms.

Wherever worn or carried, it acts as a physical and mental energizer; it also enhances and protects the aura and provides for amplification of the energy field of the body.

The Aurora Borealis Stone can stimulate mental clarity, facilitating deep meditative states and activating psychic abilities and can provide for balancing of the physical body, for stabilization and balancing of all chakras, for clearing and activation of the heart and crown chakras, and for synchronicity between the self and another.

It has also been used inclusively to cleanse and to smooth the aura and to release negativity from ones emotional, physical, intellectual, and spiritual bodies.

It helps one to maintain balance in relationships and cooperative efforts, facilitating diplomacy and discretion in all matters of import. It also enables one to curtail unpleasant situations at the onset, defeating negativity with ease.

This mineral can be used in the field of radionics to enable the user to more easily recognize the response. It facilitates the attunement of the radionics operator with the subject.

It has been used to stimulate the thyroid and parathyroid glands, being also helpful for respiratory problems such as congestion and sore throat. It can be used in the treatment of disorders of the urinary tract, motion sickness, acrophobia, and prostatic enlargement.

Aurora Borealis Stone vibrates to the number 3.

**"WRITE YOUR OWN MUSIC
WRITE YOUR OWN SONGS"**

Bob Jackson
Earth-Love Gallery
Colorado, USA

## BAUXITE [Astrological Signs of Aries, Pisces, & Taurus]

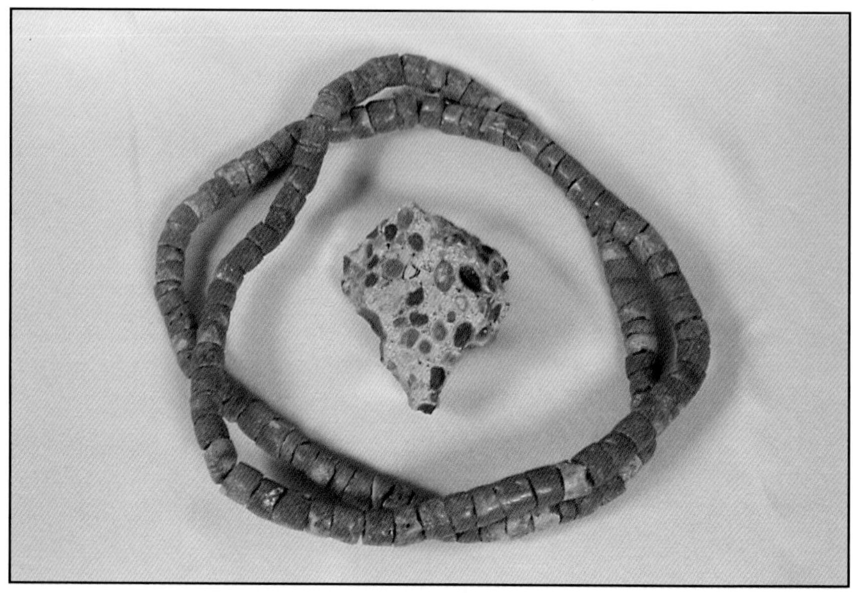

***BAUXITE*** - $Al_2O_3$♥$2H_2O$ or $Al_2O_3$♥$H_2O$; Hardness 3-7; Locality: Africa (beads), Arkansas (Rough); Photography by Jim Hughes, Assisted by ♪ Melody ♫; Collection of ♪ Melody ♫, Applewood, CO, USA.

Bauxite crystallizes as an off-white, grey, brown, yellow, or red-brown rock, comprised of a mixture of varying amorphous or crystalline hydrous aluminum oxides and hydroxides, and free silica, silt, iron hydroxides, and clay. The formation is found as concretions, as compact or earthy masses, and as small round or ellipsoidal accretionary bodies and disseminated grains in sedimentary rock. The name is sometimes (and originally was) spelled with an "e" prior to the "a". The mineral was first described by A. Dufrenoy and was named for Beaux, France, a locality where it is found.

This mineral has been used in meditation and has produced a calm and a ready channel for obtaining answers to personal questions. It assists one in connecting with the energies and the information relative to the native cultures of northern Africa, bringing knowledge of ritualistic methodology and healing practices.

The energy acts as one which does not leave ones energy field, and has not been found to be transferrable. Hence, the intensity is increased for personal use.

The energy is joyful and, when held, tends toward the suspension of anxieties and toward the heightening of ones state of well-being. It assists with adjustments and adaptation in ones life, and in the relief of feelings of anger.

Often times it can promote ease of emotional release, bringing one to the evaluation and balance of ones feelings while releasing the negativity of exasperation.

This mineral is for the young and "old"; the young, because they have not yet overlooked the knowledge which they brought to Earth during this lifetime; the "old", because they have retrieved and increased the information with which they originated prior to visiting the Earth during this lifetime.

It is quite helpful for those studying the field of medicine and can promote holistic, homeopathic, and herbal medicine studies, providing insights and, when required, the skepticism to induce further testing.

Carrying Bauxite has provided a supplemental energy to assist one in "decoding" others and in understanding exactly what is being communicated, more on an intellectual and superficial basis; subsequently, the application to the spiritual and material plane is enhanced. It furthers ones understanding of the intent of others.

This mineral has been used to relieve excess acidity in the body, to promote the assimilation of iron, to strengthen the hair and the nails, to stimulate the intestines and digestive tract, and to treat disorders of the throat. It has also been used to increase distances for sight, to further the sense of smell, to ameliorate potassium deficiency, to promote the dissipation of growths, and to enhance body-building and stability in mobility.

Vibrates to the number 1.

## BINDHEIMITE [Astrological Signs of Aquarius & Capricorn]

***BINDHEIMITE*** - $Pb_2Sb_2O_6(O,OH)$; Hardness 4-4.5; Locality: Siberia, Russia; Photography by Jim Hughes, Assisted by ♪ Melody ♫; Collection of ♪ Melody ♫, Applewood, CO, USA.

Bindheimite crystallizes in the amorphous formation as well as reniform, earthy, and as crusts. The colour ranges from earthy yellow to brown and grey. The mineral was first described by J.D. Dana in 1868 and was named for J.J. Bindheim.

This mineral can be used to stimulate sensory transmissions between the physical and ethereal body, to facilitate the re-energizing of voids in ones aura, and to support the preservation of the corporeal life force. It demonstrates a greater proclivity for action with the physical form than with the intellect, and tends to assure soundness in the aura for the complete physical system. Re-energizing of the voids within the aura, the energy also provides for protection from dangerous situations and from dis-ease associated with this world.

It provides for a bridge between the grounding energy of the Earth and the aspects of personal power which are manifested via the intuitive self.

It facilitates contemplation via inspiration. It promotes protection of oneself from emotional situations which could bring disharmony and rejection.

Bindheimite can be used to eliminate separation in relationships, withholding decomposition due to aging or lack of excitement, while providing for persistence and diligence in affiliations, and assisting in attraction where one determines exactly what is to be attracted.

It is helpful in the management of affairs, again allowing the intuitive side to predominate, with satisfactory results.

It has been used to enhance ones musical (performance) capabilities and to further ones sense of humour. It also acts to stimulate ones ability to lessen the seriousness of any situation.

Bindheimite acts to show one that which is internal to the self and to others with respect to emotional, physical, and intellectual circumstances. It can draw forth negativity from these centers while transferring the positive forces of another mineral to same; hence, performing as a expediting courier.

It can also be used in the garden and around houseplants to stimulate strength in structure and enhancement in growth.

The structure provides stimulus to the ideal of service to the world, and to the development of a humanity which is both attuned to healing and to furthering the subsequent eradication of dis-ease.

It has been used in the treatment of degenerative dis-ease, broken bones and torn ligaments, hernia and ruptures, and hysteria, and to both slow the pulse rate and lower the blood pressure. It provides an energy to stimulate the efficiency of both the immune system and ones maintenance against dis-ease.

The slight lead content of this mineral precludes its use in the normal method of preparation of an elixir.

Vibrates to the number 8.

## BINGHAMITE [Astrological Signs of Sagittarius, Gemini, & Virgo]

***BINGHAMITE*** **-** A recognized regional name for a pseudomorph replacement of acicular/needle-like Goethite and Hematite with Quartz such that the replacement with Quartz is required to be between 80% and 90% and an acicular chatoyancy is exhibited; Hardness 5-7; Locality: Cuyana Iron Range, MN, USA; Photography by Jim Hughes, Assisted by ♪ Melody ♫; Collection of ♪ Melody ♫, Applewood, CO, USA. Gift of Peter Giangrande, MN, USA

Binghamite crystallizes in the form of chatoyant masses with the colour ranging in the hues of reds and blacks. The mineral was first described by J. Sinkankas in 1959 and was named for W.J. Bingham. The mineral actually exhibits a linear-viscous behavior above a yield point and rigidness below the yield point (the differential stress at which a material begins to undergo permanent deformation).

This mineral has been said to be filled with the energies of elves and flower fairies, the energies which cultivate ones good fortune, good foresight, and good times. It tends to bring action to ones life and to stimulate a lack in isolation, replacing solitary pursuits with group pursuits and restoring community effort and environmental awareness in all activities.

It has further been used to accentuate the contact with ones spiritual friends and has been an excellent stone for use by the "child within" to access the imaginary friends of yesteryear, and by ones matured conscious self to commune with the Inner Self of today.

It also facilitates clairaudience and, sometimes, allows one to hear the music of the ethers. It enhances communication on the physical plane and strengthens the connection with other worlds and beings in those worlds. It can be used to alleviate distractions and to provide for intensified concentration.

It can enable one to predict future events and can be used to enhance the abilities of a divining rod. It can also facilitate clairvoyant experiences. In addition, it has been used to grid an area to enhance and to strengthen the energy for welcoming positive other-worldly energies.

Binghamite tends to induce amplification of the energy field in the location in which it resides. It can produce a force field of healing negative ions while clearing the surrounding atmosphere of positive ions and can further extend the energy of recovery to the totality of ones environment. Hence, it is an extremely useful mineral for sessions of healing.

It acts to stimulate the Theta brain wave pattern, activating a deeper state of ESP, enhancing psychokinesis [PK], facilitating painless surgery and dentistry, and initiating influential levels of suggestibility.

It has also been used to amplify and to direct the energies of "assistant" minerals.

Binghamite has also been used to return energy to an area of the body in which the flow has been diminished; this energy restoration can assist in the rebuilding and renewal of cells and in the dissipation of dis-ease.

It has been used in the treatment of burns, anemia, convulsive states, and disorders associated with the ears, throat, veins, alimentary canal, and esophagus.

Vibrates to the number 7.

## BISMUTHINITE

[Astrological Signs of Leo & Cancer]

***BISHMUTHINITE*** - $Bi_2S_3$; Hardness 2; Locality: Black Pearl Mine, Eureka District, Yavapai Co., AZ, USA; Photography by Jim Hughes, Assisted by ♪ Melody ♫; Collection of ♪ Melody ♫, Applewood, CO, USA.

Bishmuthinite crystallizes in the formation of foliation, fibers, and shapeless masses. The colour ranges from grey to grey-white, often with a lustrous yellowish or iridescent tarnish and metallic luster. The mineral was first described by F.S. Beaudant in 1832 (as Bismuthine), with the spelling modified by J.D. Dana in 1868, and was named for its Bismuth content.

This mineral confers an invulnerability, and favorably influences the outcome of lawsuits, petitions, and judgments. It has been used to augment the qualities of diplomacy.

It acts as a bridge between the self and other cultures such that one may readily receive information. It is a "stone of the magis", bringing information for the self and for others relative to the pre-programmed ethereal energies which are in ones energy field.

It possesses an energy which can locate energy blockages and can totally open the crown chakra, allowing for release of blockages and promoting the cleansing and activation at the same time.

When held or worn at the solar plexus, it can provide for the stimulation of total body energies, and can also increase ones emotional fields [this may/may not be desirable and is dependent upon ones emotional stability at the given moment]. It furthers the energy emitted to allow one to recognize "signs" of forthcoming events and to formulate emotional readiness.

Bishmuthinite has been used in body-zoning work, assisting the user to locate the area(s) which require regulation and facilitating the transfer of adjustment to that/those area(s).

It can be used in the practice of reflexology to stimulate energy transfer and in cranial sacral therapy to expedite movement.

It has been used as a "stone of metamorphosis", guiding one through the changes required to attain systematic conditions while smoothing the state of change and dispensing a supplemental physical stamina and mental awareness to the user.

It transforms the energy of the crown chakra to energize the base chakra [in contrast with most stones] and actualizes both the instinctual energies of preservation and the power of wisdom.

It can be used to support gridding exercises associated with the promotion and the enhancement of the condition of stability; in this case, a piece of the mineral would be placed on top of each of the other minerals chosen for the gridding.

Bishmuthinite has been used to stimulate the metabolic processes, to support ones life forces during surgery, in the elimination of toxins and excess mucoid within the body, as an anti-bacterial agent, and in veterinary work to induce an ease of willingness.

Vibrates to the number 5.

## "SUNSHINE DESCENDS UPON MORE THAN ONE PERSON A DAY"

John Crowley
California, USA

## CALCITE - ELESTIAL [Astrological Signs of Scorpio & Cancer]

***CALCITE - ELESTIAL*** - $CaCO_2$; Hardness 3; Locality: Bill Williams River, Mohave County, AZ, USA; Photography by Jim Hughes, Assisted by ♪ Melody ♫; Collection of ♪ Melody ♫, Applewood, CO, USA. Gift of Robert Poley, Jr., AZ, USA.

Calcite was first described as "Kalkspat" by A.F. Cronstedt in 1758, as "Calc-Spar" by R. Jameson in 1804, and translated to "Calcite" by J.K. Freiesleben in 1836; it was named for its Calcium content. The word "Elestial" has been coined within the last 15 years by the lapidary industry to represent a condition of overgrowth of terminations upon a crystal structure; this specific structure became apparent after one washing of the mineral. The following properties are in addition to those listed in the CALCITE section of "Love Is In The Earth - A Kaleidoscope Of Crystals Update".

This mineral is another for the "Indigo Children", encouraging the presence of the appropriate members of the angelic realm and the manifestation of same, while producing the energies of understandable complexity, protection, and love. It further assists in providing for comprehensible information transfer between the worlds, enhancing messages with exactness, simplicity, and precision, and allowing for a re-charging effect for all. The Calcite Elestial elixir is excellent for stimulating approach and for connecting one without regard to the intervals of (normal) frequency and the reserve which has occasionally been evidenced.

The mineral provides for a "lengthening" of experiences in order to facilitate and to advance the spontaneous and the deliberate receipt of knowledge such that approach to each event/condition/experience is with absolute precision, ease, and beneficial construction; the concept of approach and retrieval of information being via strategic techniques.

The Calcite Elestial also facilitates the extension of the mind back to the beginning of the Earth phase while stimulating recall of past-lives relative to this planet.

It is truly an "enchanted formation", bringing with it the abstraction of Shiva and the discernment that after conversion from one phase of life or from the physical body, the uniqueness will again be imparted. It provides the user with an embrace from the universe, promoting and allowing for ease in change and actualization.

It can be used to support ones awareness of the timeless-ness of the spiritual being within the physical body and to enhance ones life on this plane of reality. It also assists one in the comprehension of the processes of life and the levels of death. It serves to provide an entrance to information concerning the past and future of ones personal existence.

The Calcite Elestial can be used to both nourish and conserve one during transitions, preparing one for any definitive and ultimate transformation and allowing for the understanding of the justifications which sustain conditions of distress and dis-ease. It further assists one in releasing the cause; hence, decreasing or eliminating the effects of distress.

It has been used in the treatment of epilepsy and drug-related burn-out. It can assist in the restoration of emotional stability. It can further be used to diminish vertigo and symptoms associated with physical imbalances within the body.

Vibrates to the master number 55.

## CALIFORNITE

[Astrological Sign of Aquarius]

***CALIFORNITE*** - $Ca_{19}Fe(Mg,Al)_8Al_4(SiO_4)_{10}(Si_2O_7)_4(OH)_{10}$; Hardness 6.5; Locality: Happy Camp, Siskiyou County, CA, USA; Photography by Jim Hughes, Assisted by ♪ Melody ♫; Collection of ♪ Melody ♫, Applewood, CO, USA.

Californite is a green massive compact variety of vesuvianite. The mineral was first described by G.F. Kunz in 1903 and was named for California, the state location in which it was discovered.

This mineral is said to enhance "the midas touch", facilitating the connection between one and the abundance of the universal wealth - in the physical realm as well as in the spiritual realm. The connection tends to further acquisition in both domains.

It is an energy for activation of the heart chakra and for eliminating restraints upon furtherance of ones goals in relationships, groups, and altruistic situations.

It promotes clarity of purpose and removes energy blockages in the area of the heart such that one may experience the ingress of positive and loving energies from others.

Californite can also be used to assist one obtaining information relevant to the karmic burdens incurred during past-lives, helping one to both recognize and to understand the easiest methods to negate the karma; it should be noted that the "easiest methods" are truly easy if one allows ones actions to flow and does "not push the river". It can further be used to view future incarnations and to understand that which is to be achieved in this life in order to approach the lessons of the next life.

This mineral acts to activate ones inner rainbow, passing the energy through the body with an elevated frequency of vibration and allowing for the visible manifestation of the spectrum within the aura. It actually infuses ones aura with the bouquet of multi-coloured energy.

It further brings stability to the "three-dimensional" levels of awareness - the physical, mental, and emotional - and provides for communication between the "three" and the "one" of spirituality.

Californite assists one in recognizing the angelic energy which supervises each personality and each "thing" upon the Earth. It has been used to induce trance states and to guide one in petitioning the appropriate angelic being for the appropriate circumstance, person, or object. It also assists Earth-bound spirits in leaving the Earth plane, helping these beings to realize the discontinuity in their progress and providing the attraction for continuance of their cycles.

It is said to be the patron of policemen and firemen, bringing a protective energy and furthering insight into danger.

The mineral mediates any abrupt or unexpected changes such that freedom and independence are maintained and one is provided with information prior to these changes. It should be noted that one must be willing to give credence to these flashes of insight in order to eliminate the surprise-nature of same.

It is an excellent healing stone and has been used to eliminate toxins from the body, to stimulate the production of beneficial bacteria within the body, and to act as an anesthetic

Vibrates to the number 4.

## CALLAGHANITE

[Astrological Sign of Pisces]

***CALLAGHANITE*** - $Cu_2Mg_2CO_3(OH)_6$♥$2H_20$; Hardness 3-3.5; Locality: Gabbs, Nye County, NV, USA; Photography by Jim Hughes, Assisted by ♪ Melody ♫; Collection of ♪ Melody ♫, Applewood, CO, USA.

Callaghanite crystallizes in the formation of masses. The colour ranges from blue to grey. The mineral was first described by C.W. Beck and J.H. Burns in 1953, with the formula modified by G. Brunton, H. Steinfink, and C.W. Beck in 1958; it was named for E. Callaghan.

This mineral has been used to provide stimulation to the meridians which represent survival and protection of the physical and emotional bodies.

It is a stone to promote the rationality of the mind and the consciousness of speech. It produces a vitality to launch ideas and inventions from the stage of planning to the stage of construction. It provides defense from chaos and promotes organization and rationality in planning and in action.

It has been used to enhance the methods and results of Chinese herbology and tends to work well as an elixir during these tests. It has been applied to research in the fields of homeopathy and holistic healing and has supported divination techniques which provide guidance toward the method, program, or stimulus which is required.

It dissipates obliviousness, intolerance, and self-righteous attitudes, revealing to one that the highest state of "being in the body" is one in which the idea and the effects of love to all truly amplifies the positiveness of this world. It also helps to eliminate jealousy, animosity, and resentment from ones environment and from ones personality.

It assists in the removal of obstructions from ones path, provides calm confidence, and increases ones inherent strength of character. It yields insight to the equality of ones brothers and sisters and supports the understanding of respect for all and everything.

Callaghanite produces an excellent energy for administrators, clerical personnel, the ministry, and for the priesthood, and for those pursuing education. It tends to bring the ability to see all sides of issues and to support the adequate communication of same - whether for problem resolution or for understanding ones tasks and/or assignments.

The mineral has also been used to promote understanding of the "phases" that the self and/or others are "going through" and provides the perception of the reasons behind these stages of development. It facilitates an empathy with the subject of the "phase" and a knowledge that, if one is being directly affected by the action of another, that "this too shall pass". It is an excellent stone to use when one is experiencing "abandonment" issues relative to those who are considered to be good friends.

It has been used to further activities associated with therapeutic touch and integrated massage therapy where messages are transferred from the hands to the consciousness concerning malfunctions and disorders in specific locations.

Callaghanite has been used in the treatment of restrictions and constrictions within the body, to promote the healing of cellular disorders of the throat, to regulate the secretion of adrenalin, insulin, bile, and cortin, and to moderate the cholesterol levels.

Vibrates to the number 3.

## COLUSITE

[Astrological Sign of Libra]

***COLUSITE*** - $Cu_{26}V_2(As,Sn)_6S_{32}$; Hardness 4.5; Locality: Colusa Claim, Butte, MT, USA; Photography by Jim Hughes, Assisted by ♪ Melody ♫; Collection of ♪ Melody ♫, Applewood, CO, USA.

Colusite crystallizes in the form of masses and tetrahedrons. The colour ranges from bronze to metallic cream to grey. The mineral was first described by H. Schneiderhöhn and P. Ramdohr in 1931 and was named for the Colusa Claim in Butte, Montana, the locality of discovery.

This mineral is representative of the indescribable and transcendent energies of the universe. The divine force of all energy is focussed within and through this mineral, bringing conscious awareness to the user - for all times and all circumstances.

It provides a sanctuary within itself, radiating to fill ones energy fields or to fill the energy field of the environment (providing for an expansive sanctuary), whichever is necessary, while promoting the internal recognition and the outward manifestation of ones personal power to originate, to create, and to develop.

It is a "stone of samadhi", bringing the "attainment energy" and providing insight to information which will assist one in same. For example, it assists one in releasing the concept of meditation which allows for thoughts to remain or to be furthered within the mind; it is truly a mineral to bring the "no mind" state and to further ones affinity with "All That Is". The energy does not allow one to "sit" with the turbulence of overall tension and emotional baggage remaining within the mind; it actually grants the energy to allow these conditions to dissipate (at least for a time period) and to support the actualization of inner silence.

Colusite further assists one in breaking-free of self-imposed subconscious sabotage. It assists one in recognizing that which is concealed and camouflaged within ones structure of belief (which can be a multitude of "things" from ourselves and others) due to early and current experiences of conditioning, repression, inhibition, and bombardment with taboos. It assists, subsequently, to promote the release of the "beliefs" which provide sabotage to ones development. It actually produces a visual picture of each belief-system which has been formed during the course of ones present life, allowing for both understanding and eradication of those which impede.

It is also a lovely energy for promoting research in history and in theoretical areas.

The mineral has been used extensively in the area of "colour-puncture" therapy, to assist one in focusing upon the areas requiring restoration, to provide insight into the type and conditions of reconstruction or renewal which would be beneficial, and to facilitate direction of the energy toward that end while promoting the release of energetic imbalances.

Colusite has been used in the treatment of tendinitis, acidosis, anaphylactic shock, hydrophobia, cellular disorders, and to support the body during aerobic exercise. It has also been used in the diminishment of cellulite.

The slight arsenide content of this mineral precludes its use in the normal method of preparation of an elixir.

Vibrates to the number 5.

## CORAL - AGATIZED

[Astrological Sign of Pisces]

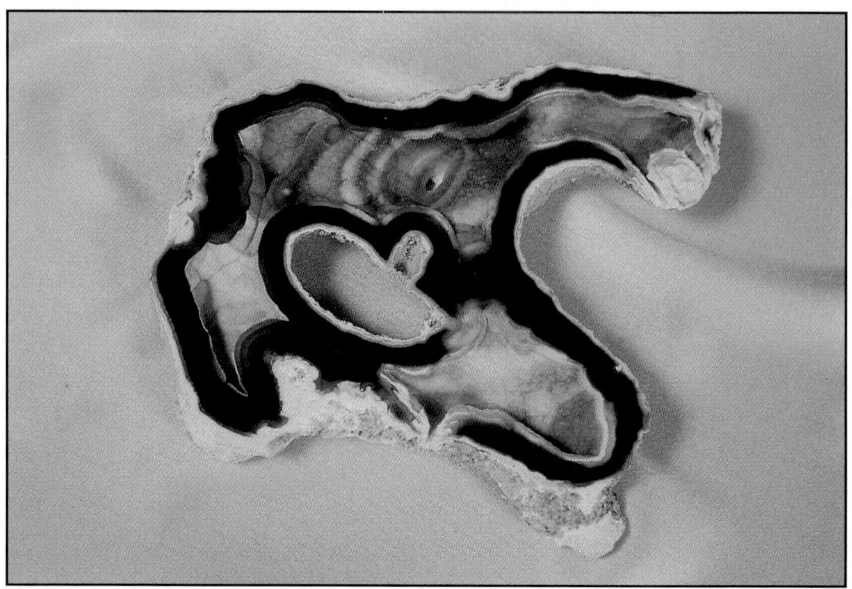

***CORAL - AGATIZED*** - $SiO_2$ with other polymorphs of silica; Hardness 7; Locality: Florida, USA; Photography by Jim Hughes, Assisted by ♪ Melody ♫; Collection of ♪ Melody ♫, Applewood, CO, USA.

Agatized Coral comes from the sea and is the lustrous vacated housing, of marine animals and sea animals, which has become agatized. The word "Coral" was taken from the Latin word "Corallum". The word "Agate" was described by Pliny in 77 A.D. and was named for an occurrence on the River Achates in Sicily. In addition to the properties listed in the AGATE, SHELL, and CORAL sections of "Love Is In The Earth - A Kaleidoscope Of Crystals Update", the following attributes apply.

This mineral has been used to support trauma therapy, assisting one to change patterns and to enter relationships which reflect ones growth. It is an excellent energy for removal of emotional disturbances which have been prompted by divorce and/or by dysfunctional families, work situations, and relationships. The mineral assists the non-utilitarian memories to be transformed to the concept of positive lessons and further assists one in relinquishing the situations to which one attributes "cause".

Agatized Coral assists in the transfer of knowledge with respect to the question "why is there suffering"; it further promotes clarity in understanding "why" one would personally need to experience suffering and "what" other avenues are available for the fulfillment of this lesson. It also promotes a high transfer-energy so that one may assist another in recognizing the alternatives to his/her personal sufferings and can direct the action of this person to the other means of attainment.

It brings the positive, active, and dynamic forces to ones actualization and styles one to follow the guise of the "white magician". Supplying impulse, it facilitates the projection of energy to create, to sustain, to change, to modify, .......

It provides the primary energy toward the activation of the divine nature and the infinite perfection which is within the self. Bringing a "right" transmission of that which is "willed", it promotes a balance of ones world of physical needs and further provides for the supplementation of the element of realization.

The mineral instills authority over ones circumstances, and promotes concentration in any endeavor which is recalled into the energy field.

It has also been used in activities associated with iridology and the study of the eyes, assisting one in interpretation of signs and symbols and in the application of reconciliation of conditions.

It has also been used to assist one in answering the question, "why do good things happen to bad people" (note the contrary context). It brings the energy to allow one to access the reasons and the bases for the occurrences and to understand the lessons involved (for both the person and for the investigator).

Agatized Coral has been used in the treatment of disorders of the spine (including alignment and meningitis), lung tissue, lymphatic glands, to enhance the skin resilience, and to ameliorate calcium deficiencies. It has been applied to strengthening the skeletal structure and to renewal of cellular tissue in the eustachian tubes.

Vibrates to the number 5.

## CUMENGÉITE

[Astrological Sign of Gemini]

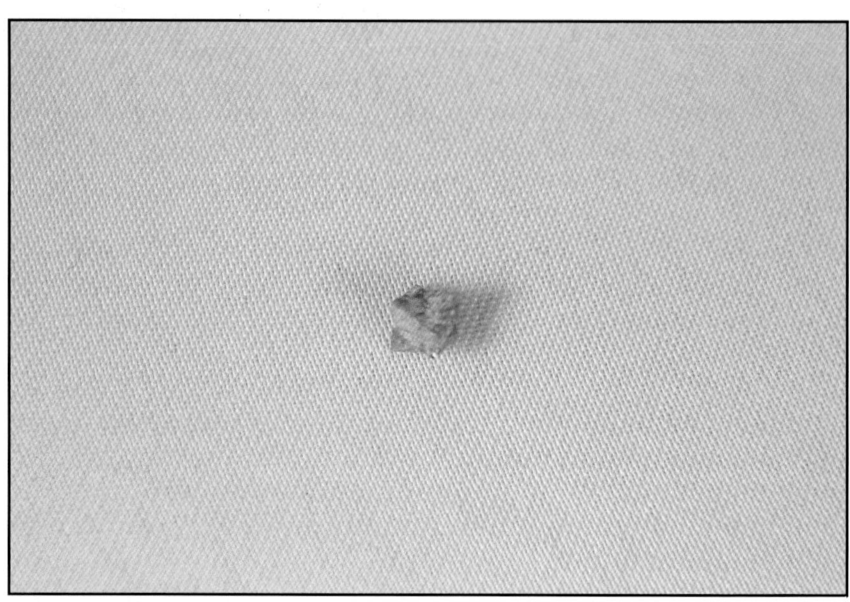

***CUMENGÉITE*** - $Pb_4Cu_4Cl_8(OH)_8$♥$H_2O$ or $Cu_{20}Pb_{21}Cl_{42}(OH)_{40}$; Hardness 2.5; Locality: Bed-3, Amelia Mine, Cumenge shaft, Boleo Copper Dist., Baja, CA, Mexico; Photography by Jim Hughes, Assisted by ♪ Melody ♫; Collection of ♪ Melody ♫, Applewood, CO, USA. Gift of Bonni MacKintosh, CA, USA.

Cumengéite crystallizes both singly, including twinned and in matrix as a tetragonal pyramidal, and as a regular intergrowth or overgrowth with Boleite. A regular grouping obscures the boleite altogether and simulates actual twinning with a fanciful star-like body composite. Crystals also are tetragonal in structure, taking a pyramidal, octahedral, or cubo-octahedral shape. The colour ranges from azure to indigo. The name is sometimes spelled without the "é" prior to the "i". The mineral was first described by E. Mallard in 1893 and was named for E. Cumengé.

Said to be "Most Powerful Medicine" by one of the miners, it supersaturates feelings of joy and gratitude and brings relief pervaded by the senses.

It furthers intimacy, has been used to facilitate yoga techniques, and stimulates the actualization of results in Jungian psychotherapy.

The mineral has been utilized to access the world soul or Akasa, upon whose memory is impressed all that happens; the process is conducive to visual contact with, and understanding of, the Akashic records. A similar exercise may be applied to the art of vision transfer; in this situation, the thought of a certain person may be held in mind while one places the mineral upon the third-eye in the expectation of seeing a vision form in its depths. The thought held in the mind provides the seed for the psychometric action via the ethereal configuration. During the act of vision transfer there is a relaxation, similar to sleep, but with the conscious self in a "stand-by" condition in the waking-state such that one may observe that which is sensed by the subconscious through the images centering around/within the crystal.

Cumengéite is filled with time-honored techniques which allow one to develop the inner abilities and to actualize them in an outward productive manner.

Based upon the premise that dis-ease is an alteration of the oscillatory state of the equilibrium of an organism which is affected in the physical and psychic fields, one may align the internal and external rays of vibration to correspond to each other via the utilization of Cumengéite, assisging in the production of a state of balance and well-being. The energy tends to ameliorate the disruptive energies to which one has been externally, or internally, exposed, in order to initiate healing on the physical and emotional levels.

It has also been used as a configuration for receiving the creativity of the universe, furthering ones pursuit of inventive and original ideas, and prompting an endless flow of relevant and insightful information to the user.

Cumengéite has been used in the treatment of microbic infections, disorders of the upper chest and dis-eases of the throat. It has promoted re-stimulation of the thymus and furtherance of the immune system.

The slight lead content of this mineral precludes its use in the normal method of preparation of an elixir.

Vibrates to the number 3.

**"IF YOU GET IT YOU GET IT
IF YOU DON'T GET IT YOU DON'T GET IT
STILL, YOU GET IT"**

Osho
"The Divine Melody"

## DELAFOSSITE

[Astrological Sign of Scorpio]

***DELAFOSSITE*** - $CuFeO_2$ or $Cu^{+}Fe^{3+}O_2$ or $Cu_2O$♥$Fe_2O_3$; Hardness 5.5; Locality: Bisbee, AZ, USA; Photography by Jim Hughes, Assisted by ♪ Melody ♫; Collection of ♪ Melody ♫, Applewood, CO, USA. Gift of Michael Alexander, AZ, USA.

Delafossite crystallizes in the rhombohedral formation and as small spherical aggregates imbedded in clay. The mineral was first described by C. Friedel in 1873 and was named for G. Delafosse.

This mineral is representative of the "trinity", the three directions encompassing the Earth, the Sky, and the four directions of the medicine wheel. It has been used in medicine wheel ceremonies to provide a synthesis of the energies and to facilitate the return of the energies to the Earth plane for the participants to share.

It is a truly positive mineral, promoting ease in fusing with another and with the spiritual beings representing the four directions. Upon this melding, it enhances balancing of the yin-yang energies, utilizing, in addition, the magnetic qualities of the energy to balance the meridians within the body and to provide a stable equilibrium between the ethereal nervous system and the physical nervous system.

It assists in the focusing of energy and emotions for balance between the body, mind, and spirit. It also assists in the dissolution of negativity, transforming the negativity, in the dissolved state.

It is a stone of the province of the Earth, conducting the magnetism of the region of the Earth in which it resides. The energy of this stone is dependent upon the negativity or positivity emitted from the environment from which it is located. Most areas are similar with respect to the amount of energy available; however, the energy accessible in the environments which are gridded for protection tend to bring the strength of renewal and rejuvenation. The energy provided is dependent upon the location of the mineral upon the Earth, facilitating the emanation of the energies of the vortex structures when placed in a medicine wheel where the force is abundant, and where this abundance does not rely upon the presence of beings; it has been placed in a medicine wheel during ceremonial work and has been buried in the same location after the ceremonial work has been completed (in addition, pieces of the mineral have been carried by each of the participants in the ceremony).

Delafossite can also facilitate the "charging" of talismen; a photograph, a drawing, or the actual talisman may be used. A photograph, drawing, or the actual object may be placed beneath the mineral, with a written missive of the feelings which the object will convey when magnetically charged. Note that the mineral will not accept negative feelings.

The mineral also provides for stimulation of the intelligence of the cellular structure of the body such that the cells may recognize the reason for malfunction in conditions of dis-ease; it further provides the vitality and creativity for the correction of the malfunction. This mineral will be made available to those who are ready for the complex energies.

It has been used as a "misting" agent when one is in the state of dis-ease. It can assist in stabilizing nervousness, shakiness, and dis-eases related to these disorders. It promotes the assimilation of iron and has been used in the treatment of arthritis and muscular pain. It is currently being tested in experiments for relieving the effects of fibro-myalgia.

Vibrates to the number 7.

***DIABOLEITE*** - $Pb_2CuCl_2(OH)_4$; Hardness 2.5; Locality: Top = Mammoth-St.Anthony Mine, Tiger, AZ, USA (Rich blue in Cerussite Matrix); Bottom = Rowley Mine, AZ, USA; (Lighter blue with Cerussite & Barite); Photography by Jim Hughes, Assisted by ♪ Melody ♫; Collection of ♪ Melody ♫, Applewood, CO, USA.

Diaboleite crystallizes in the form of micro-crystalline structures in the colour range of deep blue to pale blue to almost colourless. The mineral was first described by L.J. Spencer in 1923 and was named for the Greek word "apart", referring to its distinction from Boleite.

This mineral acts to bring consciousness to the dimensional transition to, and activities upon, the astral plane, further assisting one to actualize the conscious state during sleep, such that lucid dreaming provides for continuity between the physical and astral worlds, and between life in the physical realm and life in the realm which transcends the physical.

The transition from the physical realm to the astral dimension is not instantaneous, but is sudden and direct. One passes through the dimensional planes quickly and easily. Discarnate friends and/or incarnate friends who are also visiting the astral plane in a state of awareness, may be encountered. One may also meet incarnate friends who are not cognizant of being on the astral plane and will not, or will only vaguely, remember the encounter; one may also form new friendships, with those from other parts of the physical world and with whom problem-solving, philosophical discussions, etc., can be undertaken during future meetings.

It has also been used to enhance the production and marketing of crafts and art forms. It furthers ones pursuits in the manufacturing and retailing fields, bringing the energy to stimulate the influx of customers and the sufficiency of commodities.

Energizing of elixirs and tinctures has been amplified via Diaboleite.

It has been used in the treatment of disorders associated with less than adequate motor skills and in the amelioration of conditions associated with dysfunctions of the brain and the pineal gland. It has inhibited over-eating and over-consumption, and has facilitated the amelioration of dysfunctional metabolism.

The slight lead content of this mineral precludes its use in the normal method of preparation of an elixir.

Vibrates to the number 1.

**"CLEAVE THE ROCK AND I AM THERE"**

Gnostic Gospels

## EASTONITE

[Astrological Sign of Pisces]

***EASTONITE*** - $K_2Mg_5Al_4Si_5O_{20}(OH)_4$; Hardness 2.5-3; Locality: Easton, PA, USA; Photography by Jim Hughes, Assisted by ♪ Melody ♫; Collection of ♪ Melody ♫, Applewood, CO, USA.

Eastonite is a member of the Biotite family and usually crystallizes in the formation of thin lustrous green-grey laminae and tabular or short prismatic crystals or plates. The mineral was first described by A.N. Winchell in 1925 and was named for Easton, Pennsylvania, the locality where it was discovered.

In addition to the properties listed in the BIOTITE section of "Love Is In The Earth - A Kaleidoscope Of Crystals Update", this mineral has been used to increase the oscillatory rate for changing states of the body and the consciousness. With intent, the user is able to gain momentum for the changes and to return to the initiating location with permanent results.

It also augments the vision of the third-eye, bringing information concerning structures in ones life and structures from past times and civilizations. The pathway to channeling information from other realms is unobstructed with the application of this mineral.

Eastonite may also be used to facilitate ones understanding of present circumstances and past patterns, to allow for knowledge with respect to whether one is a "star person", to further define the lifetime in which one was a "star person", to discover the reasons for coming to Earth, and to ascertain the point of origin. The arrays also facilitate inter-planetary and/or inter-galactic communication.

It assists on in the ability to turn away from a life of non-questioning and toward a life where questioning is a common occurrence. One can find in the secrets of this life, the answers to secrets not of this life.

This is a wonderful mineral within which to "carry an angel", an angel to bring peace, to dispel chaos, etc. One can easily program Eastonite with the positivity of angelic work, subsequently giving the mineral to another. Please note that the mineral will not accept negative programming. The programming is facilitated by: first, writing that which one desires to be given; second, placing the stone on top of the paper and concentrating on sending the energy into the Eastonite. One will either feel a "tingling" or a flow of warm or cool air after the programming has been completed. It is a lovely thought and a lovely deed to facilitate this adventure.

It also brings an energy to assist one in astrology and astronomy, supporting one in decision-making with respect to correct methodology and procedures.

It has been used to help one in purchasing - assuring the "right" merchandise is available, and assuring a "good" price for value.

Eastonite provides a "fun" energy, promoting the consciousness of all sensation one experiences and/or creates, while further supporting one in the enjoyment of same.

It has been used to assist in the assimilation of potassium, in the treatment of neuromuscular disorders, disorders of the thyroid, the spleen, the adenoids, the cardio-vascular system, and the veins. It is excellent as an elixir.

Vibrates to the number 9.

# ELECTRUM

[Astrological Signs of Leo & Cancer]

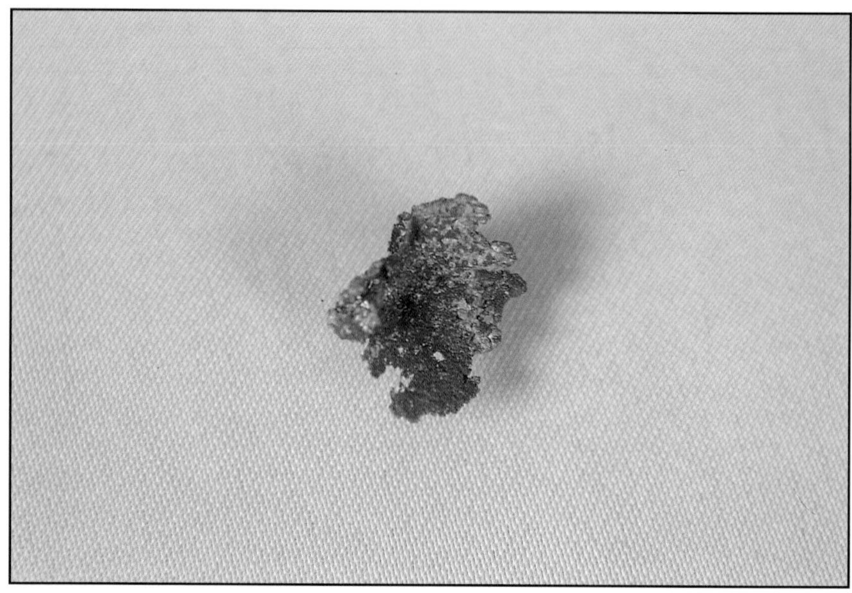

ELECTRUM - AuAg - 91% Silver, 4.2% Gold in minor Acanthite matrix; Hardness 2.5-3; Locality: Green's Creek Mine, Juneau, Alaska, USA; Photography by Jim Hughes, Assisted by ♪ Melody ♫; Collection of ♪ Melody ♫, Applewood, CO, USA.

Electrum crystallizes in the form of highly malleable strings, scales, and small plates and particles. It is usually available in its tarnished greyish state, but upon removal of the tarnish, the colour ranges from silvery white to a pale metallic yellow. The mineral must contain more than 20% silver to be classified as Electrum. The name is sometimes spelled with a "k" instead of a "c". The mineral was first described by Pliny in 77 A.D. and was named for the Greek word "amber" since, prior to tarnishing, it exhibits a golden colour. The following properties are in addition to those listed in the GOLD, SILVER, and ACANTHITE sections of "Love Is In The Earth - A Kaleidoscope Of Crystals Update".

This mineral is said to be the mythical stone (Escarmoucle) used by the Knights of the Round Table, to promote success in confrontation, in debating, and in conflict resolution. It is said to have provided communication skills, strength and fortitude, and a protective shield of energy for each holder.

It can facilitate electrical stimulation from the force fields of the Earth and has been used to expedite the receipt of information from all realms, for "tapping into" the universal source of power, and for bringing strength and determination to ones life. It represents the creative forces and advances the application of the energies of the Earth via the electrical force fields which are established within the structure of the mineral.

It can be used to open the heart, crown, and base chakras and, when focussed, can align these chakras with the ethereal system. It is also used to cleanse ones environment and to promote an atmosphere of calm.

Electrum has been used as a "touchstone" to provide verification of authenticity for messages which are given via auguries from the world of natural phenomena. The "touchstone" provides for a connection with the "absolutes of nature" which govern ones actions - i.e., honesty, purity, love, and unselfishness. If the message contains these qualities and does not contradict ones intrinsic morality, the answer may be safely implemented. The answer to all questions will also be based upon the enhancement of ones efficiency, strength, and loving progress. It should be noted that the world of natural phenomena may be incited via contact in physical of photographic form; one method is via placement of the mineral upon the object and via, subsequently, requesting the prophecy and/or information.

The energy of Electrum allows the body to heal itself by absorbing and transmuting negative energy into positive energy. It emits a sunny and bright soothing energy which helps to calm nerves and to enliven the disposition.

It is an excellent energy for healing situations. It facilitates the internal adjustment to ones external environment, providing for a direct receipt and an appropriate routing of vibratory energies to the proper nerve centers, with subsequent transmission, via the sympathetic nervous system, to the appropriate organs of the body. The stimulating vibrations are reinforceed and provide for proper metabolic responses. It has also been used to lessen fevers and to restore the optimum body temperature.

Vibrates to the number 7.

## EUCRYPTITE

[Astrological Sign of Libra]

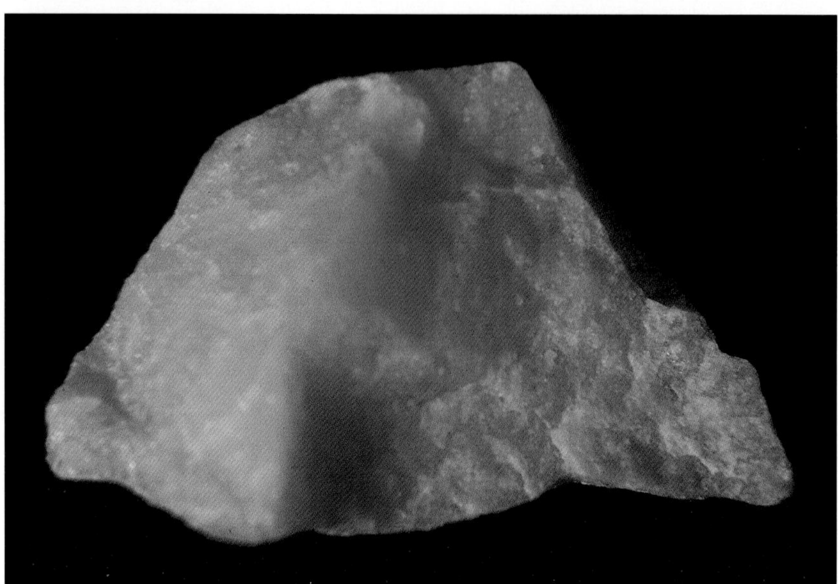

***EUCRYPTITE*** - $LiAlSiO_4$; Hardness 5.5-6; Locality: Bikita, Zimbabwe; Photography by Jim Hughes, Assisted by ♪ Melody ♫; Collection of ♪ Melody ♫, Applewood, CO, USA.

Eucryptite crystallizes in the form of hexagonal crystals and masses and is, usually, intergrown with Albite. The colour ranges from white to translucent colourless. The mineral was first described by G.J. Brush and E.S. Dana in 1880 and was named for the Greek word "well concealed", since it occurs closely intergrown with Albite. For all formations inclusive of Albite, the integration of the ALBITE section of "Love Is In The Earth - A Kaleidoscope Of Crystals Update" is suggested.

This mineral has been used to stimulates the acupressure/acupuncture meridians and to facilitate the preservation of same.

It has been used at the crown chakra to provide activation and to produce a peace which permeates the inner essence of ones being. It is an excellent stone for those who are not totally relaxed when expressing the emotions of the heart space.

It assists one in attaining deep meditative states and provides for centering in all situations; it helps one to become rather "invisible" and to remove the consciousness, when in the midst of a crowd; hence, eliminating the modes of distraction and sustaining the innate wisdom in the midst of chaos or absurdity.

It can be used during radionic analysis; holding a piece of Eucryptite and placing a piece of Eucryptite on the witness <u>or</u> using a pendulum of this stone, the energy of the stone interferes with the energy of the user and points to the problem[s] involved. It has also been used to assist in the location of energy blockages within the body; placing the Eucryptite upon the different areas of the body, one can usually feel a change in temperature at the location of the obstruction.

It is a sacred stone of the Rhodesian native cultures and has been used for centuries for communication with the physical and spiritual animal worlds. It further serves to "call-in" ones totem animal and to provide for a connected-ness in "service".

This mineral is also very useful for gridding ones environment; as a agent for producing tranquility with attentiveness, it has been used to grid classrooms; it has served successfully in gridding shopping centers, conference rooms, concert halls, etc., to lessen confusion and discordant energies. It has also been used in gridding disorderly areas of the Earth, helping to bring stability to the structure of the ley lines and of the tectonic plates.

It has assisted in the alignment of the universal energy forces to produce abundance and to eliminate or to rectify dis-ease.

It has been used to eliminate energy blockages which encourage the onset of dysfunctions within the body. It can also be used to stimulate the secretion and stimulation of endorphins and to promote the alleviation of stress, tension, and nervous disorders. It has been used for RNA/DNA structuring and re-building, to promote stability in cellular development, and to assist in the energy deflection of radiation and microwaves from ones auric field.

Vibrates to the number 7.

## EUDIALYTE

[Astrological Sign of Virgo]

***EUDIALYTE*** - $Na_{16}Ca_6Fe_3Zr_3(Si_3O_9)_2(Si_9O_{27})_2(OH,Cl)_4$ or $Na_4(CaCe)_2(Fe^{2+}MnY)ZrSi_8O_{22}(OHCl)_2$(?); Hardness 5-5.5; Locality: Chibine, Kola Penninsula, Russia; Photography by Jim Hughes, Assisted by ♪ Melody ♫; Collection of ♪ Melody ♫, Applewood, CO, USA.

Eudialyte crystallizes in the form of masses and micro-tabular and rhombohedral crystals. The colour range includes pink, rose, red, and red-brown. The mineral was first described by F. Stromeyer in 1819 and was named from the Greek words for "easy" and "to dissolve", referring to its solubility in acids.

This mineral promotes the anisotropic (variable with direction) energies of sound waves, assisting in clairaudient capabilities and in the stabilization of the variables from which they emanate. It is a directional energy which acts to block multiple transmissions and to enhance those which are definite and distinct. It serves as a fine-tuner for transmissions.

It further stimulates both the Alpha and the Beta states, supporting the discharge of the Beta brain wave pattern to the level of the conscious mind; it activates the Alpha brain wave pattern on the level of the dreaming mind, during the creative state, and with the initiation of minimal extra sensory perception [ESP] and cellular energy renewal. There is measurable increase in both the Alpha and the Beta states after holding Eudialyte for one hour.

This mineral has been used to both open and to activate the heart chakra and has been known as a "stone of the heart land", representing the perfection of the unconditional spiritual love of "All That Is" and facilitating the manifestation of this energy on the Earth plane. The energy flows from the crown to the base chakra, opening the chakras and providing for a pathway for the movement of the Kundalini. It is quite effective at the heart chakra, stimulating a resonant love which can be felt by others and which is totally "in-tune" with the vibratory energies of the perfect state of the universe.

Among the ancients it has also been known as the "stone of Hyacinthus", one which dispels jealousy and rings the "bell" in ones mind and in ones heart whenever soul-travelers reunite. Often times the reunification is for but a brief time, but the energy of the stone assists the participants in recognizing and in understanding the encounter for exactly "what it is".

Eudialyte serves to infuse the being with inspiration and confidence. The insights are astonishing when one holds the mineral and allows for the connection between the emotional body and the intellect. The energy also acts to facilitate "absent-forgiveness" such that one can separate oneself from the anger, guilt, resentment, hostility, animosity, despondency, depression, anguish, sorrow, etc., which limits ones self-love and the ability to give love to others. It should be noted that "beliefs" which are contrary to ones worthiness of self-love and/or love from others are frequently based on past feelings that one has acted in an unloving manner toward another [or others] and/or another [or others] have acted in an unloving way toward oneself.

Eudialyte has been used in the treatment of disorders of the optics of the eyes. It has also been used to exact definitive locations of disorder and to amplify the sympathetic vibration of the outer bodies in order to stimulate expeditious response.

Vibrates to the number 3.

♪ IS IT A COINCIDENCE,
OR AN IMMENSE OPPORTUNITY? ♫

## FAIRFIELDITE

[Astrological Sign of Aries]

***FAIRFIELDITE*** - $Ca_2(Mn,Fe)(PO_4)_2 \cdot 2H_2O$; Hardness 3.5; Locality: Foote Mine, Kings Mountain, Cleveland County, NC, USA; Photography by Jim Hughes, Assisted by ♪ Melody ♫; Collection of ♪ Melody ♫, Applewood, CO, USA.

Fairfieldite crystallizes in the formation of foliated or fibrous crystalline aggregates. The colour ranges from white to green-white to pale straw-yellow. The mineral was first described by G.J. Brush and E.S. Dana in 1879 and was named for Fairfield County, Connecticut, a locality where it is found.

This mineral brings the energy of global awareness on the physical and intellectual levels. It is an excellent energy for promotion of Earth-healing, Earth-restratification, and Earth-children.

It has been used to assist one in "seeing" the aura, and tends to enhance the aura and to produce a halo-effect around ones body.

It activates and energizes the heart chakra and the intellect, bringing logical thought to interactions of the emotional side of ones nature.

Fairfieldite is an energy of growth, bringing happiness and virtue and assisting in the actualization of ambitions, calmness and balance in decision-making, and discrimination in actions.

It can be used to stimulate "returning" to ones origin, immediately prior to this life or to the state of the creation of the self. It assists one in recognizing the karmic patterns and the lessons one has chosen, promoting acceptance of responsibility for ones reality. It is an excellent array for use during sessions involving ascension and meditation, providing for clarity via calming of the mind.

It assists one in building structures within ones life, organizing systems, and establishing basic foundations for personal development. It can also be used to assist one in the conservation of resources and in the attainment of prestige via tenacity and continuance of action. It assists in the relief of inhibition, providing for equilibrium of the emotions. It is an excellent mineral for those who have, or who are applying for, Security Clearances; it produces the ideal of "right action" and "right conduct" and maintains same.

It has been used to grid vegetation, to produce bountiful and healthy yields; it is a configuration for the Earth and the mountains, stimulating stability and strength.

Fairfieldite can assist in the discovery of mineral deposits and in the study of geology and geological forces. It can provide visions, given background information, with respect to locations of that which has not been discovered and/or that which has been "lost".

It has been used to promote the study of history, traditions, mathematics, and Eastern religions.

Fairfieldite has been used in the treatment of leukemia, mending of bones, disorders of the pneumogastric nerve and the vagus nerve, diphtheria, hyperacidity, and malnutrition. It has assisted in the alleviation of obesity and the causes behind the symptom. It has also been used in the energizing/stabilizing of ointments to promote longevity.

Vibrates to the number 5.

## FLUORITE - BLUE JOHN [Astrological Sign of Scorpio]

***FLUORITE-BLUE JOHN*** **-** $CaF_2$ - Vitreous banded colourless, blue, white, and purple, with film-like inclusions of petroleum and, occasionally, a fluorite/ petroleum mixed coating (in the rough state); Hardness 4; Locality: New Zealand; Photography by Dave Shrum, Colorado Camera; Collection of ♪ Melody ♫, Applewood, CO, USA. Gift of Peter & Sylvia Simpson, New Zealand.

Blue John Fluorite usually crystallizes in the form of masses with the colour ranging from white, blue, colourless, and purple, and containing film-like inclusions of petroleum. Fluorite was first described by C.A.G. Napione in 1797 and was named for its fluoride content. Blue John (Fluorite) was first described by R. Kirwan in 1785 and was a local name given to the discovery of this configuration in Derbyshire, England. The following properties are in addition to those listed in the GOLD and FLUORITE sections of "Love Is In The Earth - A Kaleidoscope Of Crystals Update".

This mineral has been used in gridding arrangements to stimulate the restructuring of the ozone layer in ones environment. Used in planetary awareness and global meditations, it can further facilitate the healing of that stratospheric layer for the Earth.

Blue John Fluorite has been used to further pursuits in accounting, computing, "Web surfing", and the martial arts. It facilitates precision and enhances ones dexterity, and competency in the chiropractic field, in the realms of chemistry and alchemy, and in healing.

It is an excellent stone for braving the unknown, acting as a catalyst for change and personal growth, and enabling one to go beyond that which is remembered. Used during physical travel, it promotes courage in experimentation of the new and promotes understanding of others. It stimulates altruistic pursuits, spontaneity, and the exploration of the "fresh". The mineral provides for an atypical perspective and encourages discovery. It can also promote visions of the future, allowing one to remain detached and as an observer. It further serves to instill trust and to assist one in considering the highest "good" during decision-making. It helps one to extricate the self from undesirable situations and acts to initiate and to provide courage for the permanence of a total departure from ones lifestyle; this facilitates and enhances the commencement of a fresh and dynamic life.

It can also be used to assist in the activities associated with "cloud-busting". During cloud-busting activities the Blue-John Fluorite has been placed at the bottom of the rod; it has also been placed upon a photograph of the desired result.

If ones power animal is in the family of the mammal, the array can stimulate ethereal and/or dream visits by same. The visitations have been conducive to immediate healing, to the awakening of the inner forces so that one may actualize that which is desired, and to the facilitation of contact between the self and ones etheric double.

When used as an elixir, Blue John Fluorite has also been said to ease fatigue and to promote the assimilation of minerals. It has been used in the treatment of chills, equilibration of body heat, hypothermia, electrolytic imbalance, emphysema, lubrication of the joints, and restoration of muscular and cellular fluids. It has also been said to assist in restoring women from the effects of "mysterious weaknesses".

Vibrates to the number 4.

## FLUORITE - ENHYDRO [Astrological Signs of Pisces & Capricorn]

***FLUORITE-ENHYDRO*** - $CaF_2$ - Vitreous transparent purple; Hardness 4; Locality: Durango, Mexico; Photography by Dave Shrum, Colorado Camera; Collection of ♪ Melody ♬, Applewood, CO, USA.

The Enhydro Fluorite has been found in the colour purple. Fluorite was first described by C.A.G. Napione in 1797 and was named for its fluoride content. The Enhydro was first described by T. Egleston in 1887, representing the inclusion of water within geodes. In addition to the properties listed in the ENHYDRO and FLUORITE sections of "Love Is In The Earth - A Kaleidoscope Of Crystals Update", this mineral introduces the "Law of Rational Counterparts", such that the "stream of change" can flow through one with the strength and rapidity one selects. It acts upon the esoteric teaching of mystery, hidden philosophies, and truths of the ages, while influencing inductive reasoning.

It is said to have been found in a grid-like pattern in the Sun and Moon Pyramids in Mexico and to promote the improvement of ones understanding of the planetary occurrences during the last thousands of years. Due to the continental drift, it appears that the grid patterns have supported the noted relationships of planetary architectural orchestration such that all of the Mexican pyramids are in position to "communicate" between themselves. Further experimentation with selected arrays of grid patterns, using this mineral, has produced communication between the spirits of the ancient members of the research teams.

The Enhydro Fluorite also represents a law in physics which states that water will reach its own level by its own weight and further supports the corresponding principle of metaphysics which states that consciousness will externalize at its own level, by its own recognition. The label for this principle can be called trust, personification, or ..., and truly responds and conforms to ones mental states.

The mineral assists one in turning away from rationalizing restriction allowing for the understanding that to acknowledge limitation is to accept it and to accentuate the state of consciousness which produced the condition.

This mineral has been used to facilitate all orders of connections and acts to strengthen same. It supports the attunement between the self and another, similar to the action produced by the Faden Crystal, the Oaxaccamer, and the Herkimer diamond. It assists in producing and in maintaining the ethereal connection which one has with another [on any plane, and in all dimensions].

It is a stone for finding ones complement on the physical plane, serving as a magnetic field to attract ones counterpart and to facilitate an unfathomable energy transfer between the self and the other. It is a stone of "seeking", assisting one in "ferreting-out" information which is either hidden or unknown. It is an excellent stone for future-telling and telepathic activities.

It has been used to promote the "turning-away" from dis-ease, without knowing the bases, but with allowing the trust; this has produced miracles which can transform the body and the world, with little comprehension of how the miracles have been accomplished. It facilitates "mending" on all levels, assisting one to trace ones actions/belief systems back to the original cause of a disorder, and subsequently, promoting the restoration.

Vibrates to the number 6.

***FLUORITE-RAINBOW*** **-** $CaF_2$ - Vitreous transparent with a variety of colours; Hardness 4; Locality: Minas Gerais, Brasil, South America; Photography by Jim Hughes, Assisted by ♪ Melody ♬; Collection of ♪ Melody ♬, Applewood, CO, USA.

Rainbow Fluorite crystallizes in the form of masses, grains, columns, cubes, octahedra, and rhombdodecahedra crystals. The colour range is endless and the mixture of colours appears never to be the same. Fluorite was first described by C.A.G. Napione in 1797 and was named for its fluoride content. The addition of "Rainbow" to the name is due to the exhibition of multi-colour bands of hues included within the mineral. In addition to the properties listed in the FLUORITE section of "Love Is In The Earth - A Kaleidoscope Of Crystals Update", this mineral is another which exhibits the energies for our "Indigo Children", encouraging the presence of the appropriate members of the angelic realm and the manifestation of same, while producing the energies of perception, simplicity, safety, and love. It further assists in providing for varied information transfers between one and the world of guides, decorating information with beauty, benefit, and enchantment, while promoting re-energization for all. The Rainbow Fluorite elixir is excellent for stimulating multiple contact and for enhancing the beauty and the protective state which is evidenced.

The mineral also promotes self-sufficiency such that one does not allow ones happiness to rest in others and such that there is no anxiety demonstrated or felt during confrontations. It also assists one to identify the differences in "love", furthering realization that "falling" in love implies some loss of balance, while "being" in love implies being in the moment with the emotions.

The energy of Rainbow Fluorite is also provides the bases for the multi-dimensional pathways used by the Ayahuasca shamen in Brasil; the mineral is used to facilitate access and to assist one in traversing the realities. It has also been used in the removal of ethereal cords and to protect and to shield one against psychic attack.

Rainbow Fluorite activates and energies all chakras and has been used in the treatment of disorders of the corpuscles, the arterial pathways, emotional trauma, and vertebrae. It has also been used in Shiatsu and in deep tissue massage to assist both the practitioner and the subject to journey to the interior of the body and to retrieve information concerning emotional and/or physical blockages.

Vibrates to the number 8.

**"A ROCK BETWEEN YOUR CHEEK AND GUM,
GEM ELIXIR, HERE I COME"**

Gary "Horsefeathers" Wallace
DC, USA

## GALAXYITE

[Astrological Signs of Gemini, Scorpio, & Leo]

***GALAXYITE*** - $(Ca,Na)(Si,Al)_4O_8$ in $(K,Na,Ca,Ba,NH_4)(Si,Al)_4O_8$; Hardness 5-6 in Feldspar (6-6.5); Locality: Quebec, Canada; Photography by Jim Hughes, Assisted by ♪ Melody ♫; Collection of ♪ Melody ♫, Applewood, CO, USA.

Galaxyite is a massive formation of micro-labradorite crystals in Feldspar. The primary difference between Galaxyite and Labradorite is that the Galaxyite contains both Feldspar and micro-crystals of Labradorite. It was first described in 1995 by a miner from Quebec as Galaxite, but the mineral Galaxite exists in a different form and is recognized by the mineralogical community. Hence, the addition of the "y", to remain with the consistency of the miner's intentions. The following properties are in addition to those listed in the FELDSPAR and LABRADORITE sections of "Love Is In The Earth - A Kaleidoscope Of Crystals Update".

This mineral is one to teach us that love does not consist of two people looking at each other, but of looking together in the same direction. It brings the positive light energy of collective consciousness, between two or more people, providing a force to guide the energies in a focussed direction, allowing for the consideration of the many facets of the focus.

Galaxyite is a stone facilitating "Self-Organized Criticality", the complex dynamical phenomena (similar to earthquakes, tides, and evolution) which has achieved growing popularity among scientists, and which is a model of a system which reaches the "critical" state without intervention, without fine-tuning of parameters, and with the absence of a single well-defined time scale. Simply stated, this mineral promotes the occurrence of events of all sizes, with insignificant events occurring frequently and with significant events occurring infrequently; the specific overall focus is defined by the user and the occurrences are based upon punctuated equilibrium. Hence, when using Galaxyite, one may focus, intend, and then wait for the subtle changes preceding the major changes (bringing preparedness, familiarization with the process which will occur, and precognizance of events).

It is a "stone for discovery", bringing the sensation and the actualization of discovery and inventiveness from the Inner Self to the conscious mind, providing the information, and the actuality, that "things are moving".

The mineral represents the galaxy, and has been used to facilitate contact with the extra-terrestrial beings of higher spirituality. Used for gridding, carried, or worn, it has provided shielding from negative energies and negative events.

This mineral has been used, with excellent results, for gridding for polarity balancing, and for transmuting that which is unwanted. It can also be used to quicken lucidity during contemplation and can enhance the stabilization of the frequency of brain wave transmissions. It can provide for a connection to the psychic self, awakening the energy of the third-eye and expediting the verbalization of that which is encountered. It has also been used as an attunement mechanism, between two or more people and between the self and the environment, the world, the galaxy, and the infinite.

It has been used in the treatment of the eyes, the alimentary canal, and the blood vessels, to release heat from fevers, to ameliorate brucellosis, and to support cellular reconstruction. It can also be used to energize additional minerals and to support the transfer of energies during healing.

Vibrates to the number 5.

# GARNET - GOLDEN AURA [Astrological Signs of Scorpio & Leo]

***GARNET - GOLDEN AURA (Top - With No Back Light; Bottom - With Back Light);*** $(Mn,Fe)_3Al_2(SiO_4)_3$; Hardness 7.5; Locality: Dinner Bucket Ridge Mine, Idaho, USA; Photography by Colorado Camera; Collection of ♪ Melody ♫, Applewood, CO, USA. Gift of Jesse Williams, Idaho, USA.

Golden Aura Garnet is a form of the Manganalmandine Garnet which crystallizes in the form of compact and granular masses and dodecahedra or trapezohedra configurations; the "Golden Aura" is effected by a special patented process which involves no addition of other minerals and no irradiation, but causes the Manganese (Mn) and the higher than normal valence state of the Iron (Fe) to migrate (in varying amounts) to the surface. The colour without backlight is a metallic gold, and with backlight ranges from red-violet to blue-violet (daylight backlight) or a raspberry (incandescent backlight). Manganalmandine was first described by J. Palmgren in 1917; "Golden Aura" was selected by the author and the miner to describe the aura-like golden colour which envelopes. In addition to the properties listed in the GARNET section of "Love Is In The Earth - A Kaleidoscope Of Crystals Update", this mineral ties together the energies of all chakras and promotes both synthesis and alignment. An elixir form is a truly energizing agent.

It has been used to assist one in connecting with the ancient civilizations of Lemuria, Atlantis, Mu, etc., and in traveling to the original cultures representing the native tribes of the world. It has been utilized to reach these territories via the accessing of parallel dimensions where the cultures continue to exist, and has promoted the receipt of information concerning the associated rites, rituals, and ceremonies. Often ceremonial instruction is presented during the dream state; "journaling" is suggested.

This "stone of universal correlation" has also been used for astral/mind travel to within this universe and throughout other galaxies. The energies stimulate cooperative efforts between those of extra-terrestrial origins and those who are experiencing life on Earth, and assist in transcendence of the illusions of life and in re-connecting with the forces which assisted ones transition to this plane. It can be used to facilitate interdimensional travel and to promote future communication with other realms.

Golden Aura Garnet has been used in the treatment of body temperature regulation, inflammations of tissue, and to remove toxins from the body. It is currently being tested to validate the use for cancer, AIDS, and degenerative disorders. It has also shown success in RNA/DNA restructuring and in the treatment of tumors.

Golden Aura Garnet vibrates to the number 1.

## GARNET - SILVER AURA [Astrological Signs of Cancer & Taurus]

***GARNET - SILVER AURA (Top - With No Back Light; Bottom - With Back Light);*** $(Mn,Fe)_3Al_2(SiO_4)_3$; Hardness 7.5; Locality: Dinner Bucket Ridge Mine, Idaho, USA; Photography by Colorado Camera; Collection of ♪ Melody ♫, Applewood, CO, USA. Gifts of Jesse Williams, Idaho, USA.

Silver Aura Garnet is a form of the Manganalmandine Garnet which crystallizes in the form of compact and granular masses and dodecahedra or trapezohedra configurations; the "Silver Aura" is effected by a special patented process which involves no addition of other minerals and no irradiation, but causes the Manganese (Mn) and the higher than normal valence state of the Iron (Fe) to migrate (in varying amounts) to the surface. The colour without backlight is a metallic silver with flashes of varying colours, and with backlight is a lovely red-violet to blue-violet (daylight backlight) or a raspberry (incandescent backlight). "Silver Aura" was selected by the author and the miner to describe the aura-like silvery colours which envelope; Manganalmadine was first described by J. Palmgren in 1917. In addition to the properties listed in the GARNET section of "Love Is In The Earth - A Kaleidoscope Of Crystals Update", this mineral is representative of the entire gateway to actualization, the "Eight-Fold Path" which includes right views, aspirations, speech, conduct, mode of livelihood, effort, mindfulness, rapture. An elixir form is a truly facilitating agent.

This mineral assists in the transfer of the low voltage vital energy to facilitate the activation of the pathway which connects the Inner Self with the Higher Self [e.g., connection activation]. The pathway is activated to facilitate the transfer of thought-forms, relative to requests and entreaties, to the Higher Self; the activation clears the pathway and furnishes the Higher Self with a connective channel which may be used in the transmittal of instant and/or miraculous response to requests for healing. It also acts to facilitate the connection between the low voltage vital energy of the body and the medium voltage life energy of the mind, activating the connection between the conscious self and the Inner Self in order to raise the energy levels and to promote the free-flow of chemistry and magnetism within the body/mind and/or to transfer the flow from one person to another person or object. It further assists in the accumulation of same and can expedite "reserve" in all permeable materials; e.g., in wood, crystals, plants, animals, fabricated articles, ones bodies, and ones thoughts. A substantial discharge of this low voltage vital energy can supply an enormous amount of energy to that upon which it is released and can supply sufficient energy to move or to affect physical objects; it has also been used to facilitate the state of "wellness".

Silver Aura Garnet vibrates to the number 3.

## GARNET - RAINBOW

[Astrological Sign of Aquarius]

***GARNET - RAINBOW*** - $(Ca,Fe,Mg,Mn)_3(Al,Fe,Mn,Cr,Ti,V)_2(SiO_4)_3$ is the general formula - the Rainbow Garnet has trace inclusions (speculated to possibly be Titanium); Hardness 6.5-7.5; Locality: Mexico; Photography by Jim Hughes, Assisted by ♪ Melody ♫; Collection of ♪ Melody ♫, Applewood, CO, USA.

Rainbow Garnet, also known As Topazolite, is an andradite garnet with specific supplementary trace inclusion minerals providing a flash of rainbow colours on the outer layers and, sometimes, on polished areas and facets. It is unknown with respect to whom first described Garnet; the name, however, was derived from "granatum", defined as pomegranate, for the resemblance of this mineral to the seeds of this fruit. The name "Andradite" was first described by J.D. Dana in 1868 and was named for J.B. d'Andrada. The name "Topazolite" was first described as a variety of Andradite by B. Bonvoisin in 1806 and was named to characterize the Topazolite of Piedmont, Italy, which was of the colour and transparency of Topaz. In addition to the properties listed in the GARNET and ANDRADITE sections of "Love Is In The Earth - A Kaleidoscope Of Crystals Update", this mineral has all of the qualities of a friend, love without conditions, honour without pomposity, generosity without condescension, humour without malice, and courage with mercy.

It activates and energies the seven major chakras, providing for a clear path through which the Kundalini can progress. It begins with the base chakra, actually opening that chakra, and progresses through the remaining chakras with the movement of the stone.

It has been known as a "stone of the seventh mansion", accelerating meditative voyages to the domain of "all knowing", while mapping for the user the passageway to higher bliss. It provides for a direct approach to intensified strength and can be used to project the self into the higher dimensional awareness; this plane of awareness yielding a limitless zone of silence containing greater peace and unity than one has ever known.

The ancient cultures of the Aztecs are said to have used the energies of this structure in shamanic ceremonies to stimulate altered states.

The outer layer of "inclusive" minerals tend to emanate both positive and negative currents. These alternating currents are linked via the ethers to the forces of "revelation" through which charisma and desire are promulgated. When a request is directed through the Rainbow Garnet to the object or to the thought form which is desired, the mineral acts as a conductor for the message - sending the message to the ethers via a closed circuit of current which penetrates the energy field related to the apocalypse of disclosure. The message is then relayed to the universal mind which, in turn, refines the information and assures that the intent is for the good of all, before sending the transmission directly toward the physical plane. The energies of this mineral surpass both intervals and distance, inducing delicately-harmonized cooperation and rewards which grow from the idea/ideal which one desires to learn (as a physically manifested lesson or as an intellectual exercise).

It can be used to learn of health disorders within the body. It has been used in the treatment for the loss of sense of taste. Use as an elixir is an excellent method of dispersing the energy throughout the body; as an elixir, the request is directed through the elixir to the visualization of that which is to be learned.

Rainbow Garnet vibrates to the number 3 and Topazolite vibrates to the number 4.

***GASPEITE*** - (NiMgFe)$CO_3$; Hardness 4.5-5; Locality: Carr Boyd Mine, West Australia, Australia; Photography by Jim Hughes, Assisted by ♪ Melody ♫; Collection of ♪ Melody ♫, Applewood, CO, USA. Gift (polished specimen) from Maria Grundner, Australia.

Gaspeite crystallizes in the rhombohedral system and primarily in massive formation. The colour is a rich limey green. The mineral was first described by D.W. Kohls and J.L. Rodda in 1966 and was named for the Gaspé Peninsula where it was first discovered. In Australia, the mineral is also known as "Allura".

This mineral is said to bring spirituality in every day living, bringing the enchantment and attraction of sanctity to the user. It assists one in removing the curtain between the distress of ignorance and a very clear view of assurance.

It is also said to be used by the Aboriginal Tribes to gain visions and to provide success to endeavors. It has been used by this culture in diagnostic healing, in raising the consciousness toward the enlightened state, and in communicating with the spirits and with those from other worlds. It is thought to bring healing powers to the user and to provide protection from all dangers occurring on the physical plane. The energy has brought about the awakening from the "dream of illusion" and to promote the experience of the self as a part of the universal spirit.

It can be used to attract people toward one for friendship or business, such that the manifested attraction is "for the good of all". Sometimes, those wearing Gaspeite grow absorbed with the enormity of successes of mundane nature such that there is little time for the sacred; hence, a "break" is often necessary to assure continuation "on the path". Use of the "Super Seven" with Gaspeite ameliorates the necessity for the "break".

Gaspeite also enhances impartiality, yet resolution, and allows one to endure individually when conditions demand. It also assists one in understanding that it is "okay" to ask for, and to accept, help from others; it contributes to the insight of reality that assistance from another is, in truth, help from the self.

It has been used in the treatment of disorders of the lungs and to ameliorate the expansion of mucous glands in the bronchial walls. It can also be used to further the application of oxygen affecting the stimulation of the senses, speech, behavior, thought patterns and memory.

Gaspeite vibrates to the number 1. Allura vibrates to the number 8.

## GEARKSUTITE

[Astrological Sign of Virgo]

***GEARKSUTITE*** - $CaAlF_4OH \heartsuit H_2O$ or $CaAl(F,OH)_5 \heartsuit H_2O$ ; Hardness 2; Locality: Jamestown, Boulder County, Colorado, USA; Photography by Jim Hughes, Assisted by ♪ Melody ♫; Collection of ♪ Melody ♫, Applewood, CO, USA.

Gearksutite crystallizes in the form of snowy-white masses and acicular crystals. The mineral was first described by G. Hagemann in 1868 and was named from the combination of the Greek word for "earth" and the mineral Arksutite, due to the resemblance (in the earthy form) to Arksutite.

This mineral assists one in recognizing and in acting upon any suspicion, distrust, or disbelief, which is built upon past events and ones past experiences. It further assists one in releasing "injustices" which know not the constraints of rationality and/or self-preservation. It can be used to support one in approaching life with an expectation, and manifestation of enjoyment, such that, to be in the presence of the user, is a true pleasure.

Promoting ones vision of justice, it can be used to assist in attaining "higher" knowledge of legitimacy, fairness, and truth. Gearksutite is a mineral to bring understanding that the "truth" may cause pain to another, and in this circumstance, it can serve to bring the holder to that recognition such that a kinder version of the "truth" is realized and communicated.

The mineral does not suggest deception, but does suggest that kindness is more significant and more meaningful than veracity which leads to pain. The user may, in such instances, find it to be "second nature" to find the words to courteously say nothing.

Gearksutite is a mineral for the crown chakra and for the connective-ness between the crown chakra and the purity of the intellect. It furthers ones understanding of the bases for resolve and continues to produce the forceful affinity of bond between the higher spiritual self and the rational mind.

This mineral is one of resilience, quite valuable in imaging [for healing and/or for attracting healing], in meditation, and in projection. It helps one to absorb from the universe, the healing which is needed, prompting adaptability and agreeability to act. It helps one to creatively change ones personal world, enhancing awareness and inducing the states of healing expansiveness and healing manifestation.

It can also be used to traverse the gap between the physical world and the spiritual world, and can help to prepare one for the transition, promoting ease, love, and calmness during the movement. Gearksutite assists in the development of patience, strength, and perseverance, allowing one to recognize the desired course and to maintain the pathway which will produce the desired goal. It is helpful in matters of opposition, promoting advice to inspire the mind in worldly matters. It can provide for an advantage in "gaming" activities, stimulating the flash of an instantaneous imprint of the suggested next move, while encouraging action.

It has been used in the treatment of disorders of the teeth, the bones, ambulatory impairment, ruptures, strains and sprains, and acidosis, and to enhance mental acuity. It has been used to enhance the T-Cell count.

Vibrates to the number 1.

## GILLESPITE

[Astrological Sign of Scorpio]

***GILLESPITE*** - $BaFeSi_4O_{10}$ with white Sanbornite; Hardness 4; Locality: Baja, California, Mexico; Photography by Jim Hughes, Assisted by ♪ Melody ♫; Collection of ♪ Melody ♫, Applewood, CO, USA.

Gillespite crystallizes in the form of red tetragonal or hexagonal crystals. The mineral was first described by W.T. Schaller in 1922 and named for F. Gillespie.

This mineral brings the power to create wisdom and the understanding of non-destruction of same.

It can be used to facilitate the understanding of the akashic records and the individual and collective karma to which one has agreed. Providing for insight to "how" ones actions and thoughts impact the recorded information, it further assists one in influencing that which is inscribed. The techniques facilitated by this mineral (via meditation with same) have been used to assist one in the examination of past lives and to expedite "new directions" during ones present life. Holding the mineral, usually in conjunction with Sanbornite, tends to place one, at the commencement of the meditative state, with the akashic records; subsequently, leading one through the processes, mechanisms, and procedures for understanding and for reorganization and restyling.

Fostering contact with the angelic realm, this mineral assists one in learning about immortality and the basis it has in ones personal life; it furthers understanding of the afterworld and assists one in determining ones next incarnation.

It helps one to learn to extract vital information from the past, sifting through the trivial and insignificant and bringing forth the relevant such that one may discover superior potentials which have not been consciously recognized for many years. It teaches one that the knowledge of others is a sign of intelligence and perception, but to "know thyself" is a sign of wisdom; going beneath the superficial, this mineral teaches one to "know thyself".

The mineral assists in transforming consciousness, providing wisdom and logic to understand the varied methods of progression. It acts to present a listing of methodology, with clarification of definitive action.

Gillespite is a "stone of foundations", providing an energy for understanding the infrastructure of that which is consciously intended. The creation of groundwork is accomplished with ease, spontaneity, and expertise.

The mineral further promotes intuitive and inspirational writing, as well as automatic writing. It is a "stone for prophesy" auguring both adeptness and mastery.

Gillespite can be used in the treatment of disorders of the intestines and for detecting where dis-ease is located. In combination with Sanbornite, it has assisted the cellular members of the body to act in a cooperative manner, bringing balance to the structure, to the autonomic and sympathetic nervous systems, and to the generative systems.

The Sanbornite with Gillespite configuration merges the energies of both to provide a very powerful energy.

Gillespite vibrates to the number 6.

♪ HAVE YOU NOTICED
HOW ONE CONDEMNS,
MOST SELF-RIGHTEOUSLY,
THAT WHICH ONE
HAS NEVER HAD
THE OPPORTUNITY TO DO? ♫

## HANCOCKITE

[Astrological Sign of Capricorn]

***HANCOCKITE*** - $CaPbAl_3(Si_2O_7)(SiO_4)(O,OH)_2$ or $(Pb,Ca,Sr)_2(Al,Fe^{+3})_3Si_3O_{12}OH$; Hardness 6-7; Locality: Franklin, Sussex Co., NJ, USA; Photography by Jim Hughes, Assisted by ♪ Melody ♫; Collection of ♪ Melody ♫, Applewood, CO, USA.

Hancockite crystallizes in the formation of tan to brownish-red lath-like crystals. The mineral was first described by S.L. Penfield and C.H. Warren in 1899 and was named for E.P. Hancock.

This mineral assists one in "mindfulness" on "new" planes. One may go either within this dimension or outside of this dimension while being totally "in the moment". It acts to dissipate critical-ness, to amplify insight, to inspire interaction and participation with others, and to augment individual power.

It is a stone to assist one in eliminating the afflictions of loneliness, dysfunctional relationships, losses on the physical plane, and grief due to "death". Providing an inner attunement with the user, ones innate strength and ingenuity are activated in order to provide focus toward ones hopes and dreams.

Hancockite produces the knowledge of a workable approach to mystical awareness, helping one to develop and to implement practical techniques for enriching ones consciousness through nourishing ones personal inner garden and through enhancing ones clarity and insight.

It provides the energy for one to recognize life after death, furthers contact and communication with those who have transcended the physical reality, and allows the illumination from the other side to be transmitted and received. It can provide the stimulus to allow one to connect with other worlds via automatic writing. It can be used to calm the emotions, to stimulate the aspect of unconditional love, and to help one to flow through stressful situations. This mineral also assists one in writing personal thoughts clearly. It is also helpful in verbal communication and in enhancing ones listening abilities.

This mineral can bring omnipresent efficiency in the course of confusion and disorder. It can accelerate constructive formation within ones life, and contributes both a balancing in associations and an eradication of criticism.

It also assists in the elimination of indications of oversensitivity.

The word "speed" is key to the energy of Hancockite; speed bringing acceleration to completion, speed bringing rapidity to results, speed bringing swiftness to the thought process.

It is helpful to teachers, providing for an optimization in teaching capabilities and bringing an energy to invoke understanding within any conference or gathering.

It is also useful to combat dehydration and fatigue, infectious conditions, and muscular cramps, to assist in weight loss, and in the treatment of disorders associated with the nervous system, mental awareness, and thyroid and parathyroid.

The slight possible lead content of this mineral precludes its use in the normal method of preparation of an elixir.

Vibrates to the master number 44.

## HOLMQUISTITE [Astrological Signs of Capricorn & Scorpio]

***HOLMQUISTITE*** - $Li_2(Mg,Fe^{2+})_3Al_2Si_8O_{22}(OH)_2$; Hardness 5-6; Locality: Sao Joao del Rei, MG, Brasil (Inclusion in Quartz Sphere) and Foote Mine, Kings Mtn, Cleveland Co., NC, USA (Rough); Photography by Jim Hughes, Assisted by ♪ Melody ♫; Collection of ♪ Melody ♫, Applewood, CO, USA.

Holmquistite crystallizes in the orthorhombic system, usually in the form of fibrous structures. The colour ranges from light to dark blue/grey and from violet to violet-black. The mineral was first described by A. Osann in 1913 and was named for P.J. Holmquist.

This mineral has been used for stress reduction and to alleviate despondency. It can enhance the generation of the life-sustaining negative ions in ones environment, activating the instinct of self-preservation and enhancing the awareness of well-being.

It can be used to locate energy blockages within the body; placing the Holmquistite upon the different areas of the body, one can usually feel a slight "tingling" at the location of the obstruction. It is also very useful for gridding ones environment; as a calming agent and to assist in stabilizing disorderly areas of the Earth, helping to bring equilibrium to the structure of the ley lines and tectonic plates.

It allows one to experience the "strength of ones own medicine", helping one to understand (and to apply the techniques for actualization) that ones faculties include the ability to achieve the perfect state.

This mineral can help to dissipate controversy and is quite useful during disputes. Placement of another mineral on this "stone" will remove discordant vibrations from the other mineral; allowing a piece of Holmquistite to be a member of ones environment will produce the removal of discordant vibrations from that environment.

Holmquistite in Quartz combines the properties of these two minerals and further produces a significant increase in energy transfer.

This mineral can assist in the relief of tension and stress-related disorders. It can also be used to promote the relaxation of wrinkles [e.g., via an elixir]. It can be used in the treatment of disorders related to tendinitis, leg cramps, "tight" shoulder muscles, and elimination. It can assist in soothing the nervous system, stabilizing the flow of blood, and in calming the heart. It can also be used in activities to restructure the RNA/DNA.

Holmquistite vibrates to the number 6. Holmquistite in Quartz vibrates to the number 1.

## HUNTITE With DAQINGSHANITE

[Astrological Signs of Scorpio & Taurus]

***HUNTITE with Daqingshanite*** - Huntite ($CaMg_3(CO_3)_4$) with Daqingshanite $(Sr,Ca,Ba)_2(Ce,La)PO_4(CO_3,OH,F)_3$; Hardness 2-4.5; Locality: Cimarron Mtns., Pima County, AZ, USA; Photography by Jim Hughes, Assisted by ♪ Melody ♫; Collection of ♪ Melody ♫, Applewood, CO, USA.

Huntite crystallizes as white chalky masses and nodules in the rhombohedral system, usually in isostructural conjunction with Daqingshanite, a rare earth mineral occurring as a vitreous pale to earthy yellow coating and/or intergrowth. Huntite was first described by G.T. Faust in 1953 and was named for W.F. Hunt. Daqingshanite was first described by R. Yingchen, X. Lulu, and P. Zhizhong in 1983 and was named for Mt. Daqingshan in Mongolia, China, where it was first discovered.

Huntite with Daqingshanite can be used to assist one in pursuits of searching and seeking.

It acts as a guide to lead one in the direction in which one will locate that which is being sought, actually operating as a significator to guide one toward the "end result".

It is a mineral for mineral collectors; bringing knowledge of the mineral kingdom and strengthening intuitive information with respect to chemistry and locality. Used with another mineral, it can provide insight to scientific information concerning the other mineral and can guide one to the habitat locality.

A mineral of "habit", it assists one in establishing or dissolving patterns and practices - depending upon the intent of the user.

It has provided for inscrutability in the behavior of "problem people", promoting the realization of ones actions and the effects of those actions upon others in the immediate environment.

Huntite with Daqingshanite is a powerful combination of the beautiful romantic poet and the huntress, Artemis. It tends to soften the male qualities and to bring the peace and blessings of the female. (Not to say that the feminine side is all peace and blessings.) It can provide for intense stimulation of the intuition; the mineral is excellent for use by those who are familiar with the avenues of psychic awareness.

The combination further assists one in projecting the impression that is desired for any situation and circumstance. This projection is for protection and not for evasion of ones inner light.

It can further stimulate a "welcome pause" to ones hectic and chaotic life, allowing one to rest quietly and peacefully while still having "thousands of "things" to "do" and to effect". It brings to play the theory of flexible adjustment, to facilitate the integration of all that transpires.

This combination of minerals can assist in instilling adhesive properties in the body, supporting mending and restoration of muscles, bones, and organs. It has been used to abate the bases of frigidity and to help one to apply resourcefulness to handle ones sexuality with tranquility.

The slight possible strontium content of this mineral precludes its use in the normal method of preparation of an elixir.

Huntite vibrates to the number 7. Huntite with Daqingshanite vibrates to the master number 99. Daqingshanite vibrates to the number 2.

**♪ SOME WOULD SAY THIS PAGE IS WHITE,**
**MY JUDGMENT TELLS ME IT IS SO,**
**BUT AM I SURE?**
**AND DO I KNOW? ♬**

I

## INDERITE

[Astrological Sign of Aries]

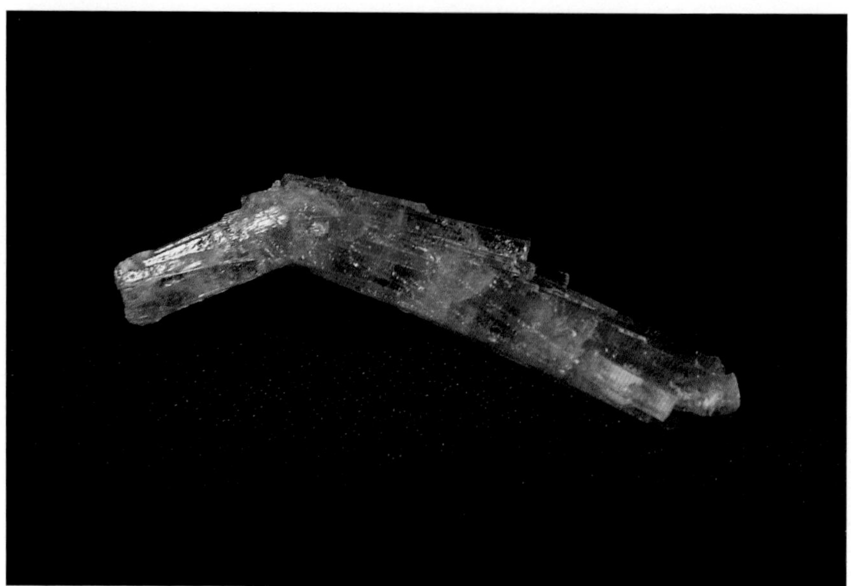

***INDERITE*** - $MgB_3O_3(OH)_5$♥$5H_2O$; Hardness 3; Locality: Near Boron, Kramer Borate Deposit, Kern Co., CA, USA; Photography by Jim Hughes, Assisted by ♪ Melody ♫; Collection of ♪ Melody ♫, Applewood, CO, USA.

Inderite crystallizes in the monoclinic system in the form of vitreous, pearly, colourless crystals. The mineral was first described by A.M. Boldyreva and E.N. Egorova in 1937 and was named for the Kzyl-tau Deposit in Inder, Kazakhstan, where it was first discovered.

This mineral is one for the crown chakra, also stimulating the mind to instill theoretical judgment.

It assists one to recognize the "fool" both within the self and within others; it further supports ones decision-making process when one is beset by skepticism such that one regains confidence in personal abilities.

Providing freedom from the strict, the orthodox that ossifies the faculties of invention and discovery, it facilitates the power of the mind to free it from shackles of fear.

Supporting also "mistakes", it helps one to discover and to name new "truths" and to avoid the trepidation in commencing adventures into unknown regions of thought or knowledge.

The energies of Inderite are likened to Socratic methodology, such that the focus of "questioning" all and everything is encouraged and latent ideas and concepts are developed. It also tends to bring the knowledge of the "right" questions and facilitates "the asking" when one is beset by confusion propagated by another.

Inderite liberates and steadies the mental faculties, helping to free negative thought patterns from the intellectual, sentient, and corporeal bodies. It helps one to identify and to apply that which is consequential to further ones progress along the spiritual path, functioning to discontinue any sensation of confinement, even if physical confinement is a reality.

It can be used allay anger, to banish discouragement, and to assuage fear. It contributes a certainty to ones feelings about oneself and helps one to courageously brave any danger which is in ones path; it also provides for realization of the wisdom to prevent dangerous situations.

Acting initially at the crown chakra, it can also be used to align the chakras with the subtle bodies, enhancing physical stability and increasing the prospects for contentment, as well as, discrimination between that which is "good" for the body and that which could be detrimental.

Inderite acts to bring the energy to assist one in the elimination of debts, to enhance conservation within ones life, and to facilitate acceptance of responsibility. It provides a greater than gentle reminder of ones economical condition and serves to pilot one to the stage of reconciliation of ones funds.

It has been used in the treatment of disorders related to the enamel of the teeth and to assist in bringing the energy to facilitate cleaning of arteries. It can also be used to support the elimination of fatty deposits and to diminish the conditions relative to leukemia and spinal dis-alignment.

Vibrates to the number 3.

**"MY LIFE CAN BE DIFFERENT**
**IN ANY MOMENT**
**I CHOOSE TO CHANGE MY CHOICES"**

Julie Murphy
Washington, USA

## JAMESONITE

[Astrological Sign of Leo]

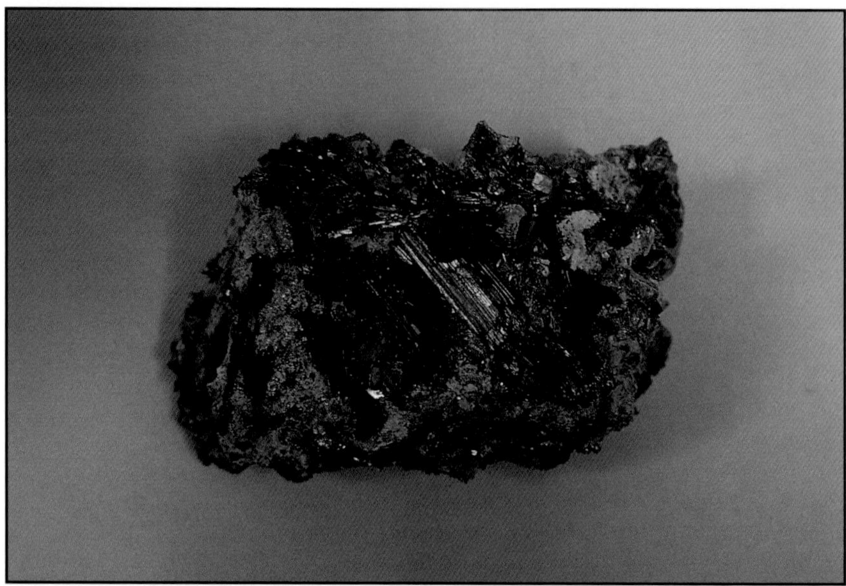

***JAMESONITE*** - $Pb_4FeSb_6S_{14}$; Hardness 2.5; Locality: Sevier Co., AR, USA; Photography by Jim Hughes, Assisted by ♪ Melody ♫; Collection of ♪ Melody ♫, Applewood, CO, USA.

Jamesonite crystallizes in the form of fibrous masses, compact masses, and acicular crystals. The colour ranges from steel-grey to dark grey. The mineral was first described by W. Haidinger in 1825, but earlier described from a Hungarian locality; it was named for R. Jameson.

This mineral has been used to ameliorate volatile energies and to assist one in emotional clarity. It further assists one by stimulating clarity in thought and by augmenting the frequency of brain wave transmissions. It can provide for a connection to the psychic self, provide the polarity adjustments which are necessary within the etheric structure to stabilize the psychic body and to facilitate the maintenance of optimum "states".

It has been used in diplomatic pursuits, to shield against incursions (hostile invasions into ones diplomatic territory), and to support the development of more efficient administrative capabilities.

The mineral brings an understanding of, and basis for, the activities of physicians, surgeons, herbologists, homeopathists, holistic healers, veterinarians, etc. It tends to produce an inner knowledge that one can access for any specific disorder, bringing also the method of remediation to the mind.

It is said to be used in Persia to assist one in performing "wonders" while within the body, also acting to dispel evil and to provide safety and preservation of the self.

Jamesonite also brings the energies of grounding, a type of grounding which assists one in clarity of thought and to encourage the practical side of ones nature. It has been used to advance one in career and to assist one in gaining employment in the field which will enhance ones growth.

It further acts to integrate the positive energy in an area and to interact with all who are present, providing for revitalization, for stimulation of ones rational side, and for the concentration of healing energy for other minerals while consolidating any group effort.

It has been used to provide for a deep state of meditation, allowing the state of "thinking" to be at rest. Prior to this utilization of the stone, one can consciously decide whether to use the meditative state as a vehicle of emptiness, or as a vehicle to further the psychic process and to provide visions with respect to pre-defined questions.

Jamesonite has been used to reduce fever and to generally cool the physical body. It has also been used to reduce swelling and to ameliorate water retention, and to assist in the treatment of multiple personalities, panic disorder, and manic depression. It can be used as an anti-toxin, can reduce inflammation and acts to protect against colds, flu, etc. It has been used for disorders of the sympathetic nervous system, the hands, adrenal glands, and the thymus.

The lead content of this mineral precludes its use in the normal method of preparation of an elixir.

Vibrates to the number 3.

## JASPER - MOOKAITE

[Astrological Sign of Leo]

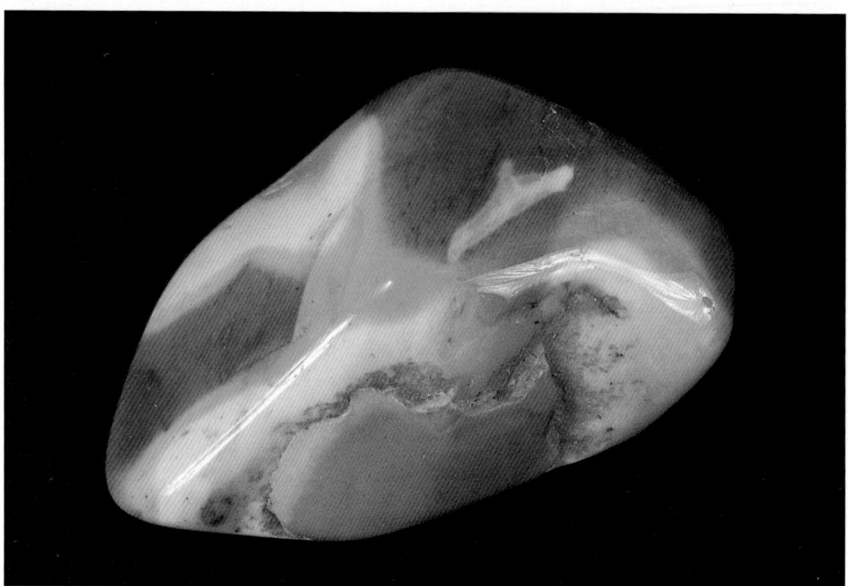

***JASPER - MOOKAITE*** - $SiO_2$ with impurities; Hardness 7; Locality: Australia; Photography by Dave Shrum, Colorado Camera; Collection of ♪ Melody ♫, Applewood, CO, USA. Gift of W.E. Hagestein, New Zealand.

Mookaite Jasper is a form of opaque, usually patterned, chalcedony and occurs in massive formations. The colour range is as shown. Jasper was first described by J.D. Dana in 1837 and was named from the Greek word for "an opaque coloured variety of quartz". The origin of the individual descriptive name of "Mookaite" is unknown to the author. The following properties are in addition to those listed in the CHALCEDONY and JASPER sections of "Love Is In The Earth - A Kaleidoscope Of Crystals Update".

This mineral has been used to enhance pragmatism in expressiveness, and to assist one to celebrate circumstances which are new, soothing any erratic excitable states and assisting one to await "the highest" in all situations. It assists one in dealing with negative situations and provides for a shield of uncompromising strength when one confronts danger. It also helps one to grow emotionally, with change.

It further assists one with decision-making in times when one is experiencing dilemma, guiding one to the best possible decision between any opposing sides. Mookaite Jasper acts as a "mentor" when one is faced with whether to "brave the path one knows not" or to "brave the path one knows". It is interesting to note that the ideal of the "new" is not always the choice in these cases where the options are in total opposition.

Mookaite Jasper helps one in the attunement to the necessities of others and inspires discretion during the assessment of problems. It promotes the balancing of ones needs with the requirements of the day, allowing one to recognize and to care for that which is of prime importance to well-being. It provides for flexibility and openness in opinions, and for faithfulness in promises. It provides companionship for those who are alone, and stimulates the inner understanding of, and a beneficial behavior modification for, children. It further assists one in being kind to oneself and to others.

It tends to promote a plethora of energy and flashes of ideas, acting as a catalyst for the employment of enthusiasm toward the fulfillment of the excellence of the self. It can help to sensitively dissipate the obstructions which tend to impede gain.

This mineral is a very shielding stone and has been used during combat; the stone can act to stimulate the optimum levels of well-being within the user, while affording protection to the body.

It also stimulates contact with loved-ones who have ascended to other planes and can be used in communication with animals.

It has also been used to eliminate distractions, in dissipating the illusions of ones reality, and in revealing that which is concealed.

Mookaite Jasper has been used in the treatment of disorders of the fatty structures and glandular structures of the body, disorders of the stomach, conditions of hernia and ruptures, and to ameliorate water retention.

Vibrates to the number 5.

## JASPER - OWYHEE

[Astrological Sign of Sagittarius]

***JASPER - OWYHEE*** - $SiO_2$ with impurities; Hardness 7; Locality: Owyhee Mountains, Idaho, USA; Photography by Jim Hughes, Assisted by ♪ Melody ♫; Collection of ♪ Melody ♫, Applewood, CO, USA.

Owyhee Jasper is a form of opaque Chalcedony, patterned with striations, and occurring in massive formations. The colour range is as shown. Jasper was first described by J.D. Dana in 1837 and was named from the Greek word for "an opaque coloured variety of quartz". The origin of the individual descriptive name of "Owyhee" is from the Owyhee Mountains in Idaho where it was first discovered. The following properties are in addition to those listed in the CHALCEDONY and JASPER sections of "Love Is In The Earth - A Kaleidoscope Of Crystals Update".

The essence (via elixir) of this stone is excellent to combine with the world of flower essences, providing a shaping and actualizing quality to the flower essence in order to support the qualities of same. It tends to act to transfer the energies from one body to the other; this quality provides the user with further information with respect to both the state of the body, mind, or spirit (whichever is being attended) and to the conditions and actions necessary for application and attainment.

It is a mineral to assist in all veterinary pursuits and in the promotion of healing in the animal kingdom.

Owyhee Jasper can also be used to energize the hand and feet chakras in order to expedite the linear arrangement of the meridians within the physical body.

It is useful in acupressure/acupuncture techniques to produce an energy flow through, and a dissipation of, the energy blockages.

It is a mineral for the outdoors-person, bringing strength and "right" action to living in immediate proximity to the Earth. An "Earth-Stone", it has been used to bring healing to the Earth via gridding and planting techniques. It fosters a loving and rekindling energy to support the growth and refurbishment of that which has been harmed.

The mineral provides one with multipurpose versatility with respect to changing environments and surroundings. It furthers ones ability to travel with spontaneity through variations in ones activities, ambience, and adventures.

It has been used by the Native American culture to act as a "locator", for producing a directional indication for that which one wishes to detect. Not an energy for finding that which is lost, but in locating something which is "new". It is quite conducive to the actualization of "visioning".

Its directional energy further enhances the process of "laying-on-of-stones", providing an energy of insight with respect to the position of placement of the other appropriate minerals upon the body or in the environment.

Owyhee Jasper has been used to help in the re-alignment of cellular structures which have become imperfect and to eliminate the dis-eased structure through normal body functions. It has also been used in the treatment of diabetes and hypoglycemia, and to eliminate parasitic infestations within the body.

Vibrates to the number 6.

## JASPER - SNAKESKIN

[Astrological Sign of Scorpio]

***JASPER - SNAKESKIN*** - $SiO_2$ with impurities; Hardness 7; Locality: Utah, USA; Photography by Jim Hughes, Assisted by ♪ Melody ♫; Collection of ♪ Melody ♫, Applewood, CO, USA.

Snakeskin Jasper is a form of opaque Chalcedony, patterned with pale to rather lime green striations, and occurring in massive formations. Jasper was first described by J.D. Dana in 1837 and was named from the Greek word for "an opaque coloured variety of quartz". The origin of the individual descriptive name of "Snakeskin" is said to be due to the snakeskin-like striations and patterns of colour of the mineral. The following properties are in addition to those listed in the CHALCEDONY and JASPER sections of "Love Is In The Earth - A Kaleidoscope Of Crystals Update".

This mineral is said to have manifested from the Earth-changes occurring during time immemorial, and to have been used in early times to assist in bringing safety to "within the realm". It protects one against succumbing to temptations which may be detrimental to ones being and further stimulates the mood of fascination in examining the protected unknown domains.

It has been esteemed by the ancient tribes throughout the world as a magical gift - one which can prompt fecundity of both the mind and body and can further guard against conspiring negative attitudes and actions.

Snakeskin Jasper is effective in sustaining the rise of the Kundalini. It produces an opening in the pathway at the heart chakra through which the Kundalini may progress (after arrival at the heart chakra), and tends to alleviate the uneasiness in this area which is sometimes associated with the movement.

Placement of the mineral at both the crown chakra and the heart chakra provides a drawing force conducive to continuing the movement, but does not open the other chakras; it is actually used as a force to draw the energy upwards while clearing any hazy areas from the heart to the crown. It is also an excellent stone for enhancing the meditative state.

It has also been used to amplify smudging activities, initiating the forces of constancy (of the clearing condition) and further imparting a uniform stability to the environment.

It is a stone to eliminate the threat of insidious enemies and constraints, preventing the penetration of psychic attack and renewing ones strength to facilitate the relinquishment of bonds and restrictions.

Snakeskin Jasper has been used to assist in the construction of the "family tree", and in the assemblage and the fabrication of geometric patterns. It also enhances the abilities in pursuits of geometry, construction, and architecture.

Providing a stabilizing energy, it has been used to grid areas of soil instability; the results being a lessened movement and a return (at least partial) to the initial condition and/or location.

It has been used to assist in the assimilation of Vitamins A and C, and in the treatment of varicose veins, poisoning (to locate the source), dis-alignment of the spinal vertebrae and, as an elixir, to smooth the skin.

Vibrates to the master number 55.

## JOHANNSENITE

[Astrological Sign of Virgo]

***JOHANNSENITE*** - $CaMnSi_2O_6$; Hardness 6; Locality: Broken Hill, NSW, Australia; Photography by Jim Hughes, Assisted by ♪ Melody ♫; Collection of ♪ Melody ♫, Applewood, CO, USA.

Johannsenite crystallizes in the monoclinic system. The colour range includes vitreous brown, grey to green, colourless, and blue. The mineral was first described by W.T. Schaller in 1932 and was named for A. Johannsen.

This mineral has been used to assist one in employing self-esteem and self-respect in an unprejudiced manner, providing both modesty and tribute for the exceptional presentation of the intellect. It allows one to understand that any effectiveness of any antagonistic force is actually less than the effectiveness within the self which may be used to combat same.

Johannsenite is a powerful stone for locating, for movement, and for ameliorating the disruption of energy within the body and within the emotional structure. It has been used successfully in the removal of energy blockages and in re-aligning the energy channels to their proper locations.

It can be used to activate and to clear the base and the heart chakras, and to provide calming action during stressful activities.

This mineral can be used to stimulate the loving feelings of ones essence and can provide assistance in survival techniques on all levels. It enhances emotional learning and couples the practical side of ones nature to both the emotions and the instincts.

Also assisting one to perceive the duality within the self, it further stimulates the regaining of the delicate side of nature, being a good stone for healing those who will not allow themselves to manifest sorrow. The energy of the mineral can allow one to mentally and emotionally detach oneself from a situation while remaining physically present; it provides a "stand-in" ability which allows intellectual or emotional discussions to continue while the user connects and enjoys the meditative state (truly wonderful for argumentative encounters). It can also provide for the fortitude necessary for one to withdraw from any endangering or impairing physical situation.

It is favorable to the dream state and stimulates the state of awareness bringing lucidity during dream time; hence, enriching the dream state and further providing access to the angelic realm.

Johannsenite has been used in the study, and comprehension, of European languages, assisting one in understanding the communication of same by others and facilitating an ease in learning to communicate in the other language. It further symbolizes the powers of communication and interpretation.

It can also provide insight to allow one to recognize and to accept the multi-dimensionality of ones nature, inciting one toward self-assessment, originality, self-realization, and self-restoration.

It acts to provide for an increase in strength to all parts of the body, to increase muscular structure, to treat physical weakness, fatigue, and psychological disorders, to dispel pain, and to eliminate the cause and the symptoms of migraine headaches. It has also been used to calm pets.

Vibrates to the number 8.

**"LIFE IS A PATH, NOT A REST STOP"**

Kimi "Fire Within" Nichols
Washington, USA

## KAERSUTITE

[Astrological Sign of Scorpio]

***KAERSUTITE*** - $NaCa_2(Mg,Fe)_4Ti(Si_6Al_2)O_{22}(OH)_2$ and $NaCa_2(Mg,Fe^{2+})_4TiAl_2Si_6(O,OH)_{24}$; Hardness 5-6; Locality: Boulder Dam, Mohave County, Arizona, USA; Photography by Jim Hughes, Assisted by ♪ Melody ♫;Collection of ♪ Melody ♫, Applewood, CO, USA.

Kaersutite occurs in the formation of black to brown crystalline titanium amphibole, crystallizing in the monoclinic system with columnar or fibrous prismatic crystals. The mineral was first described by V.I. Vasil'ev in 1987 and named for the Kadyrel deposit in Tuva, Russia, where it was first discovered.

This mineral can assist one in the validation of values and in the presentation and fortification of ones personal values. It assists one in minimizing egotism and pomposity with respect to ones abilities and/or possessions.

Providing a stimulus for the mind, it further enhances ones structure of thought and bases for ideas and conceptions. Enhancing adaptability, attentiveness, and consistency, it is also a stone for expression, reflection, writing, debating, and traveling. It assists one in charismatically attracting that which one desires and in amplifying practicality and freedom. It further acts to reduce sycophantic behavior.

Removing the ambiguity from ones nature, it fosters the ability to dispel hesitancy, vacillation, and uncertainty in ones decisions and actions. Kaersutite serves to reinforce the creation of harmony, unison, and beauty.

It assists one to act in a gentle, kind, and free manner, bringing romance to ones life, through the stimulus to be courteous, accommodating, and refined, without "giving away" ones own power.

It facilitates the energies to stimulate one in the adeptness of love and the social arts. It has been used in socio-emotional situations to stimulate harmonious partnerships and to progress toward the gain of possessions and money.

Kaersutite has been said to have been used by the early Greek civilizations to bring both riches and comfort.

The mineral has assisted one in the ability to empathize with others and to understand exactly what is being felt, more on a spiritual plane; subsequently, the application to the mental and material plane is enhanced.

Blocking all aspects of the ludicrous, it stimulates reasoning capabilities and is excellent in promoting success in rationality. It tends to provide the energy to assist ones intelligence to reassert itself over emotion, no matter how invidious ones position. It also produces non-discriminatory action.

Kaersutite has been used in the treatment of emotional disorders, to ameliorate disorders associated with choking, and with the regulatory organs, the circulatory system, and the feet. It has also been used in the correction of dis-ease associated with the upper spine, the esophagus, the bladder, and the parathyroid glands. It can be used in the elimination of free-radicals from the body.

Vibrates to the number 3.

## KAURI GUM

[Astrological Sign of Leo]

***KAURI GUM*** - Fossil Resin; Hardness 1.5-2.5; Locality: New Zealand; Photography by Jim Hughes, Assisted by ♪ Melody ♬; Collection of ♪ Melody ♬, Applewood, CO, USA. Gift of Richard Two-Bears and Martine, New Zealand.

Kauri Gum, also known as Kauri Copal, is a fossil resin of the coniferous tree of the same name (Kauri Pine), Agathis Australis, of the far north of New Zealand's North Island. The colour ranges from translucent to transparent, varying from deep honey to straw-colour. Kauri Gum was first described by J.C. Willis in 1973. Kauri Gum is also known as Agathacopalite; the mineralogical name, Agathacopalite, was first described by J. Paclt in 1953 and was named for the content of agathic acid ($C_{20}H_{30}O_4$) and from the species Agathis Australis. Like amber, it becomes charged with electricity when rubbed and will pick up small pieces of paper. However, it is softer than amber, has less polymerization, and melts at a lower temperature. Most Kauri Gum is also fluorescent.

This mineral can bring one solace in times when one feels besieged, engulfed, or overwhelmed by conditions. It further instills the energy for one to surmount these submerging forces and imparts an energy to assist one in both action and completion. The energy acts to dissipate the feeling of "waiting at the station for a train that is long overdue", helping in the realization that the "time will come" for the end result to become a reality.

Kauri Gum has been used in prophetic pursuits, to assist one in receiving the whole of the principal parts of the pursuit. It is the "stone of the sibyl", possessing the energies for prophecy and divination, while allowing for the return from prophetic ecstasy to the "ordinary" self which still exhibits the flickering of the fire of divination.

It has also been used to further syllogistic reasoning and forethought, bringing rationality. It is a mineral for both the intellect and the crown chakra, stimulating logical knowledge of the spiritual paths.

Kauri Gum produces an energy conducive to bringing the connection of the sentient self to infinite purity. It helps one in the art of seeing that which is required in order to facilitate that which is desired.

When consciously directed, it also converts the energy of physical endurance toward the mobilization of unconditional love, and provides an energy to incite the awareness and subsequent response of choice, helping one to select and to be selected.

It is a sacred stone to the Maori native culture of New Zealand. It has also been used in the fire ceremonies of the Maori healers. It was also burned for "smudging" and as an incense to clear the atmosphere of negativity. It cleanses the environment in which it rests and is an excellent mineral for use in purifying. It has been said to bring good luck to warriors.

The mineral has been used to promote healing of infection, stimulating the absorption and transmuting of disordered energy into healing energy. It emits a tranquilizing energy which helps to calm nerves and to enliven the disposition, and has been used to enhance the dexterity of the feet.

Kauri Gum vibrates to the number 2 and Kauri Copal vibrates to the master number 44.

## KNEBELITE

[Astrological Sign of Cancer]

***KNEBELITE*** - $(Fe,Mn)_2SiO_4$; Hardness 6.5; Locality: Blue Bell Mine, British Columbia, Canada; Photography by Jim Hughes, Assisted by ♪ Melody ♫; Collection of ♪ Melody ♫, Applewood, CO, USA.

Knebelite crystallizes in the formation of compact and/or granular masses, grains and, rarely, as crystals. The colour ranges from grey to black to brown. The mineral was first described by J. W. Döbereiner in 1817, analyzed by A. Erdmann in 1849, and was named for Major von Knebel.

This mineral has been used to stimulate the capability to "talk", on all levels and both in and out of the mysteries of time. It is useful for the physical reality in assisting one in the formation of words - from the infant to the adult.

Knebelite represents the essence of pragmatism, of gaining a discernible "hands on" awareness of the self so that one is able to understand and to expedite determinations. It further assists in multi-dimensional shifting of the consciousness such that one can initiate the processes which are required.

The mineral can facilitate the past "life" experience(s) which are significators for this incarnation. The experiences may be from ones days of youth (during this incarnation), during the time of "yesterday" (also during this incarnation), or from a past personification.

The energy tends to attract generosity due to the enthusiasm that others feel about one who is attending the energy of Knebelite. It reduces the insecurity of the self and promotes a methodology of "soft sell".

It is a "stone for transitting", assisting each challenge to be met with the length of cycles determined by ones decision. When one wishes to not continue a specific cycle of experience, Knebelite can assist in expediting its completion.

It is an excellent stone for use with astrological and astronomical pursuits, to provide precision of discretion with respect to problems which are encountered and further providing an insight to the many facets of resolution.

It has been used to promote the observation of subtle changes of adiabatics when one is experiencing either meditation or the trance state. One is able to scrutinize, for example, the actual temporary loss of body weight and a nearby drop in the temperature of the environment; this is an ectoplasmic phenomena which has been measured.

Knebelite represents "life growth", which can be visualized as a four-dimensional doorway to a three-dimensional experience, with the basis of "time and space" being the extra variable so that one is enabled to experience three-dimensional events in varying time periods and in varying environments, by employing the Knebelite energy distinctions of intervals and location.

It has also been used to purify ones body, mind, and spirit when worn, carried, or used as an elixir. It has also been successful in the treatment of disorders of the kidneys and bladder and to assist in the rejuvenation of brain tissue. It acts to assist in the assimilation of iron and manganese.

Vibrates to the number 2.

**"IT IS DIFFICULT TO EXPLAIN - BUT I'M HERE BECAUSE OF YOU AND YOU'RE HERE BECAUSE OF ME"**

Mulla Nasruddin

## LÖLLINGITE

[Astrological Sign of Sagittarius]

***LÖLLINGITE*** - $FeAs_2$; Hardness 5-5.5; Locality: Shaft 321 Pohla Dist., Saxony, Germany (This mine was the largest U-mine in the world, kept a secret by USSR until 1992); Photography by Jim Hughes, Assisted by ♪ Melody ♫; Collection of ♪ Melody ♫, Applewood, CO, USA.

Löllingite crystallizes in the formation of masses. The colour ranges from whitish to silver-white to steel-grey. It occasionally contains silver, bismuth, and antimony. The name is sometimes spelled with an "e" added prior to the first "l". The mineral was first described by W. Haidinger in 1845 and was named for Lölling, Carinthia, Austria, where one of the first discoveries of Löllingite was made.

This mineral produces an energy to transform attacking qualities to defending qualities and is an excellent preventive which will shield one from many forms of negative energy. Simply placing the mineral in ones environment brings in the protective, shielding aspect of this stone which works on the physical, etheric, and emotional levels. It can help to keep out the negative vibrations of pollutants at the physical level, due to an energy field which it creates within the aura. It is a unique protector and is an excellent stone to keep in ones environment when performing hazardous work; it helps to keep-away all forms of negative resonance and can work to allay bodily danger.

Löllingite can assist one in the "painless" retrieval of ideas; it acts to bring ideas to one during the state of dreaming.

It also assists one in perceiving pretenses, promoting discernment of that which lies beneath expressions and deeds. It can be used to awakening the powers of the mind, amplifying memory and maintaining recall of pertinent knowledge, when required.

The mineral has also been used to assist in the formation of opinions and conclusions in connection with orthodox explanations, providing the energy to favour both the non-arbitrary and non-authoritarian explication.

It assists in explaining that the written word and conventional beliefs are not the "law" (although they may be required by society), but experience, itself, is each persons personal "law".

Löllingite has also been used in the abstract world of composites - bringing one an opportunity to see that which one encompasses; e.g., the segments of souls one has met in other lifetimes or in other worlds. And from this information, the mineral acts to further the information describing each segment, also producing information concerning the method and means of synthesis.

It has been used to assist in the prevention of RNA/DNA damage and can be used in repair of same. It can be used in the treatment of bronchitis and disorders of the lungs. It has been used in the treatment of violent and/or highly infective dis-ease, as well as by others who are working with those affected, in order to provide protection from the affectation. It has also been used to regulate the body temperature, to reduce inflammation, and to assist in the amelioration of hydrogenated products.

The arsenide content of this mineral precludes its use in the normal method of preparation of an elixir.

Vibrates to the number 7.

♪ YOU ARE THE DANCE ♫

## MACFALLITE

[Astrological Sign of Capricorn]

***MACFALLITE*** - $Ca_2(Mn^{3+},Al)_3SiO_4Si_2O_7(OH)_3$ or $Ca_2Mn_3(SiO_4)(Si_2O_7)(OH)_3$; Hardness 5; Locality: Expl. Mine, Copper Harbor, MI, USA; Photography by Jim Hughes, Assisted by ♪ Melody ♫; Collection of ♪ Melody ♫, Applewood, CO, USA.

MacFallite crystallizes in the form of silky sub-adamantine fibrous plates and overlays. The colour range includes yellow, red-brown, and maroon. The mineral was first described by P.B. Moore, J. Ito, and I.M. Steele in 1979 and was named for R.P. MacFall.

This mineral has been used to provide an armour of knowledge to facilitate protection from that which is fraudulent. It brings strength and courage to confront falsity and provides the "gypsy's warning" to "not run away".

It is quite useful in instilling consideration within the minds and hearts of the young. There have been a multitude of successes with the correction of impertinence, impudence, and brazen-ness, and the further facilitation of changes which reflect the lovely states of courtesy and respectfulness.

It also assists one in infallible mortality; specifically in being error free with respect to living in and on our Earth.

It is a mineral to assist with the remediation of repression. Although initially repression is shallow and that which is repressed keeps trying to attain release, as time passes, the repression becomes reinforced and is often "beneath the layers of many veils". MacFallite assists in removing the "veils" and in assisting one in the examination of the repression - helping one to look at the result with logic and understanding, in order to release it.

When one feels that some event or condition has deprived one of some need (basic or superfluous), although the immediate reaction would be to retaliate, MacFallite assists one in remembering that one is totally responsible for oneself and that no one else can either give or take that responsibility. Hence, it acts to instill an understanding and a forgiveness of both the self and any outside influence.

It has been used to enhance the study of psychology, psychiatry, and the mystical. It has also been used to assist in the study and the reading of the tarot, the Runes, and the "stones".

MacFallite is a "stone for reunions" (class, family, friends), for gatherings of those one has not seen for some time. It brings, not necessarily recognition (by name), but a truly lasting popularity and an enduring regard - shown by all participants in the assemblage. It is interesting to note the difference in perception by one who carries MacFallite when attending all types of social events.

It also assists a person in perceiving oneself as others view him/her - allowing the "mask" to remain, but allowing one to see both through and behind it.

This mineral has been used in the treatment of narcolepsy, insomnia, gout, and myopia. It has been conducive to success in ameliorating disorders of the adrenal glands, and in the treatment of asthma and mononucleosis.

Vibrates to the number 1.

## "MALACHITE - RED" [Astrological Sign of Libra]

***"MALACHITE - RED"*** **-** $SiO_2$ with impurities; Hardness 7; Locality: Mexico; Photography by Jim Hughes, Assisted by ♪ Melody ♫; Collection of ♪ Melody ♫, Applewood, CO, USA. Gift of Angel Torrecillas, Mexico.

"Red Malachite" is actually a red banded (dark bands) jasper which crystallizes in the massive and fibrous layered structural formation, providing for swirls and curved lines as exhibited in Malachite. The name was coined by the Torrecillas family due to the Malachite-type patterns and the red colour.

This mineral is truly a stone for the "new age". It has been known as the "stone of reminding" - dates, times, etc., as well as reminding one of the learning from prior experiences and conditions so that one need not "fall into the trap" of repeating same. It tells the story that one can learn from a one-time occurrence of a lesson and need not repeat lessons over and over without learning.

It is likened to the biblical words "Cleave the rock and I am there", revealing the "All" and the "Everything".

It has been known as the "firestone" bringing only the construction of "good" and transmuting that which is not "good" to that which is "good". It has been said to have been the material used to build the oval dome of Atlantis (the dome used for receipt of advanced healing information), the material being only in the hands of the initiates; the energy of the stone was said to purify all those who experienced its touch. It is truly an exceptional purifier and has been applied to the physical, mental, emotional, and the higher planes of thought.

It has further been used for diagnosis, to allow one to look within to determine the cause of any specific condition; e.g., providing insight to the basic disorders within the body, mind, and emotional structure, and to the conditions which are associated with interaction with others in this reality.

It further assists one in determining the molecular structure of the body and of other physical forms.

The energy of "Red" Malachite also assists one in bringing the image to "in front of the eyes", permitting not the loss of the memory, but stimulating the remembering.

Used also by the ancient Aztecs in building the gateways to temples, the mineral is revered as sanctified and consecrated. The gateway often represented the entry into ones beginnings.

"Red" Malachite is an equalizing and balancing agent, structuring the meridians of the body and aligning them with the meridians of the Higher Self; it can create an unobstructed path, leading to a desired goal. It stimulates instinctive and intuitive reasoning, allowing for change which facilitates advancement.

It is said to protect against radiation and can be used in the treatment of the cellular structure and to enhance the immune system. It has been used in the treatment of tumors, dysfunctional cellular structures, torn muscles, cataracts, the structure and function of the veins, and to regulate the RNA/DNA structures.

Vibrates to the number 9.

## MARTITE

[Astrological Sign of Taurus]

***MARTITE*** - Iron sesquioxide under an isometric form; Hardness 6-7; Locality: Mapimi, Durango, MEXICO; Photography by Jim Hughes, Assisted by ♪ Melody ♫; Collection of ♪ Melody ♫, Applewood, CO, USA.

Martite crystallizes in the formation of sub-metallic iron-black, occasionally with a tarnish, octahedral crystals. The crystals are often in a matrix of massive sesquioxide. The mineral was first described by A. Breithaupt in 1828 and named for Mars or Martis, the alchemist name for Iron.

This mineral acts to align the ethereal energies to the physical, mental, and emotional bodies, providing for an even flow of perfect order to the requirements of the Earth plane while balancing the electromagnetics of the physical body.

It acts to stimulate mental attunement, memory enhancement, original thinking, and technical knowledge.

It assists one in mathematical pursuits and in the development of both mental and manual agility. While enhancing the mental aspects, it provides for a calming atmosphere, helping one to realize that the only limitations which exist are those self-limiting concepts within the mind.

It facilitates the balancing of the yin-yang energies, employing, in addition, the magnetic qualities of the energy to balance the connections between the body and the astral plane and between the astral plane and the ethereal plane, to provide a stable equilibrium between the ethereal nervous system and the physical nervous system.

Martite provides for a connection between the user and the nurturing aspects of the Earth, facilitating grounding and balancing between those bodies. The grounding cord, usually running from the base of the spine to the core of the Earth, is strengthened; hence, all manners of situations are afforded focus, and the environment of a healer during healing situations is provided further security and stability.

It is a mineral to produce sustained effort; as has been recounted, "a good first effort is capable of a sustained second effort"; e.g., when the veteran marathon runner "hits the wall", breaks through, and finds a "second wind".

The Martite crystals are also excellent for the dissolution of negativity, transforming the negativity, in the dissolved state, to the purity of the universal light of love.

It has been said to attract personable, bonding, and companionable love. It is truly a "stone of attraction", also helping one to "attract" the healing energies necessary for recovery from disorders.

It is also capable of helping the body to remain cool, or of dispelling heat at the physical level (use at the throat and at the third-eye are recommended). An elixir is also expedient. It can be used in the treatment of muscular cramps, blood disorders [such as anemia], nervousness, and restlessness. It can also be used to assist in the healing of breaks and fractures and in the adjustment of the vertebrae of the spine.

Vibrates to the number 5.

## MERWINITE

[Astrological Sign of Sagittarius]

***MERWINITE*** - $Ca_3Mg(SiO_4)_2$; Hardness 6; Locality: Riverside Co., CA, USA; Photography by Jim Hughes, Assisted by ♪ Melody ♫; Collection of ♪ Melody ♫, Applewood, CO, USA.

Merwinite crystallizes in the form of grains and granular masses. The colour range includes colourless to white, pale green, and blue-grey. The mineral was first described by E.S. Larsen and W.F. Foshag in 1921 and was named for H.E. Merwin.

This mineral provides a solid foundation with respect to bonds to ones family and unification within a group. Advancement and cultivation in information transfer has been recounted; both for inter/intra family formations, employment climates, social environments, and other macrocosms. It can serve one in presenting an openness from the heart space, to exhibit authentic emotions of love and altruism, and to maintain composure.

It has further been used to awaken the crown chakra and the throat chakra and to produce concurrent grounding.

It has been used for thought-shifting between the realm of speech and the realm of awareness and is an excellent stone for centering and for meditation.

It functions analogous to an electrified conductor and can be used during healing activities to promote the energy transfer from a healer, or from other minerals, to the subject of the healing.

It can be used to order the chakras and to direct the alliance between the ethereal and physical nervous systems. It is an excellent energy for pendants and for the interior of wands.

Merwinite has been used during the state of reflection to produce stellar communication with the eminent order of angels, assisting one to gain information which is inordinately appropriate and of broad relevance to the users. Used at the crown chakra, it has aligned the chakras and has bestowed a centering effect. At the throat chakra, it seems to clean the area and to promote protection (from non-mindful speaking) and centering concurrently. It assists one in gaining sensitivity to the stages of ones life and furthers insight into the modifications required to advance harmony and pleasure within ones life.

It has acted to clear the brain from the "fog" and to promote the intergrowth of new ideas from old ways. It furthers the elimination of trivial sophistry, the beguiling but fallacious method of reasoning, bringing soundness to ones rationality and adroitness in effectiveness of execution of same.

This mineral provides for an internal warmth and can accelerate circulation as well as well-being. This attribute applies to both the emotional and physical bodies - the outer world of associations <u>and</u> the inner world of physical composition. It can be used in the treatment of osteoporosis and grinding joints, disorders of the eyes, disorders of the gall bladder, and to lessen muscular cramps. It can also be used to improve circumstances which may cause excessive anguish and/or anxiety.

Vibrates to the number 8.

## METEORITE - NANTAN [Astrological Sign of Aquarius]

***METEORITE - NANTAN*** - $Fe_2O_3$; Hardness - not available; Locality: Nantan Iron Meteorite, Lihu, Nandan Co., China (1516 A.D.); Photography by Jim Hughes, Assisted by ♪ Melody ♫; Collection of ♪ Melody ♫, Applewood, CO, USA.

The Nantan Meteorite is from a 9 ton meteorite which came to Earth in 1516 A.D. and was named for the location in which it was first discovered. The black oxidized portion is primarily maghemite (with a very high-magnetism); the orange-yellow is akaganeite, goethite & lepidocrocite; cohenite and schreibersite is also present due to corrosion. When coupled with the orange-yellow, the reader may include the properties of the relevant minerals.

This mineral is one which enhances ones power to create wisdom and to restrict the destruction of same.

It is a mineral which assists one in exhibiting an interior-based charm which "shines" through ones own projection; its clarity and centered-ness being received with same. It focusses on the "particle" of ones being which is known as charm and tends to draw other finer particles toward it, acting in a similar manner to the all encompassing "magnetic attraction".

It assists one in recognizing that no matter how much one has forgotten, one, most likely, retains an advantage over those who never knew anything in the beginning.

It further promotes the observation of subtle changes of adiabatics when one is experiencing either meditation or the trance state. One is able to scrutinize, for example, the actual temporary loss of body weight and a nearby drop in the temperature of the environment; this is an ectoplasmic phenomena which has been measured. This phenomena has also been noted during healing - with the energies of this mineral, the meditative and or consciousness state of the subject can become such that the protoplasmic structure of the disorder loses both form and density, sometimes leaving the subject's body via ectoplasmic extrusion (producing the same temporary weight-loss occurrence and a drop in temperature of the environment). This situation has been shown to occur in controlled situations by the Kahuna practitioners of Polynesia.

The Nantan Meteorite assists one understanding the emergence of form from the formless. It can promote the receipt of information to further ones psychic and "magical" abilities.

It is the emissary of a space-time continuum; both representing and providing for the three spacial coordinates (within itself) and facilitating the connection with the extension of time.

It assists in alleviating encumbrances and in bringing to accomplishment that which is "wanted". It encourages maintaining clarity of ones intention, suspending chaos of mission and stabilizing unanticipated incidents. It also promotes incentive and faith in oneself, eliminating uncertainty and dependency upon others.

It has been used to align the astral body to the etheric body to stimulate ease in astral travel.

The Nantan Meteorite assists in the removal of energy blockages which are existing in states of dis-ease, inducing the unconstrained flow of the strength of the body to renew itself.

Vibrates to the number 3.

## MEYERHOFFERITE

[Astrological Sign of Aries]

***MEYERHOFFERITE*** - $2CaO \bullet 3B_2O_3 \bullet 7H_2O$ or $CaB_3O_3(OH)_5 \bullet H_2O$ or $Ca_2B_6O_{11} \bullet 7H_2O$; Hardness 2; Locality: Mt. Blanco, Death Valley, Inyo Co., CA, USA; Photography by Jim Hughes, Assisted by ♪ Melody ♫; Collection of ♪ Melody ♫, Applewood, CO, USA.

Meyerhofferite crystallizes in the triclinic system in prismatic and tabular crystals and as fibers. The colour ranges from colourless to white. The mineral was first described by W.T. Schaller in 1914 and was named for W. Meyerhoffer.

This mineral brings a fusing between the self and another (person, place, or thing) such that the unification exhibits sturdiness and an intumescent growth between the two.

It rids one of the state of "thoughts and fears crowding the mind" and brings a carefully cultured languor and sophistication which is not susceptible to callous battering.

One may observe incidents with interest, the mind seizing upon any incident as a relief from ones own mental chaos, and rising to a height of which one thought incapable. It assists one in solving difficulties with a humorous element for each stage.

It is a "stone of alteration", assisting the "good" in remaining during the transformation. It promotes the ability to "call" with earnest desire for the assistance of the Higher Self and the Inner Self, or to make an appeal to other worlds for assistance in guidance or actualization of a thought form.

The mineral tends to assist one in remaining inviolable, freeing one from the energies of violence and providing a sanctuary within ones immediate energy field.

Meyerhofferite has been used to release one from the bonds of others who are those who can "only have one friend at a time" and who, during the remaining time when one is not considered a friend, the other considers one to be "the enemy". The energy facilitates the recognition of the "game" and encourages one to release the necessity to "play".

It assists one in dealing with negative situations and provides for a barrier of unassailable strength when one confronts danger. It also helps one to grow emotionally, with change.

It has been used to stimulate the imaginative forces for design and for fabricating ones creations. It acts as a stimulus for promoting effort in producing a "finished product". It is an excellent energy for composing (music, the written word, etc.) and for the creation of poetry, clothing, and style.

It enhances the desire for, and facilitates the attainment of, those ideals which assist in the evolution of ones spirituality.

It has been used in the treatment of bodily changes involving a lessening of activity, especially organs which tend to slow during "middle age". It has assisted in the assimilation of Vitamin A and in Calcium. It has also been used in the treatment of disorders of the lungs (breathing), the total respiratory system, and the spleen.

Vibrates to the number 5.

## MINIUM

[Astrological Signs of Leo & Cancer]

***MINIUM*** - $Pb_2PbO_4$; Hardness 2.5; Locality: Tonopah-Belmont Mine, AZ, USA; Photography by Jim Hughes, Assisted by ♪ Melody ♫; Collection of ♪ Melody ♫, Applewood, CO, USA.

Minium crystallizes in the form of crystalline scales. The colour ranges from bright to dark orange-red in/on matrix. The mineral was first described by J. Smithson in 1806 and is named from the Latin word meaning "red lead".

This mineral can be used to promote leadership qualities and is an excellent stone for facilitating tact and cooperation within groups, bringing an interactive harmony to the collective relationships. It also guides the "leader" toward understanding and toward leading with harmony, assuring sensitivity to the wishes of the group and in the methods of decision-making. Minium provides an energy such that even in the midst of tribulation, the thoughts of general (and group) philosophy occur, providing for a modicum of manners to prevent the making of any reprehensible demonstrations. It is a wonderful stone to present to a leader, to a committee chairman, etc.

It is extremely supportive for those studying within the discipline of medicine and can promote holistic, homeopathic, and herbal medicine applications, providing insights and knowledge of testing.

Minium can help to amplify the functions of emotional and intellectual regeneration <u>and</u> the processes therein; in order to achieve the integration of experiences and the acceptance of emotions, with subsequent renewal of the aspects of self-discovery, one must re-affirm the direction of inherent thoughts and feelings.

It is a useful energy for commercial-travelers, as well as pleasure-travelers. It allows one to easily adapt to situations and to change as is required; it enables one to realize that these changes are transient and, hence, the energy helps one to be accommodating.

It can be used to assuage introversion, to provide diplomacy to situations, and to impart the techniques and advantages of cooperation.

It is excellent to use in the ceremonial aspect, promoting a bond between participants while sustaining grounding of the energy centers. It also provides for guidance and assured-ness to activities. It can also be used in ceremonies of the medicine wheel to bring a stronger connection between the four directions, to connect those around the wheel, and to stimulate totem connections.

Minium is useful in helping one to recognize those who have been a part of ones past-lives. The mineral can also facilitate access to a connection with other-planetary beings, allowing for the remembering of other worlds and other times.

It has been used to diminish infections and to heal skin lesions on the body, and to provide beneficial assistance to conditions of disorderly blood and olfactory systems. It can be used to increase the assimilation of selenium and zinc, to stimulate circulation.

The lead content of this mineral precludes its use in the normal method of preparation of an elixir.

Vibrates to the number 7.

***MISERITE*** - $K(Ca,Ce)_4Si_5O_{13}(OH)_3$ or $KCa_5Si_8O_{22}(OH)F$; Hardness ?; Locality: Vanadium Mine, Hot Springs, AR, USA; Photography by Jim Hughes, Assisted by ♪ Melody ♫; Collection of ♪ Melody ♫, Applewood, CO, USA.

Miserite crystallizes in the form of the triclinic system as translucent to opaque pink to pink-grey masses, fibres, and needle-like crystals. The mineral was first described by W.T. Schaller in 1950, was originally named natroxonotlite, and was renamed (because it was not related to xonotlite) for H.D. Miser.

This mineral has been used to assist one in never underestimating another; the energy tends to bring astute rationality such that the user is given the insight to "right" judgment and the capability to see through facades and/or to see that the facade is not present.

Miserite allows one to avert pandemonium, bringing order and systematic action.

It has been used for gridding areas which are known to be chaotic, to instill tranquility and to induce mediate disruption. It acts to produce the effect of positive behavior modification and has been seen to allow those who are disorderly to be "borne precipitously toward the door".

The mineral assists one in the accumulation of reserves for the proverbial "rainy day". It acts to induce a realism with respect to ones financial state and resources, and promotes the energy with which one may devise strategies to facilitate gain.

The energy of Miserite is a sacred energy for temples, both personal and public. It elevates privacy protection and the quiet protected state of those who are visiting and/or who are a part of the temples.

It has been used quite effectively to provide a preservation capability for that to which it is applied; it is inclined toward the maintenance and perpetuation of a condition - the condition being supported as it is "today". For example, it would only bring forth the energy of the fountain of youth if one were youthful - please note, this energy maintains and does not assist in the reversion to that which has been.

Miserite has been used to assist one in gaining appointments and in obtaining reservations (when none were available). The energy acts to elevate the probability of success when one is attempting to secure tickets for events and travel, a table for dinner, or a location for rendezvous.

It further provides for a "unity" between the self and the unified materiality, conveying the boundless energies which endlessly inundate the universe to insure this interaction and to elevate movement in the direction of attainment. It is emblematic of the general unity which moves gently, but steadily, in the direction of unified physical interaction. Hence, one actually melds (with "right" intent) with the energy which one desires to inspire and to motivate, bringing reassurance to that which is desired.

It has been used to assist in the assimilation of potassium and in the treatment of disorders of potassium deficiencies. It can also assist in preventing degenerative disorders and can promote the elimination of blockages within the body.

Vibrates to the master number 44.

## MOONSTONE - RAINBOW

[Astrological Sign of Cancer]

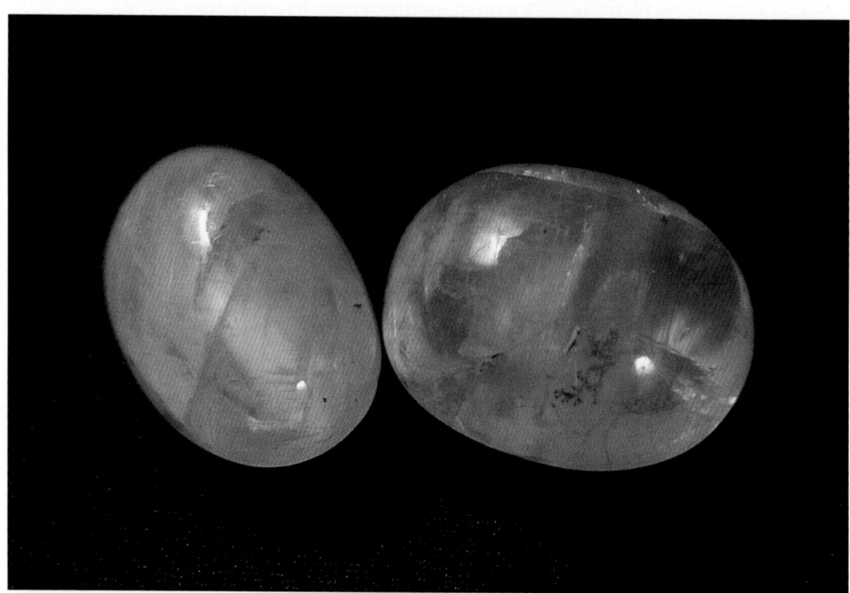

***MOONSTONE - RAINBOW*** - Combination of Orthoclase and Albite - Chatoyant opalescent reflection or schiller; Hardness 6; Locality: Sri Lanka; Photography by Jim Hughes, Assisted by ♪ Melody ♫; Collection of ♪ Melody ♫, Applewood, CO, USA.

Rainbow Moonstone is found in the orthoclase [adularia] and the albite families [both members of the feldspar group]. The properties characterizing moonstone are a chatoyancy, a milky-sheen, and a flash of rainbow colours, usually predominated with an intense blue. Moonstone was first described by A.G. Werner in 1780 and was named to describe the lustre of the stone; the term "Rainbow Moonstone" was coined by the lapidary industry within the last 10 years to describe the flashes of colour within the natural Moonstone. The following properties are in addition to those listed in the ADULARIA, ALBITE, FELDSPAR, and MOONSTONE sections of "Love Is In The Earth - A Kaleidoscope Of Crystals Update".

This mineral has been used to assist one in influencing the origination of personal and universal/world-wide progress and improvement; it acts to combine the energies of non-restraint with the employment of a diligent endurance, and furthers the development and growth intended. The energy provides indication of a succession of chronological stages, each interconnected to each other and to the "heart of the light" which radiates from the center and perpetually gives birth to the illumination of life. It assists one to recognize the interdependence of each flash of the "fountain", and promotes the acknowledgment of the permeation of each cycle with the other cycles; hence, bringing an orderliness to ones planning and interaction with the differing stages of ones life.

Rainbow Moonstone assists in carrying rainbows into ones life and is a very unique contribution from the wraith within the formation; the energy assist one in examining that which is contrary and in sustaining the perpetual realization that humanitarianism and love are ever-present in ones life. It brings the white light of healing and perfection and the multi-colours of the spectrum for activating the corresponding chakras.

The mineral contains within itself the mirror to all cycles, operating at differing levels of reality, which one has or will experience, and allows for the flow of life information and life movement to the user. Hence, one may access that which "has been" and that which "will become" with respect to ones personal lives. It presents to one the concepts of perpetual movement and energetic relationships in the unfolding of ones personal "great plan".

Rainbow Moonstone has also been used to assist one in recognizing the difference between "seen" phenomena (accessible to the senses) and those which are "unseen" or of another nature (accessible via the intuitive system). It promotes coherence in "reading" symbology which is presented and furthers the use of rigor in building correspondences with ones frame of reality reference. It is a remarkable symbolic instrument for deciphering "the world" and for promoting contact with the Higher Self.

This mineral has been used in the treatment of disorders relative to the interior of organs (e.g., intestinal digestion and cleansing, blockages in arteries and ducts, secretion capabilities of the liver, pancreas, and gall bladder, muscular toxicity, and retina deterioration).

Vibrates to the master number 77.

**"THE TURTLE MAKES PROGRESS
ONLY WHEN
HE STICKS HIS HEAD
OUTSIDE OF HIS SHELL"**

Kimi "Fire Within" Nichols
Washington, USA

## NEWBERYITE

[Astrological Signs of Taurus & Pisces]

***NEWBERYITE*** - $MgHPO_4$♥$3H_2O$ or $Mg(PO_3OH)$♥$3H_2O$; Hardness 3-3.5; Locality: Skipton Caves, Ballarat, Victoria, Australia; Photography by Jim Hughes, Assisted by ♪ Melody ♫; Collection of ♪ Melody ♫, Applewood, CO, USA.

Newberyite crystallizes in the orthorhombic system in the colour range of white to tan in a guano ranging from grey to green. First described by G. vom Rath in 1879, the mineral was named for J.C. Newbery, who first discovered it.

This mineral has been used in the stimulation of astral travel, bringing the user "quick flight" and safe and easy return. The traumas associated with leaving the body are alleviated, the return is achieved with no delay when desired, and premature return is reduced (the mineral has a buffering effect on outside noises but also provides instinctual awareness on the astral plane so that if danger is perceived, the user becomes aware and may return immediately).

Acting on the energies of flight, Newberyite stimulates second-sight and reduces error in interpretation of visions, prescience, and divination. It actually assists one in being in the visionary area of that which is stimulated by the intuitive capabilities. It has further been used to facilitate contact for channeling activities and to assure the maintenance of ones awareness during the contribution of information via the spirit world; using this mineral rather provides a "guarantee" that one need not relinquish ones awareness, ones strength, or ones power during any channeling activities. It also advances the reciprocal nourishing which is present between the physical and spiritual realms and promotes active participation through the differing levels of reality.

It is a refreshing mineral, bringing invigoration to ones energy levels and eliminating lethargy. It provides an inspiring and innovative energy for authors and acts as a central pillar from which thoughts and ideas tend to radiate in an upward winding spiral.

It has been used to stimulate upward mobility in organizations and in ones career.

Newberyite can help to combat oversensitivity and critical-ness, providing for discriminating judgment. It helps one to "stand-up" for that which is "right" in ones moral structure. It can be used to expedite a resonant meditation, and to assist one in the acquisition of the complete focus of the self upon that which is intended.

It can also be used to produce a "nesting" instinct, assisting ones return from any destination and promoting safety in both the return and in the location/structure to which one returns.

It has been used to stimulate the growth of plants and in the furtherance of agricultural pursuits to prompt a higher yield of crops.

This mineral has been used in the promotion of assimilation of Vitamin C, to promote clarity and extension in night vision, and in the treatment of stomach ulcers, olfactory degeneration, and disorders of the arms and motor capabilities.

The solubility of the matrix of this mineral precludes its use in the normal method of preparation of an elixir.

Vibrates to the number 9.

**"ALL THAT ONES NEEDS IS A SPOONFUL OF MEDITATION"**

Osho
"The Divine Melody"

## **ONYX - PERFORATED** [Astrological Signs of Scorpio & Capricorn]

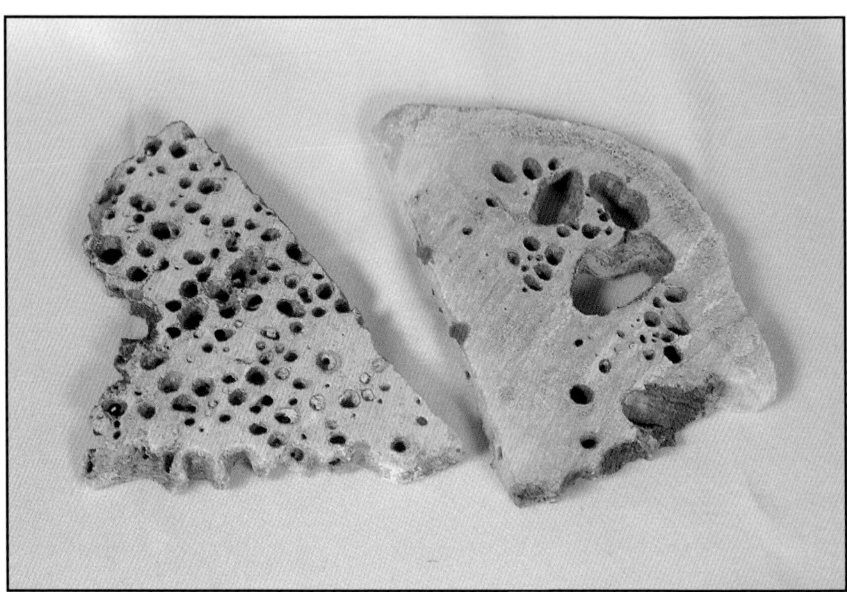

***ONYX - PERFORATED*** - $SiO_2$ with impurities; Hardness 7; Locality: Minas Gerais, Brasil; Photography by Jim Hughes, Assisted by ♪ Melody ♫; Collection of ♪ Melody ♫, Applewood, CO, USA; Gift of Natalino Oliveira, Minas Gerais, Brasil.

Perforated Onyx is a type of Chalcedony which occurs with many perforations. This mineral is also indicative of "Growth Interference". Onyx was first described by Pliny in 77 A.D. and the name is from the Greek word which was descriptive of the colour. The following properties are in addition to those listed in the ONYX section of "Love Is In The Earth - A Kaleidoscope Of Crystals Update" and in the GROWTH INTERFERENCE section herein.

This mineral has been used to assist in alleviating the state of grief, allowing it to pass like "the shadow of a leaf floating in the wind". Whatever the intensity, the duration is predisposed to be concise and condensed.

It has been used to place one in the king's chamber of the great pyramid, transporting one into ages past such that ones consciousness is unlocked and the door to another time is both revealed and opened; it further promotes movement through one universal and/or personal mystery after another, bringing startling truths and memories surging to the surface of the conscious mind.

It is an excellent mineral for use in removing the ethereal cords which tie one to another, allowing for release from interference of the energy of others and for release of others from the interference of ones own energy. Placing the mineral upon each chakra (independently and separately) promotes "seeing" the cords of others which have been sent toward one <u>or</u> the cords which one has sent to others, and further enhances either the retrieval of the cords one has sent to others <u>or</u> the following of the cords (which have been sent to the user) to the originating location and promoting the subsequent removal of same.

Perforated Onyx facilitates thought transmission and telepathic endeavors. It has been used by the Brasilian shamen to stimulate visioning and to provide a pathway for journeying (both within the body and to outside locations).

It has also acted to induce the bringing-together of those of like minds and like goals. It stimulates the growth of the roots of projects and ventures and allows the origin of evolutionary development to be mirrored in the pattern of accomplishment.

It is an excellent energy for balancing the physical energy and for stimulating the release of the non-essential; in the release of that which is not essential, it tends to bring the hidden aspects of any problem or condition to conscious recognition.

This mineral is one of higher thought and higher consciousness. It both stimulates and facilitates the increase in ones awareness (on all levels) and brings the user to the understanding of ones own essential nature (hence, promoting realization of that which one personally intends).

Perforated Onyx has been used in the treatment of neuralgia, arthritis, rheumatism, senility, arterial constriction, bruising, and cysts. It also an excellent activating agent for other minerals.

Vibrates to the numbers 9 and 6 (inclusive of Growth Interference).

## OPAL - LEMON

[Astrological Signs of Leo & Aquarius]

***OPAL - LEMON*** - $SiO_2$♥$nH_2O$; Hardness 5.5-6; Locality: Nevada; Photography by Jim Hughes, Assisted by ♪ Melody ♫; Collection of ♪ Melody ♫, Applewood, CO, USA; Gift of Bob Bleily, MT, USA.

Lemon Opal crystallizes in the form of delicious lemon colour masses. It is uncertain who the first person was to describe Opal; however, it was named from "opalus", the ancient name for the mineral. The addition of "Lemon" to the name was due to exhibition of the delicious lemon colour. The following properties are in addition to those listed in the OPAL section of "Love Is In The Earth - A Kaleidoscope Of Crystals Update".

This mineral is "a stone to provide "the key" to all problems, enigmas, and mysteries". It acts to assist one in accessing that which is hidden in any situation. One can place the mineral on letters, photographs, etc., in order to gain admittance to disguised or enigmatic messages which are inherent.

It can also be used to expedite systematic problem resolution; placing the Lemon Opal upon a publication, which contains the details necessary to arrive at a solution, has stimulated the inner comprehension of the answer.

Lemon Opal presents a holographic energy which stimulates the recognition that one is comprised of fundamental units which are always the same whether divided into a million sections or allowed to remain as one integral element; it furthers the comprehension that any of the units are the organizing principle of reality as we perceive it. When one employs the mineral to alter the consciousness, the basic hologram evolves and produces an analysis and timing which is often the key to the real solution for any serious or unbalanced problem. It assists one in separating radically from the physical plane in order to experience other dimensions, while returning in the same corporeal form to regain touch with the Earth plane.

The mineral has been used to solve the "riddle of humanity" and brings the awareness of Norse mythology to ones cognizance. It actually facilitates the action of "going in many directions" at the same time, bringing focus for all directions and eliminating the "scattered" feeling that excessive work often brings. The energy makes visible the lines of growth for completion.

Lemon Opal radiates a lovely energy and has been recognized as a constant source of the brilliant light for the crown chakra. When one holds or carries the mineral (or uses an elixir of same), the energy tends to surround the body, providing for a protective barrier. It acts as a fountain of energy, emanating from the crown (or apex of a structure or building) and continuing the enclosure to the location where the Earth is encountered.

It can be used to clear an area of negativity, to create protective barriers, and to transfer healing energy to the self or another.

It has been used as an astringent for the interior and the exterior of the body in the form of an elixir, promoting the dissipation of infection, contamination, and harmful bacteria. It can also be used in the treatment of disorders of the eyes (near-sightedness), lymph glands, and the spleen.

Vibrates to the number 5.

## OPAL - CAT'S EYE [Astrological Signs of Leo, Capricorn, & Scorpio]

***OPAL - CAT'S EYE*** - $SiO_2$♥$nH_2O$ with impurities; Hardness 3.5-4.5; Locality: Minas Gerais, Brasil; Photography by Jim Hughes, Assisted by ♪ Melody ♫; Collection of ♪ Melody ♫, Applewood, CO, USA. Gift of Bob Jackson, Applewood, CO, USA.

Cat's Eye Opal crystallizes in the form of fibrous plates and masses exhibiting chatoyant yellow to green colours. It is uncertain who the first person was to describe Opal; however, it was named from "opalus", the ancient name for the mineral. The addition of "Cat's Eye" to the name was due to exhibition of the dazzling chatoyance. The following properties are in addition to those listed in the OPAL section of "Love Is In The Earth - A Kaleidoscope Of Crystals Update".

This mineral can help one to observe from many directions and to integrate the knowledge coming from each; for example, looking within oneself from outside the self, looking into ones environment from within the environment, and looking within the Earth from upon the Earth, looking into the auric field from within the auric field, can present answers concerning well-being and evolution. The other possibilities are endless and are left to the reader.

It has also been used as a symbol for continuation of marriage pledges and to assure commitments in personal alliances, in spiritual growth, and in business relationships. Cat's Eye Opal brings the energy of the heart chakra, the crown chakra, and the intellect, providing for love with rationality and no conditions, and for reason with an altruistic concern for others. It stimulates an "outreach" energy to bring love to one and to allow one to recognize compassion and caring. The radiant light emitted by this mineral brings an enhancement of ones aura and a shining reflective nature to ones being.

It provides for a reciprocal openness, giving a radiance of energy while allowing for an exchange of "something" (positive) to return to the user. By the action of the energy, it assists the "giver" and the "receiver" to both maintain each other and to act in the manner of reciprocity; one providing the radiant energy and one receiving the blessings of all that is needed or desired. Please note that one would be wise to be "sure" that one truly desires "something" prior to asking to receive same - in addition, being specific is absolutely necessary; it is suggested that any desire which is requested be requested in the written precise form.

This mineral has been used by the Brasilian shamen to automatically align the chakras and to provide grounding concurrently.

It facilitates the transforming of states from Alpha, to Beta, to Gamma, and enhances lucidity in dreaming and memory of same.

It stimulates communication and psychic awareness on all levels. It dispels estrangement, resentment, and frustration and helps to facilitate intelligibility with respect to mental perception and linear rationality. It induces one to persist in endeavors and in situations which will further ones progression, and to desist in endeavors/situations which are detrimental.

It has been used in the treatment of broken bones, disorders of the skeletal system/nervous system/circulatory system, to dispel chills, to promote coagulation, and to extend ones peripheral vision.

Vibrates to the number 5.

## OZOKERITE

[Astrological Signs of Cancer & Gemini]
***Also Known as Moldavite***

***OZOKERITE-*** $Ca_{14}Nb_2(Si_2O_7)_4O_8F_2$; with a Melting Point of 95-100 degrees Centigrade; Locality: Soldiers Summit, Utah, USA; Photography by Jim Hughes, Assisted by ♪ Melody ♫; Collection of ♪ Melody ♫, Applewood, CO, USA.

Ozokerite is a rare exotic white to brown to black natural and native paraffin wax; the colour range depends upon the inclusion of impurities (the white form is rarely found prior to processing). The geological community hypothesizes that the mineral separated from a paraffin-based petroleum and formed when the petroleum containing it percolated through rock fissures. It is usually found in veins filling fractures in the rocks which are in turn exposed by mining. The configuration is truly unique. The name is sometimes spelled with a "c" replacing the "k". The mineral, under the name "Ozokerite", was first described by E.F. Glocker in 1833 and was named from the Greek words "to smell wax". It is interesting to note that the name "Moldavite" was coined for Ozokerite by Cobalescu and by Istrati in the late 1800's; this "Moldavite" was mined in Moldavia, Romania during that same period.

Ozokerite has been used to enhance ones voice, to promote or to correct tone and pitch, and to reinforce the arts of music and song.

It has facilitated record-keeping of ideas and inventions and has prompted communication with those of other physical worlds.

Placing the mineral at the feet, there has been a slight grounding effect as energy was directed toward the lower body and the Earth, tending to maintain more efficient grounding and assisting one in retaining harmony with the Earth. Holding the mineral at the solar plexus, a small increase has been noted in the energy in front of the body, with large increases on the sides. Kirlian photography has shown that if one holds the mineral in the receiving hand, the celestial fields of the body can be increased.

It has been used to provide protection during lightening storms and for those who work with electricity. It further assists one in activities associated with water (e.g., divers), precluding harm from same.

Ozokerite has assisted in stimulating the recall, promoting a photographic memory capability.

It promotes a "sparkle" in ones intellect which truly shines through ones life.

It allows one to live the fantasy of childhood with the intelligence of the adult, bringing illusions which are desired to realities which are requested. This is facilitated without struggle and without explosive occurrences.

It furthers romantic pursuits and assists one in attaining the compatibility of congruity and appropriate-ness, without substitution for any pre-determined criteria. The inherent magnetism within the aura of the mineral acts to bring to one that which is always within ones reach.

It has been used in the regulation of body temperature, to increase the abilities of the sense of smell, to smooth creases in the face, to alleviate insomnia, to treat disorders of the stomach and intestinal lining, to promote negative (beneficial) ion stimulation, to stimulate dexterity, to relieve multiple-personality disorders and multiple-chemical sensitivities (MCS), and to cleanse toxins and free-radicals from the body.

Ozokerite vibrates to the numbers 7 & 8.

**" IT'S JUST SPONTANEOUS,
YOU CAN'T CONTRIVE"**

Jude Painton
Oregon, USA

***PETALITE*** - $LiAlSi_4O_{10}$; Hardness 6-6.5; Locality: Ribicon, Namibia (Large white to pink Rough) and Minas Gerais Brasil (Small white to colourless fragments); Photography by Jim Hughes, Assisted by ♪ Melody ♫; Collection of ♪ Melody ♫, Applewood, CO, USA.

Petalite crystallizes in the form of the monoclinic system, masses, and cleavable foliates. The colour range includes colourless, white, grey, pink, reddish-white, and greenish-white. The mineral was first described by B.J. d'Andrada in 1800 and was named from the Greek word for "a leaf", referring to the natural cleavage of Petalite. The inclusion of Petalite again in this supplement is due to the "new" forms available; the following properties are in addition to those listed in the PETALITE section of "Love Is In The Earth - A Kaleidoscope Of Crystals Update".

The small white to colourless fragments of Petalite have been found to be quite powerful with respect to energy release and focus. When the mineral shows the pinkish-colour, it has stimulated release of the heart-energy and to promote focus for love.

The mineral both allows one to experience the Earth, and to tap into heavenly realms via use of messengers. It has been known as a "stone of the angels", bringing calm and peacefulness while assisting one in maintaining a central and centered focus.

The main "difficulty" of this stone is:

## "THE ENERGY HAS NO RULES"

This does not imply that it is unruly, but it does signify that there are no "rules" for using the energy - the energy tends to be quite orderly and directional and acts to focus on that which one proposes. A magnitude of respect is required while using this mineral; one <u>must</u> (a rule?) be mindful and prudent in making the determination with respect to focus of the energy, for "that which one thinks" will direct the flow.

Petalite has also been used to render negative energy impotent, to dissolve enchantments and spells, and to destroy all black magic.

This mineral has been used to calm disorderly energy within the physical body and within emotional states, to provide relief from stress and tension, to alleviate muscular tightness, and to regulate heart beat.

Vibrates to the number 7.

## POLLUCITE

[Astrological Sign of Aquarius]

***POLLUCITE*** **-** $(Cs,Na)(AlSi_2)O_6$♥$nH_2O$ or $(Cs,Na)_2Al_2Si_4O_{12}$♥$H_2O$; Hardness 6.5; Locality: Mt. Mica Mine, Paris Hill, ME, USA; Photography by Jim Hughes, Assisted by ♪ Melody ♫; Collection of ♪ Melody ♫, Applewood, CO, USA.

Pollucite crystallizes in the isometric system and, usually, in masses. The colour ranges from colourless to milky-white. The mineral was first described by A. Breithaupt in 1846 and was named after Pollux, who was immortal and was one of the twin sons of Zeus.

This mineral represents "brotherly" affection, and the stabilizing of kinship between all of humanity. It helps one toward mental clarity and stimulates and clears the heart chakra.

It is an excellent energy for Reiki and all hands-on healing, to direct ones actions and to stimulate the proper response to the energies applied. It also assists one in determining which minerals would be most conducive in application for a specific problem or condition.

Pollucite has been used to facilitate transition between the mortal and immortal worlds. It can be used to assist one in the release of the material world <u>or</u> to assist one in gaining information about the material world from the immortal world.

It has been used as a mineral to assist in the protection of sailors and all sea-faring activities.

It has also provided protection against the impurities and contaminants in ones environment, assisting in the dissipation of same. Hence, it is a very positive energy to have residing within ones environment and to have in ones energy field during any type of travel.

It is an excellent stone for supporting one during the stages of "lesson learning", providing insight to the diminishment of limitations and to those responsibilities which are not necessary. It also furthers ones abilities to maintain cooperation and tact in all situations.

Kirlian photography has shown that, when activated, this mineral emanates the total spectrum of colour, and can hence, be applied to all energy medians for activation, stimulation and cleansing - and can be used in the restoration of all centers.

Pollucite has been used to initiate a chain-reaction of energies within the body, allowing one to sustain oneself for long periods. Endurance, perseverance, and tenacity are enhanced. In addition, it has assisted in journeying to the interior of the body in order to facilitate diagnosis and to remediate disorders, bringing clarity to insights and methodology for procedures which would enhance the results.

It has been used to allay weakness in the body, to provide strength to atrophied muscular structures, and to produce an energy conducive to stabilization. It can be used in the treatment of hypoglycemia and pancreatic secretory functions, to assist in the alleviation of botulism, radiation, and other contaminants, and to promote recovery after chemical/radiation treatments for cancer.

The slight content of cesium in this mineral precludes its use in the normal method of preparation of an elixir.

Vibrates to the number 5.

## **PORPHYRY - IMPERIAL** [Astrological Signs of Scorpio & Libra]

***PORPHYRY - IMPERIAL*** - An igneous purple rock quarried in Egypt and characterized by phenocrysts of alkali feldspar; Hardness 6-6.5; Locality: Egypt; Photography by Dave Shrum, Colorado Camera; Collection of ♪ Melody ♫, Applewood, CO, USA. Gift of Jean Jacques Eclancher, Paris, France.

Porphyry Imperial is a pinkish-violet igneous rock containing phenocrysts of alkali feldspar. It is found in Egypt. There is no record of the first description of this mineral; the name is from the Greek word for the colour "purple". The following properties are in addition to those listed in the FELDSPAR section of "Love Is In The Earth - A Kaleidoscope Of Crystals Update".

This mineral represents both the "City of The Sun" (the location where King Tutankhamen ruled) and the "Valley of The Kings" (the location where his body was buried). The mineral was found in both locations upon discovery and archeological excavations of same.

It represents the "solution of life" and the advance to the infinite realm of wisdom. It has been used for dowsing, to enhance creativity, to enhance fertility in both mind and body, and to bring long life.

The phenocrysts act to bring forth the light of the universe, integrating it with the light of the Inner Self, such that one may speak, act, and perform the will of the enlightened.

The total structure has been used as an amulet/talisman, the phenocrysts depicting a type of hieroglyphics which represent "that which rules the Earth". It was used for protection during the time of Tutankhamen and is said to have provided a link between those of the Earth and those of other planes. Any natural or polished shape has facilitated these qualities.

It has also been used to assist one in translation of all types of symbology and ancient languages which are not constructed with the normal English letters.

Porphyry Imperial has been known as "a stone of material wealth", bringing the actualization of abundance and prosperity to the user. It further stimulates the energies of acquisition and accumulation and also assists one in not "being attached". The focal points of the phenocrysts tend to exhibit a multi-dimensional and multi-focussed energy to reach out to bring unity to the multi-facets of the material objectives.

It also tends to reverse "exclamations of impatience" such that one is provided with patience when necessary. However, the energy of the mineral is such that patience is seldom needed; the actualization is not dependent upon patience or persistence, but rather on intent.

The results of connecting with others on the spiritual plane, of connecting oneself to the higher spiritual levels, and in physical plane connections are both swift and timely.

Porphyry Imperial also tends to provide for a peeling effect to uncover that which is hidden. It also acts to assist one in connections with that which is obscured or concealed.

The mineral has been used to balance the red cell count with the white cell count, to assist in transitions, to combat growths, to lessen traumas associated with physical growth, and to ameliorate dyslexia.

Vibrates to the number 8.

## PRASIOLITE

[Astrological Signs of Capricorn & Scorpio]
***Also Known As "Green Amethyst"***

***PRASIOLITE (In Quartz)*** **-** Aluminosilicate of Mg and Fe (in Quartz); Hardness 7-7.5; Locality: Montezuma Mine, Minas Gerais, Brasil (also from Upper Amazon); Photography by Jim Hughes, Assisted by ♪ Melody ♬; Collection of ♪ Melody ♬, Applewood, CO, USA. Gift of Tony Swerus, Brasil.

Prasiolite crystallizes as a soft green fibrous mineral. The inclusion of this mineral within quartz provides the necessary iron such that the structure could theoretically be named "Green Amethyst". The name is sometimes spelled with an "e" replacing the first "i". The mineral was first described by A. Erdmann in 1840 and was named for the Greek word meaning "leek", referring to the green colour.

This mineral brings appreciation, approval, and acclaim to the user. It promotes recognition of ones accomplishments and furthers the completion of same.

It has been known as the "celestial root", bringing ancient knowledge of illumination, germination, and growth. It assists one in determining when the beginning will commence and promotes the "lighting of the fuse" to celebrate ones own fireworks, helping one to be both wise and noble with full understanding of the process. It further provides for sufficient tranquility of the mind to assist one in contemplating metaphors without vulnerability to the unknown.

Prasiolite is reminiscent of the "Green Man", who has an origin in remote antiquity. It produces the light flowing spiral energy conducive to orderly growth, and the progression of transfomation, allowing for awakening from restrictive "old ways". The energy both promotes and quickens growth and is associated with a revival of the spirit in a vigorous form.

The mineral is one of the great goddess and the reinterpretation of the past, melding with the masculine energy of protection and growth of strength and power in the intellect. It introduces the fresh conception of humanity as being comprised of an individual soul which contains the marks of personal history and experience.

It is an excellent mineral for assisting one in expressing emotions and in facilitating accuracy and power of observation unparalleled in our age.

It furthers the interdependence of human minds which is actually greater than the interdependence of other living things and advances the prophetic capabilities of all who experience the energies, the energies of continual movement and exchange.

Prasiolite has also been used to bring forth a polarizing prismatic energy, which engenders a spectrum of energy to clear and to activate all of the chakras and to create both connections and communication between the self and the consciousness from other galaxies. It has also been used in ceremonial celebrations to bring forth the healing capabilities of the participants.

This mineral has been used to stimulate healing on the spiritual level and to assist one in regaining the connection with the perfection of the self and the physical body. It has assisted in cleansing the body and in ameliorating all conditions of disorderly growth.

Prasiolite vibrates to the numbers 4 and 7. "Green Amethyst" (Prasiolite in Quartz) vibrates to the numbers 1 and 8.

## PRICEITE

[Astrological Sign of Virgo]

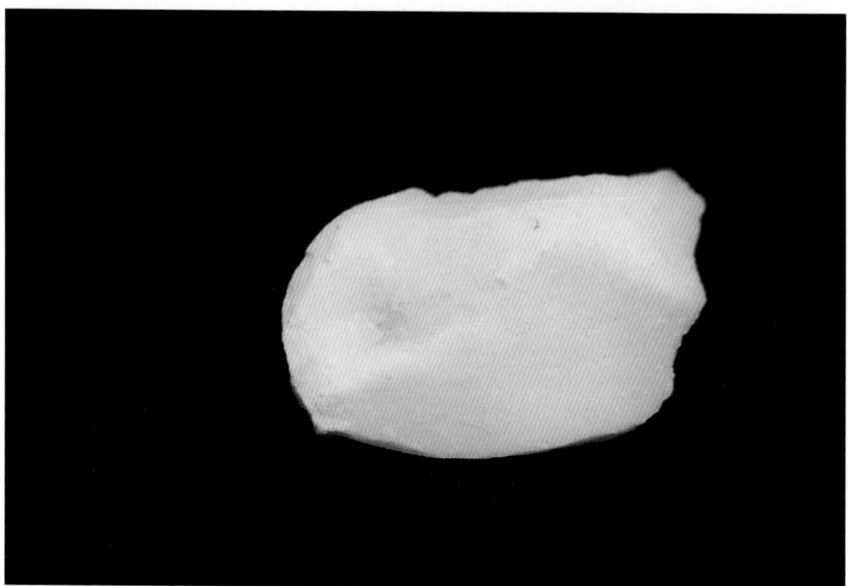

***PRICEITE*** - $Ca_4B_{10}O_{19}$♥$7H_2O$; Hardness 3-3.5; Locality: San Bernadino Co., CA, USA; Photography by Jim Hughes, Assisted by ♪ Melody ♫; Collection of ♪ Melody ♫, Applewood, CO, USA.

Priceite crystallizes in the formation of snow-white earthy porcelanous masses, sometimes with clay inclusions, and in plate-like arrangements. The mineral was first described by B. Silliman, Jr., in 1873, where he named the "unnamed" mineral discovered by A.W. Chase in 1972. Priceite was named for T. Price.

This mineral has been likened to an intact Pandora's Box, allowing for the access of same by the user. Hence, it is necessary to prepare for the release of the "blessings of the gods" which have been preserved for the human race. Preparation includes centering and circular breathing; the Guangdong Tektite has also been used to elevate ones consciousness during this time of access with the energies of Priceite.

It has been used to enhance the "chase", assisting one in tracking and in pursuing that which is desired while eliminating fatigue and apathy. It assists one with speed and endurance and is excellent for runners.

Priceite has been used to promote gain during negotiations, to instill progress during arbitrations, and to support all forms of mediations.

It is a mineral for polarity balance via exchange between the physical structure and the ethereal individual equilibrium. It brings support for transition from one level to another and assists one in retaining the foundations of balance. It acts to bring together all of the images of perfection such that the physical, emotional, or intellectual structure maintains the precision of purification.

It has been used to access the "underworld" of cosmic energies where one may draw upon the ultimate reality as the source of all life and the manifested world.

Used in tantric meditations, Priceite facilitates the flow of the inner state of meditation to the outer actualization of spirituality.

It can also assist one in obtaining bargains and in retaining monies. The energy equips one to understand that the acceptance of responsibility to the self leads to virtue in ones enterprises and in the regulation of money.

One who receives a vision from either the visible world or from the nourishing invisible world, can sustain and preserve visions of the dreamer, and can employ the energies of Priceite to assist in realizing those thoughts. It actually assists one in appreciating ones desires, and facilitates the building of ones dreams in this physical reality.

It releases ones limitations such that permission is granted which allows one to actualize aspirations and to attain limitless achievements. It inspires, motivates, and induces ambition toward the accomplishment of objectives.

Priceite can help one to achieve a bodily construction which resists physical disorders. It is said to enable one to consume alcohol without exhibiting the effects. It has been used in the treatment of chromosome dysfunction and fever producing disorders, and to lessen fatty deposits.

Vibrates to the number 4.

## "PUDDING STONE" [Astrological Sign of Gemini]

***"PUDDING STONE" -*** A conglomerate stone exhibiting differing materials in a lovely display of colours (it usually contains Jasper, Chert, Quartz, etc.); Hardness Variable; Locality: Ontario, Canada; Photography by Jim Hughes, Assisted by ♪ Melody ♫; Collection of ♪ Melody ♫, Applewood, CO, USA.

The origin of the individual descriptive name of "Pudding Stone" has been said to be due to the mixture of colours. The following properties are in addition to those listed in the JASPER, CHERT, and QUARTZ sections of "Love Is In The Earth - A Kaleidoscope Of Crystals Update".

This mineral has been used to expedite the rectification of unfair or biased situations; meditation with the mineral can provide insight to the method of amelioration. The energy conveys the theme that all alternatives are uniquely ones liability. It can also assist in providing for release during states of peril.

"Pudding Stone" can facilitate the reiteration of dreams to allow the dreamer to remember the aspects which could be consequential in ones life. It seems to replicate the dream on a video-type mechanism for access during states of meditation.

It can also be used to prevent "set-backs" in disorders. The mineral assists in helping one to learn to progress, and to eliminate the aspects of digression.

"Pudding Stone" can be used to assist in, and to augment, the state of composure. It can be supportive in eradicating anxiety, allowing one to recognize that this type of thought process does not change a situation and that appropriate action can modify results; it also assists one in gaining insight to beneficial action, eliminating distress and depression and increasing ones feeling of well-being. It is an excellent stone for bringing mental clarity to any predicament.

It can serve to activate the imagination and to promote faith in, and acceptance of, ones elemental proclivities and instinctive energies.

This mineral is important in the ceremonies of the Canadian Indians. It is said to have been used as an implement with which to request the presence of the spirit guides from each direction. It also acts to provide a bridging of worlds such that one may cross-over and/or others may approach the user.

It can be quite helpful during the state of accessing other worlds, to maintain one during the traversal of disquieting situations, and in gaining a stronghold in the "new". During the meditative state, it has produced contact with the keepers of the four directions, with information imparted which was extremely relevant and of vast importance to the users.

It can also be instrumental in both astral and mind travel, again providing the "countersign" for entry.

At the base chakra, it has provided both grounding and survival instincts; at the crown chakra, it can stimulate the melding of advancement of spirituality with protection.

It can be used in the treatment of chemical imbalances, to soothe allergic reactions, to stimulate the production of beneficial bacteria within the body, and to act as an anesthetic during times of pain.

Vibrates to the number 4.

***PYRARGYRITE*** - $Ag_3SbS_3$; Hardness 2.5; Locality: Mexico (Top) and Atacama, Chile, S.A. (Bottom); Photography by Jim Hughes, Assisted by ♪ Melody ♫; Collection of ♪ Melody ♫, Applewood, CO, USA; Top Specimen - Gift of Angel Torrecillas, Mexico; Bottom Specimen - Gift of LizBeth Christensen & Peter Bane, CO, USA.

The mineral was first described by E.F. Glocker in 1831 and was named from the Greek words meaning "fire" and "silver", referring to the colour and composition. This is another of the "Ruby Silvers", similar to Proustite, but with differing properties.

It can be used to further the advancement of the conscious connection between the higher levels of intuition and heart-felt love, producing compassion in both communication and decision-making.

Pyrargyrite is known as a "stone of royalty", both collecting and accumulating energy while elevating and inspiring intellectual concentration. It can cultivate ones mastery in contentions and conflicts, encouraging sensitivity and dissuading disorder. It is an excellent shielding stone, defending on all levels and preserving ones consciousness from psychic attack.

It has also been likened to the energy required for one to ascend from martyrdom, bringing a foundation to further ones recognition of the options which exist with respect to the need to experience suffering, distress, and/or hardship.

In Mayan cultures, it was used in the practice of fortune-telling, to assist in the determination of resolutions and decisions. It was also considered to be one of the "fire" stones, bringing cause for effects, to the mind of the user. It has further acted to terminate leakages of energy from the chakras and to transmute/transform negative energy. It can also assist one in maintaining a bond with another person, with another area of the world, or with the Earth - allowing for the transmission of information and energy to the defined location (excellent for Earth-healing).

Pyrargyrite has been used for aeons to present results prior to actualization such that one may view the results prior to experiencing the reality.

It has been used to ameliorate the intake of caffeine and to serve as an opposing force to stimulants. It can also be used in the treatment of obesity and circulatory disorders, and to enhance digestion/elimination.

Vibrates to the number 9.

## PYRITE - ISIS & OSIRIS ©

[Astrological Signs of Aquarius, Leo & Scorpio]

***PYRITE - "ISIS & OSIRIS"© - $FeS_2$;*** Hardness 6-6.5; Locality: China; Photography by Jim Hughes, Assisted by ♪ Melody ♫; Collection of ♪ Melody ♫, Applewood, CO, USA; Gift of Jean Jacques Eclancher, Paris, France.

The name Pyrite was first described by Dioscorades in approximately 50 A.D. and came from the Greek word for "fire" since the mineral produces sparks when struck with steel. The addition of "Isis & Osiris" to the name was suggested by J.J. Eclancher due to the matching and/or teaming of the two configurations -one with the druse and one with the larger cubic configuration. It should be noted that some single specimens combine both the druse and the larger cubic configuration into one stone. The following properties are in addition to those listed in the PYRITE section of "Love Is In The Earth - A Kaleidoscope Of Crystals Update".

The "Isis & Osiris" © pyrite configuration has been known as "the emperor's new stone", promoting retrieval of ancient writings concerning the esoteric precepts of sacred movements, the formation and characteristics of mystic knowledge, and details from the akashic records relative to the advancement of the innate psychic and astral abilities. It is a energy which represents the "ruler", balancing the yin and yang qualities and facilitating equilibrium of energy throughout the physical body as well as the mind and the emotions. It has also been used in single-parenting to facilitate duality in ones character such that the child receives both the feminine and masculine energies of growing.

It should be noted that the stones are of the Isis configuration (smooth, constant, and representative of the solar disk), of the Osiris configuration (erratic in structure, unpredictable, and representative of a crown of many facets), and of the androgynous (containing both characteristics).

The combination is an assurance of ones immortality, and is used to dissipate control from exterior influences while dispensing protection throughout ones aura and constructing a shield to allay negative energies.

It has been used as a disk-like conveyor for stratospheric electricity, providing for passage, to the Earth and to the user, of electrical and magnetic forces. The energy further assists one in the conscious access of ethereal consciousness, providing a medium through which an understanding <u>and</u> an actualization of healing processes can be manifested. It serves to automatically order the chakras and the energy fields and to consolidate the qualities of the chakras such that "higher work" can be performed with ease. It actually aligns all chakras automatically and immediately, with no conscious direction. If directed with the consciousness of the user, it can also open the chakras.

The "Isis & Osiris" © stones are said to have been used in Atlantean ceremonial activities to maintain the psychic energies of that time period. They are regarded as having regenerative power and are said to reinforce the genesis of both the inner and the outer selves, promoting a catalytic energy to accelerate the modification of ones world while producing the qualities of expansiveness, creativity, and awareness in the realm of knowledge which is conducive to the art of realization.

The energy further acts to align the bodies - auric and physical - to the full light spectrum, encouraging the optimum state of health and being. The stones have also been used in tissue regeneration and to promote recovery from degenerative disorders.

Vibrate to the master number 55 and the number 4.

## PYROLUCITE - VELVET

[Astrological Sign of Aries]

***PYROLUCITE (VELVET)*** - $MnO_2$; Hardness 2-2.5; Locality: Minas Gerais, Brasil; Photography by Jim Hughes, Assisted by ♪ Melody ♫; Collection of ♪ Melody ♫, Applewood, CO, USA. Gift of Roger Trontz, FL, USA.

Velvet Pyrolucite crystallizes in the formation of a fibrous and radiating structure. The colour is iron-black. The mineral was first described by W. Haidinger in 1827 and was named from the Greek words meaning "fire" and "to wash", due to its use in decolourizing glass. The inclusion of Pyrolucite again in this supplement is due to the "new" velvet form available; the following properties are in addition to those listed in the PYROLUCITE section of "Love Is In The Earth - A Kaleidoscope Of Crystals Update".

This mineral initiates "painless" realization of, and complete healing via, ones karmic cycle.

It promotes the acceptance of an internal approval and grants one the view and the understanding of the length of ones stay in the physical form, bringing to recognition those karmic debts and learning situations of which one has previously agreed to be a part; hence, producing an understanding of ones current circumstances, as well as those which will manifest due to ones "past" situations. Hence, if one wishes not to return to the physical form, one may access and apply this information.

It further promotes a suspension of barriers in ones path, catching and dispersing the obstacles and clearing the way. It also acts to promote stamina and an open mind in all endeavors.

It has been used to foster super-human strength, to assist one in diversification in areas of quests, and to encourage, during meditative states and astral projection, a range of locations, settings, and messages for consideration to the user.

Velvet Pyrolucite activates the base chakra, while providing for crown chakra stimulation, and further induces a clear connection to the powerful basis of any venture one endeavors. It inspires synchronicity in transformation, bringing collective initiative toward the application of ones goal(s).

This mineral can be used to induce analytical capabilities and accuracy. It provides for discernment in situations and revives ones innate potentials and proficiencies.

It is also used to produce revelation from, and connected-ness with, the entities residing in, or transitioning to, the spiritual worlds.

It is another truly "warm, fuzzy" stone of the new age, bringing light to the darkness and illumination to the obscure. It furthers ones action in a calm and stable fashion such that the tranquility and flexibility of ones character is foremost, while ones tenacity produces results.

The mineral can be used in the treatment of eruptions (internal and external), compulsive behavior, nervous stomach, trauma, and to stabilize conditions of disorder. It has been used for protection against the over-production of red blood cells. It is also a stone to enhance the protection of ones environment against the infiltration of dis-ease.

Vibrates to the master number 77.

# A FANTASIA ESTÁ DENTRO DE VOCÊ

## QUARTZ - With BLACK SNOWBALLS

[Astrological Sign of Taurus]

***QUARTZ - With BLACK SNOWBALLS*** - alpha-$SiO_2$ with Inclusions of Hematite, Carbon, Manganese, or etc.; Hardness 7; Locality: Minas Gerais, Brasil; Photography by Jim Hughes, Assisted by ♪ Melody ♬; Collection of ♪ Melody ♬, Applewood, CO, USA.

Quartz with Black Snowballs is configured as Quartz (crystalline or massive), with the inclusion of black snowball-like formations. Quartz was first described as "Crystallus" (representing the crystalline formation) by Pliny in 77 A.D. and was further described by U.R. von Kalbe in 1505 to present the history of the name. The name "Quartz" was originally spelled "Quertz" and represented Quartzite (the compact granular massive configuration); it was named for the Saxon word "cross-vein ore". In the late 1700's, the two configurations (crystalline and massive) were found by T. Bergman to have the same chemical composition and, hence, were consolidated and provided with one name (Quartz). The addition of "Black Snowballs" to the name is due to the exhibition of the micro-black-snowball-like inclusions within the mineral. The following properties are in addition to those listed in the QUARTZ section of "Love Is In The Earth - A Kaleidoscope Of Crystals Update".

This mineral is a "stone for peace and healing", allowing one to go to the center of the Earth, to the center of ones being, and/or to the center of any stress or conflict in order to initiate the self-healing properties of the energy of perfection.

It is a "stone of consequences", allowing conclusions to follow intentions with a magnitude of distinction and significance in their effect. It assists one in swaying to the path which will bring realization of that which is desired. It assists in clairaudient endeavors, affording lucid, distinct, and articulate verbalization of the messages received. In this manner, it can help one to achieve that which would be helpful as the end-product of manifestation, and to recognize the difference between worldly manifestation and a manifestation which would further ones development.

It has also been called the "Stone of the Whirling Dervishes", supporting the maintenance of the meditative state. It is a stone for balance, acting as an equilibrant to outside forces, and stabilizing the yin-yang values within ones energy field. It assists in the alignment of the n-dimensional energy centers with those of the ethereal domain, and promotes continence in clearing and perfecting the chakras.

Quartz with Black Snowballs has been used to assist one in refinement with respect to decisions and to bring confidence, pleasure, and peace of mind. It allows one to recognize and to exhibit sufficient sensitivity to appreciate that each person does not wish to have the same patterns in life, and that for each person the choices are different. It sometimes appears that the stone is inhabited by the "sprite of providence"; the dismissal of worries, the freedom of movement, and the energetic pursuit of intangibility being fostered - with clarity of, and approval by, the intellect.

It has been used in the treatment of disorders associated with the eyes, the lymph glands, the white blood corpuscles, and the throat. It has assisted in alleviation of hypertension, stress, and anxiety, and has helped to facilitate a decrease in high levels of blood pressure. The configuration has also been useful in treating Meniere's Dis-Ease, ameliorating and helping to regulate both dizziness and hearing loss.

Vibrates to the number 6.

## QUARTZ - With FELDSPAR STRATIFICATION

[Astrological Signs of Scorpio & Aquarius]

***QUARTZ - With FELDSPAR STRATIFICATION*** - alpha-$SiO_2$ with Inclusions of Feldspar [$(K,Na,Ca,Ba,NH_4)(Si,Al)_4O_8$]; Hardness 7 (Quartz) and 6-6.5 (Feldspar); Locality: Minas Gerais, Brasil; Photography by Jim Hughes, Assisted by ♪ Melody ♫; Collection of ♪ Melody ♫, Applewood, CO, USA.

Quartz with Feldspar Stratification crystallizes in masses; complete crystals have not yet been seen by the author. Quartz was first described as "Crystallus" (representing the crystalline formation) by Pliny in 77 A.D. and was further described by U.R. von Kalbe in 1505 to present the history of the name. The name "Quartz" was originally spelled "Quertz" and represented Quartzite (the compact granular massive configuration); it was named for the Saxon word "cross-vein ore". In the late 1700's, the two configurations (crystalline and massive) were found by T. Bergman to have the same chemical composition and, hence, were consolidated and provided with one name (Quartz). The name, Feldspar, was first described by D. Tilas in 1740 as "Feldtspat", was described by J.G. Wallerius in 1747 as "Felt-Spat", and was modified by Brünnich in 1770; it was named from the Greek word "feldspath".

In addition to the properties listed in the QUARTZ and FELDSPAR sections of "Love Is In The Earth - A Kaleidoscope Of Crystals Update", this mineral can be used to enhance communication on the physical plane and to strengthen the connection with other worlds and with beings in those worlds. It assists one in traversing the layers of the ethers and in uniting with the realm that is chosen with intent.

It is a "stone of growth", bringing progress and development to that which is desired to be manifested. It tends to preserve or to germinate the "seed" of the thought pattern, assisting one to determine the "right" time for fruition while obliterating any barren ground of resentment, frustration, or despair. Bringing a strength of concentration, it alleviates astonishment, allowing one to "remember" and providing one with "the advantage".

Quartz with Feldspar Stratification assists one in realizing that the human mind brings the gift of memory, to be celebrated and revered, while allowing for inspiration and creative flow as the Mother of the Muses.

When used in meditation, the mineral facilitates a cleaner and easier entry and assists one in attaining the state of "no mind". When holding the mineral, the energy tends to provide for protection within an encircling many-layered spiral; in meditation, the spiral is predisposed to become the Kundalini - rising, and surrounding the essence of physical body as well as the outer bodies during the same time it is within ones body. It further separates one from fear and any sense of isolation projected from within the mind, allowing for an analytic evaluation of all situations.

The mineral has been used in the study of cereology [the analysis of crop circles/markings], bringing information concerning purpose and methods. It can also provide details concerning interrelationships which were awakened during the time of construction.

Quartz with Feldspar Stratification has been used in the treatment of the autistic, to assist (as an elixir) in the control of arterial plaque, and in regeneration of the tissues of the skin. It has also been used in Diagnostic Imaging to determine location and cause of dis-ease.

Vibrates to the number 5.

## QUARTZ - With MICA INCLUSIONS

[Astrological Sign of Cancer]

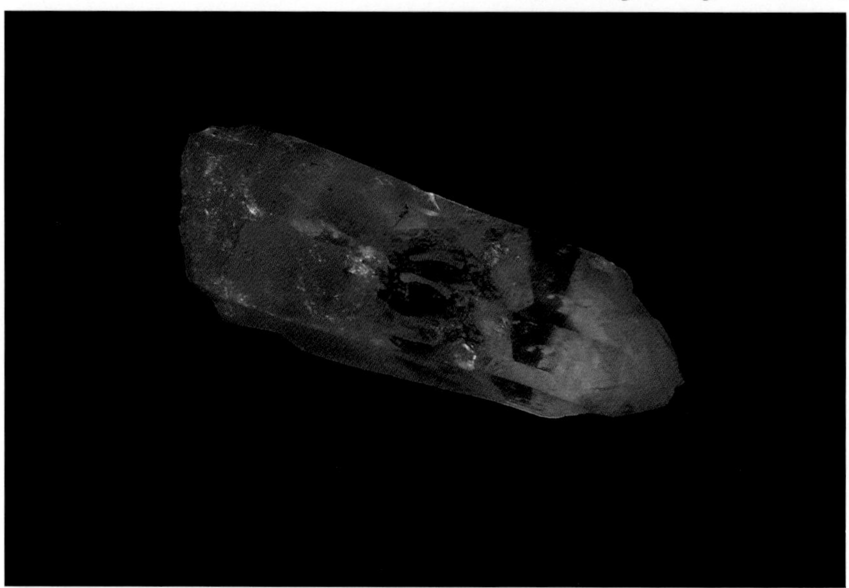

***QUARTZ - With MICA INCLUSIONS*** - alpha-$SiO_2$ with Inclusions of Mica; Hardness 7 (Quartz) and 2-2.5; Locality: Minas Gerais, Brasil; Photography by Jim Hughes, Assisted by ♪ Melody ♫; Collection of ♪ Melody ♫, Applewood, CO, USA.

Quartz included with Mica is configured as Quartz (crystalline or massive), with the inclusion of Mica (in any form). Quartz was first described as "Crystallus" (representing the crystalline formation) by Pliny in 77 A.D. and was further described by U.R. von Kalbe in 1505 to present the history of the name. The name "Quartz" was originally spelled "Quertz" and represented Quartzite (the compact granular massive configuration); it was named for the Saxon word "cross-vein ore". In the late 1700's, the two configurations (crystalline and massive) were found by T. Bergman to have the same chemical composition and, hence, were consolidated and provided with one name (Quartz). Mica was first described by J.D. Dana in 1850 and was named for the Neo-Latin word for "crumb, grain, little bit".

In addition to the properties listed in the QUARTZ and MICA sections of "Love Is In The Earth - A Kaleidoscope Of Crystals Update", this mineral assists one in recognizing, and in acting upon intuitive impulses, while also recognizing and rejecting action for compulsions. It tends to combat the primitive instincts which are unfaithful to the benefit of reason, bringing prompt reactions and actions to the genesis of thought.

It also augments the vision of the third-eye, bringing information concerning patterns in ones life and arrangement from past times and civilizations. The pathway to channeling information from other realms is unobstructed with the application of this mineral.

It is a stone of the crown chakra, bringing connected-ness with the Higher Self and heightening ones true consciousness. It assists one in changing ones ideas, preconceived notions, and beliefs, such that advancement toward the realization of the spiritual self is enhanced.

Quartz included with Mica can also assist in cleansing and repairing confused, entangled energy which induces retrogression in ones life. It helps in the determination of contrast, elevating the refinement of the will to further cohesiveness with unconditional love. It further acts to align the chakras, and to influence the optimum attitude of association between the self and others. It is an excellent stone for re-birthing and for releasing blockages which restrict one from the spiritual path. It acts also to arrest leakages of energy from the chakras and to transmute negative energy. It can assist one in maintaining a connection with the Earth and to promote cleansing of the atmospheric energies, and has been used in shamanic ceremonies for that purpose.

It is said to have been used in ancient ceremonial activities and to maintain the psychic energies of that time period. It promotes dreaming and stimulates the connection with, and transmission of information from, that time period.

It has been used in the treatment of both bulimia and anorexia, to assist in the remediation of macular degeneration, and to treat motor abilities. Used during acupuncture and acupressure, it has assisted in increasing the flow of energy to the directed locations. As an elixir it has also been found to be effective in the treatment of skin abrasions and silicosis.

Vibrates to the number 3.

# QUARTZ - BLUE PHANTOM

[Astrological Signs of Sagittarius & Aquarius]

***QUARTZ - BLUE PHANTOM*** - alpha-$SiO_2$ with Inclusions of (speculated) Blue Tourmaline; Hardness 7 (Quartz) and 7-7.5 (Tourmaline); Locality: Minas Gerais, Brasil; Photography by Jim Hughes, Assisted by ♪ Melody ♫; Collection of ♪ Melody ♫, Applewood, CO, USA.

Blue Phantom Quartz is recognized by a "blue phantom" crystal form within the Quartz crystal. The phantom is comprised of a blue mineral and may be partial or complete. Quartz was first described as "Crystallus" (representing the crystalline formation) by Pliny in 77 A.D. and was further described by U.R. von Kalbe in 1505 to present the history of the name. The name "Quartz" originally represented Quartzite (the compact granular massive configuration) and was spelled "Quertz"; it was named for the Saxon word "cross-vein ore". In the late 1700's, the two configurations (crystalline and massive) were found by T. Bergman to have the same chemical composition and, hence, were consolidated and provided with one name (Quartz). The word "Phantom" was named for the Late Latin word "Phantasma", with usage in mineralogy beginning in the 1800's. In addition to the properties listed in the QUARTZ and PHANTOM sections of "Love Is In The Earth - A Kaleidoscope Of Crystals Update", Blue Phantom Quartz assists one to be aware of the hinderance of anger and to realize the concept that anger is an intoxicant of the mind which numbs ones rationality. It assists one in both releasing anger and in perceiving that a "cause" for the anger can never exist "in the moment".

This mineral serves to actuate the throat chakra and to advance the expression of that which is in ones mind. It further acts to integrate the consciousness to the connected-ness of the brothers and sisters of the planet, detaching one from introversion and apprehension, while promoting experiences which are original and pristine. It actually assists one in transforming the fear of reaching-out to others, and brings awakening to new alliances. It produces a comforting resonance, generating a confidence with dignity during states of interruption and bewilderment, allowing one to enjoy the actions of being self-reliant and spontaneous.

It assuages anxiety, helping one to see that the basis of anxiety is only deficient knowledge; it assists one in achieving fulfillment of this knowledge. It can be used to inspire courtesy and attentiveness and is supportive of relationships. It further combines the elimination of constraint with the dedication to a steadfast vitality. The synthesis of the quartz and the blue phantom brings the correspondence to the conscious awareness of all within each dimension. The concept of unrestricted completion is revealed within this mineral.

The Blue Phantom Quartz has been used in telepathic endeavors to maintain connection with an object and to assist one in communicating the result. It has also been used to increase verbalization of knowledge and understanding during the utilization of Tarot Cards, "gazing", and other fortune-telling attendants.

In addition, it has been used in the treatment of disorders of the spleen, the endocrine system, and the blood, and to stabilize the metabolic processes. It can also assist in the treatment of the branching blood vessels within the body and, when consciously directed, to sustain the lowering of homocysteine within the body.

Vibrates to the master number 77.

## QUARTZ - YELLOW PHANTOM

[Astrological Signs of Leo & Scorpio]

***QUARTZ - YELLOW PHANTOM*** **-** alpha-$SiO_2$ with Inclusions of Limonite; Hardness 7 (Quartz) and 5 (Limonite); Locality: Minas Gerais, Brasil; Photography by Jim Hughes, Assisted by ♪ Melody ♫; Collection of ♪ Melody ♫, Applewood, CO, USA.

Yellow Phantom Quartz is also known as Limonite Phantom Quartz. The phantom crystal is recognized by a "phantom" crystal within the crystal. The phantom is comprised of a yellow mineral and may be partial or complete. Quartz was first described as "Crystallus" (representing the crystalline formation) by Pliny in 77 A.D. and was further described by U.R. von Kalbe in 1505 to present the history of the name. The name "Quartz" was originally spelled "Quertz" and represented Quartzite (the compact granular massive configuration); it was named for the Saxon word "cross-vein ore". In the late 1700's, the two configurations (crystalline and massive) were found by T. Bergman to have the same chemical composition and, hence, were consolidated and provided with one name (Quartz). The word "Phantom" was named for the Late Latin word "Phantasma", with usage in mineralogy beginning in the 1800's. Limonite was first described by J.F.L. Hausmann in 1813 and was named for the Greek word "meadow" because it had been found in meadows. The inclusion of the Yellow Phantom Quartz again in this supplement is due to the extensive new information available; in addition to the properties listed in the LIMONITE, YELLOW PHANTOM QUARTZ and the LIMONITE-INCLUDED QUARTZ sections of "Love Is In The Earth - A Kaleidoscope Of Crystals Update", this mineral promotes "quick thinking" with surprising answers to ingenuous questions and postulated problems. It assists one in selecting that which is in the mind such that stray unwanted and/or unwarranted thoughts are dismissed, and such that one does not misread the intent or meaning of personal or non-personal (i.e., belonging to others) thoughts.

It is a strange and complex mineral, providing for simplicity in the recognition of the intricacies of the functioning of the mind. It assists one in being open and honest, and in smiling such that the smile reaches the eyes and the heart, bringing with it a sensation of discovery from the depths of the consciousness and impressing upon one that "things are moving".

It holds extensive potential, for immediate interdimensional admittance to higher dimensional galactic energies, and to attract to the Earth plane those contemplative-patterns and resonances of light which are both paragon and suitable to ones preparation for ascension and elucidation. It expedites diverse, lucid, and distinct interdimensional interconnectedness between ones consciousness and the significant planes of light. It augments the extent and the eminence of the resonant spectrums which one can encounter, while empowering one for a transcendent and encompassing avenue to those spectrums of which one already has access; that is, one will "perceive" more explicitly and will "perceive" with an magnification of discernment within the vibrational domain to which one has ventured, and/or one will be furnished with the inter-alliance with the myriad of other-dimensional frontiers not yet experienced.

Yellow Phantom Quartz has been used in the treatment of the Epstein Barr Virus, to relieve complications from exposure to agent orange, and to provide protection (used as an elixir) from pollen and airborne allergies. It has also been employed in therapy for pancreatic, liver, and intestinal disorders, and for mental cellular rejuvenation.

Vibrates to the numbers 3 and 8.

## QUARTZ - CANDLE

[Astrological Signs of Pisces & Gemini]

***QUARTZ - CANDLE*** - alpha-$SiO_2$; Hardness 7; Locality: Madagascar; Photography by Jim Hughes, Assisted by ♪ Melody ♫; Collection of ♪ Melody ♫, Applewood, CO, USA. Gift of Bob Isaacs, MO, USA.

Candle Quartz is an elestiated formation of Quartz. Quartz was first described as "Crystallus" (representing the crystalline formation) by Pliny in 77 A.D. and was further described by U.R. von Kalbe in 1505 to present the history of the name. The name "Quartz" was originally spelled "Quertz" and represented Quartzite (the compact granular massive configuration); it was named for the Saxon word "cross-vein ore". In the late 1700's, the two configurations (crystalline and massive) were found by T. Bergman to have the same chemical composition and, hence, were consolidated and provided with one name (Quartz). The word "Candle" is used to convey the image of the dribbling wax after a candle has burned sufficiently to cause same; the appearance is rather a "soft elestiation".

The following properties are in addition to those listed in the ELESTIAL (QUARTZ) section of "Love Is In The Earth - A Kaleidoscope Of Crystals Update".

Candle Quartz is a "stone for the luminaries" of our Earth, providing for thought transmission within the physical realm and between the luminaries of other worlds. The intent to contact a specific realm is not necessary; the focus is determined by the mineral with respect to the level of ones spiritually. The information received is, usually, relative to the enhancement of the development of Earth beings, for the furtherance of this development by facilitating the connection with the total structure of humanity, and for healing of our planet.

It has been used to provide insight into the significance of the physical body as a vehicle for the lessons to be learned during this life. It conducts one to the interior of the being and fosters regard for the body as a "mansion for comprehension". It produces a realization of the damage one consciously allows to occur to the physical body and helps one to be more in control of the issues, recognizing the path to ameliorate and to discontinue negative self-fulfilling prophesies. Similar wisdom is also made accessible for the emotional and intellectual bodies.

This mineral has been used for all "gazing" activities. Prior to the mobilization of the mineral for "gazing", conscious instruction of the mind is required - otherwise, one may observe situations and ventures which are of no relevance or significance to the user.

Candle Quartz is a very tranquilizing stone which can be used to dissipate the tedious and oppressive from ones character or environment. The presence of the stone in an environment acts as a clarifying agent "to dispel the shadowy" and to "acclaim the interior illumination".

It acts to induce prudence and sensitivity, and to enhance confidence, benevolence, and the appreciation of grace.

Candle Quartz can assist in the efficient conversion of carbohydrates to energy and in the regulation of the proper flow of insulin to the blood stream. It acts to strengthen the entire anatomy, can be helpful in the absorption of nutrients, and can act to increase circulatory flows to the muscular tissue. It has been used in the treatment of headaches and in the repair of physical damage which has impacted the body.

Vibrates to the number 7.

# QUARTZ - CONSUMMATION

[Astrological Sign of Pisces]

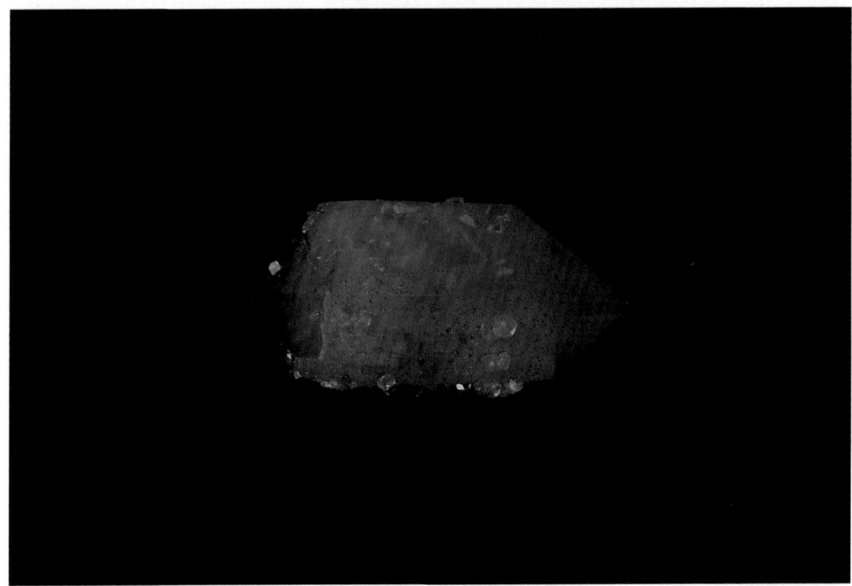

***QUARTZ - CONSUMMATION*** - alpha-$SiO_2$; Hardness 7; Locality: Minas Gerais, Brasil; Photography by Jim Hughes, Assisted by ♪ Melody ♫; Collection of ♪ Melody ♫, Applewood, CO, USA.

Consummation Quartz is configured as one crystal being in the process of consumming (engulfing) another. Quartz was first described as "Crystallus" (representing the crystalline formation) by Pliny in 77 A.D. and was further described by U.R. von Kalbe in 1505 to present the history of the name. The name "Quartz" was originally spelled "Quertz" and represented Quartzite (the compact granular massive configuration); it was named for the Saxon word "cross-vein ore". In the late 1700's, the two configurations (crystalline and massive) were found by T. Bergman to have the same chemical composition and, hence, were consolidated and provided with one name (Quartz). The word "Consummation" was used to convey the structure. The following properties are in addition to those listed in the QUARTZ section of "Love Is In The Earth - A Kaleidoscope Of Crystals Update".

This mineral is a "stone for metamorphosis and progression". It can help one to flow with constant regulation through the many fluctuations necessary in the physical world. It is also a stone for equilibrating the physical, emotional, and intellectual bodies, as well as the male/female qualities [both within themselves and between each other]. It provides for an open channel to the spiritual world, facilitating communication with those on that plane and yielding access to the akashic records.

This mineral incites the feminine aspects of a person, allowing for liberal locution of emotions. It encourage both love and a happiness with the life one has chosen.

It also assists one in writing personal thoughts clearly. It is helpful in verbal communication and in enhancing ones listening abilities. It can furnish a stimulus to allow one to connect with other worlds via automatic writing. It can be used to compose the emotions, to inspire the aspect of unconditional love, and to help one to migrate through stressful conditions.

Consummation Quartz is helpful to stimulate originality in the musician, both in the field of performance and in the area of creation.

It can further be used to surmount reservation in speech and to rectify a dissenting outlook with respect to possessions and the material aspects of ones character. It provides for grounding within communication and activates and energizes the crown chakra, culminating in the realization of ones proficiency to explicate and to clarify on all levels with discretion and alacrity.

The mineral can act as a catalyst to assist one to pursue aspirations with no restraint, bringing an energy for ending the processes of finite thought.

It has been used to reinforce ones strength, to treat spasmatic conditions, to regulate the acidity within the body, and to ameliorate discomforts associated with nervousness, mental dis-continuity, and stress. It can be used in the treatment for loss of smell and for decreasing an overabundance of mucus in ones system. It is also helpful for stabilizing ones growth patterns and for treating disorders associated with disruptive physical states.

Vibrates to the number 8.

***QUARTZ - GROWTH INTERFERENCE***
alpha-$SiO_2$; Hardness 7;
Locality: Modernertal, Canton Uri, Switzerland

***Photography by Jim Hughes, Assisted by ♪ Melody ♬***
***Collection of ♪ Melody ♬, Applewood, CO, USA***

***QUARTZ - GROWTH INTERFERENCE***
alpha-$SiO_2$; Hardness 7;
Locality: Minas Gerais, Brasil

***Photography by Jim Hughes, Assisted by ♪ Melody ♬***
***Collection of ♪ Melody ♬, Applewood, CO, USA***

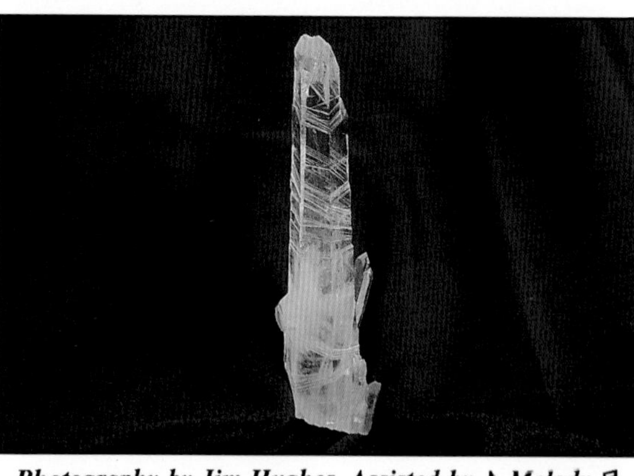

***QUARTZ - GROWTH INTERFERENCE***
alpha-$SiO_2$; Hardness 7;
Locality: Dalnygorks, Primorie, Russia

***Photography by Jim Hughes, Assisted by ♪ Melody ♬***
***Collection of ♪ Melody ♬, Applewood, CO, USA***

# QUARTZ - GROWTH INTERFERENCE

[Astrological Signs of Taurus, Scorpio & Capricorn]

Growth Interference Quartz is configured such that the structural interference of another mineral is quite obvious during the growth of the Quartz. Quartz was first described as "Crystallus" (representing the crystalline formation) by Pliny in 77 A.D. and was further described by U.R. von Kalbe in 1505 to present the history of the name. The name "Quartz" was originally spelled "Quertz" and represented Quartzite (the compact granular massive configuration); it was named for the Saxon word "cross-vein ore". In the late 1700's, the two configurations (crystalline and massive) were found by T. Bergman to have the same chemical composition and, hence, were consolidated and provided with one name (Quartz). The words "Growth Interference" are used to convey the structural interference exhibited. The inclusion of the Growth Interference Crystals in this supplement is due to the extensive new information available; the following properties are in addition to those listed in the QUARTZ - GROWTH INTERFERENCE section of "Love Is In The Earth - A Kaleidoscope Of Crystals Update".

Growth Interference Quartz allows one to penetrate the exterior layers of a difficulty or an enigma, allowing for the essence of the problem to become evident, and further providing insight to the solutions which would be most appropriate. Used alone, it further assists one in accessing the bases of any difficulties which one is experiencing. It emits an energy conducive to balancing the energy fields [personal and those with which one experiences contact] and to assist in the suspension of actions which are ineffectual and/or unavailing.

It further aligns and balances all chakras, and has served to enhance and to promote "journeying"; the energy transfer, being simultaneously multi-directional, has easily facilitated the trance state, and has enhanced all activities associated with psychic communication, astral travel, future-telling, and past-life ascension. It further assists one in the elimination of the need to chase trivia during detection activities.

It assists the energy from the third-eye to be transported throughout the body, producing an intuitive understanding of the complete cellular structure. It has been used in the treatment of disorders of spinal alignment, in the treatment of circulatory disorders, to disseminate and disperse growths, to ameliorate toxicity, and to enhance and to strengthen the structure of the veins.

Growth Interference Quartz vibrates to the number 1. To determine the vibratory number for other minerals showing Growth Interference, one may add 105 to the sum of the numbers representing each letter of the name of the other mineral.

# QUARTZ - LINEATED

[Astrological Sign of Virgo]

***QUARTZ - LINEATED*** - alpha-$SiO_2$; Hardness 7; Locality: Minas Gerais, Brasil; Photography by Jim Hughes, Assisted by ♪ Melody ♫; Collection of ♪ Melody ♫, Applewood, CO, USA. Top photograph shows lineation on face; Bottom photograph shows lineation on body.

Lineated Quartz is configured to show the presence of a parallel raised or indented rectilinear structure on the face or sides of the crystal; the indented rectilinear structure is not etched, but is caused by growth occurring against another pattern formation. Quartz was first described as "Crystallus" (representing the crystalline formation) by Pliny in 77 A.D. and was further described by U.R. von Kalbe in 1505 to present the history of the name. The name "Quartz" was originally spelled "Quertz" and represented Quartzite (the compact granular massive configuration); it was named for the Saxon word "cross-vein ore". In the late 1700's, the two configurations (crystalline and massive) were found by T. Bergman to have the same chemical composition and, hence, were consolidated and provided with one name (Quartz). The word "Lineated" is used to convey the structure. The following properties are in addition to those listed in the QUARTZ section of "Love Is In The Earth - A Kaleidoscope Of Crystals Update".

This mineral has been used by the Native Americans to both trace their heritage and to ensure correctness of same. It has also been used during the Native American ceremony of the vision quest, to provide for a connection between the physical realm and the realm of the vision. It has been dedicated to the Fox, the bringer of rapidity, dexterity, and Machiavellian tendency to that which is the focus.

It can be used for spiritual journeying to protect and to assist one in choice of option. It has also been used to induce the hypnotic state and to facilitate divination. It further instills a knowledge of "right action" and dispels reaction.

It has been used to enhance boyth working environments and business relationships, to promote adeptness in business and to bring inspiration from worldly goods.

Lineated Quartz can be used to dissipate infections, to purify the blood and the kidneys, and to regulate insulin production. It can also be used to alleviate fevers, to ameliorate emphysema, to clarify and to strengthen the eyesight, to assist in the recovery from Parkinson's dis-ease, and to provide comfort and ease during childbirth.

Vibrates to the number 2.

## QUARTZ - PLATES

[Astrological Signs of Gemini & Libra]

***QUARTZ - PLATES*** - alpha-$SiO_2$; Hardness 7; Locality: Minas Gerais, Brasil; Photography by Jim Hughes, Assisted by ♪ Melody ♬; Collection of ♪ Melody ♬, Applewood, CO, USA.

Quartz Plates are configured as a flat plate of smokey-coloured drusy lamellar matrix either:

1- between the crystal structure such that the crystal structure is on both sides of the lamellar matrix which holds the clustered structure together, or

2- on one side of the crystal structure such that the crystal structure is only on one side of the lamellar matrix which holds the clustered structure together, or

3- on both sides of the crystal structure such that the crystal structure is "sandwiched" between the matrix.

Some of these Quartz Plates exhibit phantoms. Quartz was first described as "Crystallus" (representing the crystalline formation) by Pliny in 77 A.D. and was further described by U.R. von Kalbe in 1505 to present the history of the name. The name "Quartz" was originally spelled "Quertz" and represented Quartzite (the compact granular massive configuration);

it was named for the Saxon word "cross-vein ore". In the late 1700's, the two configurations (crystalline and massive) were found by T. Bergman to have the same chemical composition and, hence, were consolidated and provided with one name (Quartz). The word "Plate" is used to convey the structure. The following properties are in addition those listed in the QUARTZ and QUARTZ CLUSTER sections of "Love Is In The Earth - A Kaleidoscope Of Crystals Update".

This mineral acts to provide for a continual attunement between two people, or more, and works quite well when applied to groups working together. Placement of a portion of a cluster in two locations can provide for attunement to the activities and/or the energy of both environments. It can accept and retain information which can be retrieved at a later time; information can also be stored within the structure prior to giving the mineral to another [the reason for the gift ranging from healing facilitation to the transfer of thoughts of love]. After implanting thought-forms of love (it will not accept negative thought forms), it has been used in gridding environments to facilitate healing and well-being for others and for the Earth.

Quartz Plates also stimulate clairvoyant and clairaudient abilities and can assist one in prescience and in telepathic communication.

This mineral is excellent for use when one is experiencing highly explosive changes; it assists one in the stabilization of the emotions and in the recognition and understanding of that which is needed in order to continue progress.

It is a lovely stone to bring a joyful feeling, as well as a feeling of being accompanied.

Quartz Plates have been used in the treatment of cellular renewal, water retention, ruptures, hernia, strains, sprains, acidosis, for disorders of the cortex of the brain, and hearing problems. They have also been used to increase flexibility in the arms and legs and to assist in the amelioration of arthritis. They can help to align the network of the nervous system and to provide for free flow of energy.

Vibrates to the number 5.

## QUARTZ - REVERSED SCEPTOR [Astrological Sign of Aquarius]

***QUARTZ - REVERSED SCEPTOR (Sceptre) -*** alpha-$SiO_2$; Hardness 7; Locality: Minas Gerais, Brasil; Photography by Jim Hughes, Assisted by ♪ Melody ♫; Collection of ♪ Melody ♫, Applewood, CO, USA.

The Reversed Sceptor Quartz exhibits a small top termination on a larger body of quartz crystal structure. Quartz was first described as "Crystallus" (representing the crystalline formation) by Pliny in 77 A.D. and was further described by U.R. von Kalbe in 1505 to present the history of the name. The name "Quartz" was originally spelled "Quertz" and represented Quartzite (the compact granular massive configuration); it was named for the Saxon word "cross-vein ore". In the late 1700's, the two configurations (crystalline and massive) were found by T. Bergman to have the same chemical composition and, hence, were consolidated and provided with one name (Quartz). The word "Sceptor" is used to communicate the configuration of a wand with a handle; "Reversed" is used to communicate that the handle is larger than the termination. The inclusion of the Reversed Sceptor Quartz again in this supplement is due to the extensive new information available. In addition to the properties listed in the QUARTZ, SCEPTOR, and REVERSED SCEPTOR sections of "Love Is In The Earth - A Kaleidoscope Of Crystals Update", the

Reversed Sceptor Quartz can be used to assist one in surmounting emotional burdens, to transport the heart and the intellect into a similitude of action, and to help one to examine the thoughts and emotions within in order to discover the regard and respect that has eternally been there. It can further act to prompt the actualization of the conscious self, allowing for astute recall of sagacious action, while exhibiting a successive affiliation with the spiritual realm and assisting one in access of same.

The mineral carries the inherent memory of that which was in existence prior to the development of humanity. It can be used to help one to become cognizant of the timeless-ness of the spiritual being within the self and to embellish ones life on this plane of tangibility.

It further assists one in the understanding of the processes of life and the levels of mortality. It serves to provide an entrance to information concerning the past, present, and future of ones personal existence.

It has been used by the Ayahuasca Shamen of Brasil to encourage visions of both spiritual nature and for healing diagnosis and for restoration of the stable state. It is sometimes placed in the center of a group, while the group is involved in healing or spiritual issues, in order to facilitate the connection with the energy between all members. It is a "stone of immortality", assisting one to both surmount difficulties and to advance toward virtues of quality. It ennobles ones sense of self-worth and helps one to discern and to achieve the indigenous states of excellence which are available.

It can further help one to become attuned to the Earth and can provide direction to assist one in directing the energy to promote increasing the ionization of the atmosphere.

Reversed Sceptor Quartz has been used in the treatment of disorders involving imperfect form and function. It allows one to recognize the perfection and beauty within the self and to manifest the totality externally, bringing a change in consciousness and conditioning with the aspects of healing.

Vibrates to the numbers 7 and 8.

## QUARTZ - STARBURST

[Astrological Sign of Cancer]

***QUARTZ - STARBURST*** - alpha-$SiO_2$; Hardness 7; Locality: Minas Gerais, Brasil; Photography by Jim Hughes, Assisted by ♪ Melody ♫; Collection of ♪ Melody ♫, Applewood, CO, USA.

Starburst Quartz exhibits a starburst imprint on quartz. Quartz was first described as "Crystallus" (representing the crystalline formation) by Pliny in 77 A.D. and was further described by U.R. von Kalbe in 1505 to present the history of the name. The name "Quartz" was originally spelled "Quertz" and represented Quartzite (the compact granular massive configuration); it was named for the Saxon word "cross-vein ore". In the late 1700's, the two configurations (crystalline and massive) were found by T. Bergman to have the same chemical composition and, hence, were consolidated and provided with one name (Quartz). The word "Starburst" was used to communicate the engraved configuration of a "starburst" on the crystal. The following properties are in addition to those listed in the QUARTZ and ETCHED QUARTZ sections of "Love Is In The Earth - A Kaleidoscope Of Crystals Update".

The ancients believed that the etched crystals exhibiting a "starburst" configuration were a result of the Pleiadian gift of the capability of transformation, delivered to the Earth in a exclamation of joyful assistance to those in the society below. A "stone of transformation", it has also produced a link to those ancient thoughts and procedures for actualization, both within this world, and from this world to another. It further maintains ones concentration, allows for discernment between logic and fantasy, and helps one to affect the ability to find the subsequent "open door" as another door closes. It is conducive to assisting one in changing situations, and dispensing sacrosanct information leading to spiritual progression; it assists one in progressing to ones highest selected elevation, to introduce ascension to a higher facet of the self, and to remember that no action unwarranted - but that all actions bring one to ones highest purpose.

Starburst Quartz can also be used to provide a link with the "star people" of this planet and with those quiescent "star people" from the other realms. The link can produce physical perception induced from the other realms, and can help to bring those like-minded others of this plane into ones physical reality. It also acts to impart a community alliance, promulgating shared experiences and actions. The energy can facilitate advancement with balance, allowing for "right" thought followed by "right" action. It assists one in listening with intention and in acting with intensity.

The mineral can, in addition, stimulate ones growth toward the lunar side of ones nature, allowing for the pathway toward evolution to be clearly marked and resonant with inner joy. It cultivates a nurturing quality and assists one to grow easily and in synchronicity with "All That Is". The energy is one of bliss and harmony, and is especially helpful during times of great stress. It helps to stimulate ideas and to give substance and continuity to thought. It is used to manifest the "enchanting" into ones life. It also allows one to recognize that, within each person and situation, there is accord and radiance.

Starburst Quartz has been used in the treatment of degenerative and addictive behavioral disorders, in the amelioration of disorders of the skeletal and muscular systems, for intestinal disorders, and for dis-ease of the nervous system.

Vibrates to the number 7.

## QUARTZ - WATERFALL

[Astrological Sign of Aquarius]

***QUARTZ - WATERFALL*** - alpha-$SiO_2$; Hardness 7; Locality: Rio Grande do Sul, Brasil; Photography by Jim Hughes, Assisted by ♪ Melody ♫; Collection of ♪ Melody ♫, Applewood, CO, USA.

Waterfall Quartz occurs in Smokey Quartz, Rose Quartz, Clear Quartz and combinations of these colours. Quartz was first described as "Crystallus" (representing the crystalline formation) by Pliny in 77 A.D. and was further described by U.R. von Kalbe in 1505 to present the history of the name. The name "Quartz" was originally spelled "Quertz" and represented Quartzite (the compact granular massive configuration); it was named for the Saxon word "cross-vein ore". In the late 1700's, the two configurations (crystalline and massive) were found by T. Bergman to have the same chemical composition and, hence, were consolidated and provided with one name (Quartz). The word "Waterfall" is used to convey the configuration of the cascading crystal structure. The following properties are in addition to those listed in the QUARTZ section of "Love Is In The Earth - A Kaleidoscope Of Crystals Update".

This mineral can act to dispel depression and to both cleanse and refresh both the aura and the chakras. It tends to protect one from depression and despondency. The cleansing of the aura is a natural process which occurs when the mineral is in ones environment, providing an energy of consistent and uniform "sweeping" while transforming any negativity which is "swept" from ones form.

The natural energy flow of Waterfall Quartz assists in stimulating analytical capabilities and precision. It provides for perceptiveness to situations and awakens ones inherent talents and adroitness. It is also used to produce inspiration from, and connected-ness with, ones Inner Self.

It is said to have been used in mystical rites and ceremonies by the ancient ones of Peru.

It is representative of the composition of the sacred condition of individual life, the sanctified progression which is directed upon, and within, the Earth, and the celestial order of the universe. The concepts and implementation of societal organization and systematic solutions are concentrated within this configuration.

It can be used to assist in businesses associated with navigation, prisons, hospitals, artistic endeavors, religious ministries, dancing, and poetry. It has also been used to eliminate erratic and careless behavior.

This mineral can be used to enhance travel and the prospects of travel, and to protect one during travel. It can assist one in intuitively knowing the acceptable customs and lore of the location visited and can guide one to areas which will be of immense importance to the furtherance of oneself.

Placed by ones bed or under ones pillow, it is a mineral for dreaming, bringing flashes of insight through dreams which concern travel and study.

Waterfall Quartz has been used in the treatment of motor capabilities, arterial flow, and dehydration, to stimulate orderly growth of tissues, to control body temperature and fevers, and to re-build and to re-structure.

Vibrates to the master number 66.

## QUARTZ - FLAME AURA [Astrological Sign of All]

***QUARTZ - FLAME AURA*** - alpha-$SiO_2$ with Titanium and Niobium; Hardness 7; Locality: Quartz (Minas Gerais, Brasil) with creation world-wide; Photography by Jim Hughes, Assisted by ♪ Melody ♫; Collection of ♪ Melody ♫, Applewood, CO, USA.

Flame Aura Quartz crystals are clear/cloudy quartz crystals which have been enhanced with a combination of Titanium and Niobium; the molecules of Titanium and Niobium adhere to the natural electric charge which surrounds the quartz crystal, and are not removed by rubbing or by scraping. The colours produced are a shown. Quartz was first described as "Crystallus" (representing the crystalline formation) by Pliny in 77 A.D. and was further described by U.R. von Kalbe in 1505 to present the history of the name. The name "Quartz" was originally spelled "Quertz" and represented Quartzite (the compact granular massive configuration); it was named for the Saxon word "cross-vein ore". In the late 1700's, the two configurations (crystalline and massive) were found by T. Bergman to have the same chemical composition and, hence, were consolidated and provided with one name (Quartz). The word "Flame Aura", introduced by the author in 1995, represents the range of intensity of the flame-like colours present. In addition to the properties listed in the QUARTZ section of "Love Is In The Earth - A Kaleidoscope Of Crystals Update",

Flame Aura has been used in emotional/spiritual applications to assist one in traversing the interval between the mineral kingdom and the self such that the energies meld into an orderly system for use and energy transfer.

The combination of the Quartz with the Titanium and Niobium brings a violet and/or golden ray to the aura in such a way that even if the colours of the aura are not predominately in this range, the violet and/or the gold tend to "show through" (Kirlian photography has been used to determine and to validate this occurrence).

The mineral assists greatly in meditation and has stimulated the movement of the Kundalini to the crown chakra, aligning the chakras during the excursion. Flame Aura Quartz has promoted contact, during meditation, with the ancient Greek civilizations.

It has been used to maintain situations in homeostasis (when consciously directed), <u>and</u> also assists in movement "toward ones path of change" (when consciously directed). Hence, it appears to have the ability to act in the method one chooses in these cases, and to further assist one in the dedication to a single cause, crusade, or aspiration.

Carrying the mineral has assisted in the increase of "reading" people and in understanding exactly what is being communicated, more on a spiritual plane; subsequently, the application to the mental and material plane is enhanced.

It has been used to provide for reduction in body temperature when fever is present, for elimination of water retention and elimination of dehydration (tending to provide a balance of the water in the body, acting as a preservative to well-being and healthful-ness (e.g., maintaining same and tending to integrate with the body to allow cellular recognition of the perfect state of well-ness). It has also been shown to stimulate the production of negative ions to assist in the maintenance of well-being, to assist in the assimilation of minerals, and to support treatments for both cellular and bone cancer, including, promoting release of toxins through the body. It is currently being used in experiments for multiple sclerosis and AIDS.

Vibrates to the number 1.

## QUARTZ - TANGERINE [Astrological Signs of Leo & Libra]

***QUARTZ - TANGERINE*** - alpha-$SiO_2$ with ?; Hardness 7; Locality: Amazona, Brasil; Photography by Jim Hughes, Assisted by ♪ Melody ♫; Collection of ♪ Melody ♫, Applewood, CO, USA.

Tangerine Quartz is a quartz crystal which exhibits a tangerine colour; the colour appears to be on the outside of the crystal and has not been removable in the usual acid baths. Quartz was first described as "Crystallus" (representing the crystalline formation) by Pliny in 77 A.D. and was further described by U.R. von Kalbe in 1505 to present the history of the name. The name "Quartz" was originally spelled "Quertz" and represented Quartzite (the compact granular massive configuration); it was named for the Saxon word "cross-vein ore". In the late 1700's, the two configurations (crystalline and massive) were found by T. Bergman to have the same chemical composition and, hence, were consolidated and provided with one name (Quartz). The word "Tangerine" is used to convey the colour. In addition to the properties listed in the QUARTZ section of "Love Is In The Earth - A Kaleidoscope Of Crystals Update", this mineral has been used to promote Inner Self evaluation and evolution. It brings one the strength and the loving essence to continue in any and all pursuits. It is an energy for psychic research, assisting one to transport and to retrieve [on both the tangible and intangible levels] patterns of force, movement, and space-time relationships. It also allows one to re-trace any negative energies which attempt to penetrate ones protective shield, providing information with respect to the reasons for, and the origin of, the negativity.

Tangerine Quartz further stimulates the sacral chakra and enhances creativity, intuition of the physical plane, and sexuality; it also provides for a leveling of emotions and a furthering of desire - the direction of the desire being facilitated by the intellect.

The mineral acts to expand the vision etherically, and to enhance encounters with others such that sharing and giving are accentuated. It further dispels isolation and dis-connectedness and abates unwarranted fears. It also has been used to activate mysticism, bringing total experiences of the body, mind, and spirit and allowing one to integrate with the known and the unknown.

In addition, the energy brings to one the tendency to feel less vulnerable, more dispassionate, and calm, when evaluating the need, the creativity required, and the actual path for "change".

This mineral can also be used to align the outer bodies, to provide grounding, and to create a pathway to the Higher Self energy.

Tangerine Quartz has been used in the treatment of disorders related to the reproductive system, to infertility and/or frigidity, and to intestinal disorders. It has been used to assist in the assimilation of vitamins and minerals, to assist the body in maintaining the proper acid/alkaline balance, and to enhance the solubility of alkaline deposits within the body. It has assisted in the removal of free-radical oxides from the body, providing for stability within ones own temple. It has also been used to promote weight loss. It is currently being used in the treatment of Parkinson's dis-ease. It has also been used in the amelioration of the rash associated with agent orange and to diminish the presence of this toxin. In addition, it is said to provide for an increased T-cell count in AIDS patients.

Vibrates to the number 7.

**♪ THINGS ARE MORE LIKE TODAY THAN THEY'VE EVER BEEN BEFORE ♬**

## RHODIZITE

[Astrological Sign of All]

***RHODIZITE*** - $(K,Cs)Al_4Be_4(B,Be)_{12}O_{28}$ or $CsAl_4Be_4B_{11}O_{25}(OH)_4$; Hardness 8; Locality: Tsilaisina, Madagascar; Photography by Dave Shrum, Colorado Camera; Collection of ♪ Melody ♫, Applewood, CO, USA. Gift of Margaret Julian, Evansville, IN, USA.

Rhodizite crystallizes in the formation of vitreous/adamantine clear to white and grey to yellow translucent dodecahedral configurations. The mineral was first described by G. Rose in 1834 and was named from the Greek word meaning "to be rose-coloured", for the rose flame colour it reveals in the blowpipe test. The name is sometimes spelled with a "c" replacing the "z".

This mineral, when used in meditation, facilitates an orderly and effortless entry and assists one in realizing the state of "no mind". When holding the mineral, it tends to provide for an enveloping spiral; in meditation, the helix-directed energy is predisposed to become the Kundalini - rising, and surrounding ones essence while remaining within ones body.

During third-eye placement of Rhodizite there is stimulation of resplendent and vibrant "cinema" depictions which can serve in self-regulation; i.e., conveying views and displays from projected time periods, both individual and ubiquitous. Observing the advice that one truly has the ability to perceive, the facility to affect major determinations and to extend oneself to others, on this and other planes, is advanced.

When holding the mineral, one may see the inextinguishable enchanting light, which will radiate for the user through all circumstances and conditions of same. The energy of the stone shows no negativity or even neutrality - it is a positive stone, and, one of the stones, recognized to-date, of the mineral kingdom, which never needs cleansing or energizing (the ethereal energy connected to the mineral conveys an infinite supply of positive energy.

It has been used extensively in "cloud-busting" [initiating rain]; it has also been used by shamen of Madagascar to control the influx of rain during torrential rain [focus of the energy upon the specific areas of intent].

The mineral has been used in the study of cereology [the analysis of crop circles/markings], to determine times, dates, and return cycles.

It is also a stone for astral travel, helping one to access the information desired, more than facilitating the state. It assists in precision, especially during memory recall of the information. It also balances the speech factors of male/female qualities, exhibiting a delicate energy filled with vitality, and allowing for understanding avantgarde topics of conversation.

In healing, Rhodizite brings a clear energy similar to the quartz crystal and can be applied to further the transference of other energies to the affectation. In addition, it can be used in the treatment of cellular disorders, cancer, and inflammation of tissue, in stabilizing incontinent brain waves, and to balance the acidity of the body. It has been used with the fragile to provide intuitive guidance with respect to objective and rationale, and to assist in the reconstruction of determination.

The slight possible content of Cesium in this mineral precludes its use in the normal method of preparation of an elixir.

Vibrates to the number 6.

## RHODONITE - GEMMY

[Astrological Signs of Taurus, Sagittarius & Leo]

***RHODONITE - GEMMY*** - (Mn,Fe,Mg,Ca)$SiO_3$; Hardness 5.5-6.5; Locality: Minas Gerais, Brasil, South America; Photography by Jim Hughes, Assisted by ♪ Melody ♫; Collection of ♪ Melody ♫, Applewood, CO, USA.

Gemmy Rhodonite crystallizes in cleavage masses and in the colours ranging from rose to brown and yellow-brown. This mineral was discovered in the late 1980's and was originally defined to be Rhodonite with additional iron and was described as Pyroxmangite and/or Pyroxferroite; however, after further research and subsequent recognized and approved changes in the mineralogical formulas, the Rhodonite formula was modified to include this mineral.

Rhodonite (without Iron) was first described by C.F. Jasche in 1819 and was named for the Greek word "a rose", for its colour. The first published description of the newly formulated Rhodonite was observed by the author to be by Earnest H. Nickel and Monte C. Nichols in 1991.

The following properties are in addition to those listed in the Rhodonite section of "Love Is In The Earth - A Kaleidoscope Of Crystals Update".

This mineral can instill the aspect of trust to relationships and situations, bringing confidence to ones emotional and intellectual characteristics, and bringing fidelity to interpersonal associations.

It has been used to the remove voids from ones aura and to fill the emptiness with a loving energy of clarity. The energy inspires creativity, imagination, ingenuity, inventiveness, and sagacity in the world of the "new".

Gemmy Rhodonite has been used to activate the heart chakra and to bring self-love to the user such that the energy permeates the heart chakra to cleanse and to assist one in understanding matters of the heart. It acts to instill a permanence to ones loving nature. Placement of the mineral in ones environment, using the energies in an elixir, and wearing and/or carrying the crystal all stimulate the loving breath of existence. It can also be used to enable the opening of the heart center, allowing for the dissolution of stress and tension.

This mineral assists one in accessing the essence of a problem, serving to support the transformation of the heart to love. It further enables one to exhibit control of ones life, promoting the actualization of the preferred reality. It promotes rationality in the processes of life, while providing for an opening to a pathway for entry into the sensuality of nature and the creativity of the heart. It can further be used to transmit messages within the physical realm.

Gemmy Rhodonite can be used to clear fluids in the cells of the body and to advance the release of pollutants. It has been used in the treatment of vertigo. It provides for help in the diminishment of disorders of the kidneys and adrenal glands, and has been used in the treatment of Lupis. It can be used [as an elixir] to clear the skin and is said to reduce wrinkles and to provide the wearer/carrier with a soft complexion. Placed upon the heart chakra, it can diminish pain, can calm, and can stimulate the proper functioning of the heart. Placed upon the area of the thymus, it has decreased coughs and soothed the bronchial and lung areas of the body. It has also been used to diminish burns and to relieve and to vanquish blistering due to heat.

Vibrates to the number 9.

## ROSASITE - GREEN BANDED

[Astrological Signs of Virgo & Libra]

***ROSASITE - GREEN BANDED (in Rhyolite)*** - $(Cu,Zn)_2CO_3(OH)_2$; Hardness 4.5; Locality: Mexico; Photography by Jim Hughes, Assisted by ♪ Melody ♫; Collection of ♪ Melody ♫, Applewood, CO, USA.

Green Banded Rosasite crystallizes in the form of layered (in Rhyolite) green Rosasite (crystalline and/or plate-like) with, occasionally, small crystals imbedded on the top tier. Rosasite was first described by D. Lovisato in 1908 and was named for the locality (Rosa, Sulcis, Sardinia, Italy), where it was first discovered. This configuration is included herein due to the additional qualities due to the structure. The following properties are in addition to those listed in the ROSASITE section of "Love Is In The Earth - A Kaleidoscope Of Crystals Update".

This mineral can be used to incite analytical capabilities and precision. It provides for perceptiveness to situations and awakens ones inherent aptitudes and adroitness. It is also used to produce revelation from and connected-ness with the entities residing in the spiritual worlds.

It tends to bring the quality of virtue, stimulating and propagating virtuous conduct throughout the many facets of ones life. It further acts to assist one in gaining "what is due", to bring to fruition the many levels of ones beliefs and to assist one to accomplish that which is "planned". It has been used to decrease vacillation and to augment tenacity, acting to attract friends and good fortune, and to encourage self-control.

Green Banded Rosasite can heighten good will, enhance ones moods, relieve mood swings, and diminish dissention. It is excellent in remediation of the feeling of abandonment, inducing ambition and autonomous unconstrained thought. It is contributory to awareness and to supporting one in the celebration of situations of isolation. It helps one to discern that one is always remembered by others who can, usually, be called upon to provide wisdom to examples of those who send loving energy toward ones physical manifestation.

It is a stone which provides for protection. It protects against negativity and helps one to be grounded to the stabilizing energies of the Earth.

Green Banded Rosasite brings composure and a tranquil effect to the whole being, with specific focus on the connection between the heart chakra and the third-eye. It inspires communication and psychic perception on all planes. It helps to expedite lucidity and exactness with respect to cognitive awareness and logical thinking. It encourages one to abide in endeavors and in circumstances which would, generally, reduce ones vitality; it provides a stimulating energy and supports one in the continuation of projects. It also assists in dispelling confusion arising from emotional, spiritual, and intellectual issues.

It can be used during radionic analysis; holding a piece of Green Banded Rosasite and placing a piece of Green Banded Rosasite on the witness or using a pendulum of this stone, the energy of the stone interferes with the energy of the user and points to the problem[s] involved.

It can be used in the treatment of disorders of the skin, both deep and superficial, to stabilize the skeletal structure, and the muscular composition, to calm the nerves during stressful situations, and to increase ones energy and stamina. It has also been used in general healing and in tissue regeneration.

Vibrates to the number 5.

**♪ THE FACTS, ALTHOUGH FASCINATING,
ARE INCONSEQUENTIAL
TO REALITY ♫**

## SALÉEITE

[Astrological Sign of Capricorn]

***SALÉEITE*** - $Mg(UO_2)_2(PO_4)_2$♥$10H_2O$; Hardness 2-3; Locality: Lake Boga Quarry, Swan Hill, Victoria, Australia; Photography by Jim Hughes, Assisted by ♪ Melody ♫; Collection of ♪ Melody ♫, Applewood, CO, USA.

Saléeite crystallizes in the orthorhombic system as small almost tetragonal crystals, usually enclosed partially within a rhyolitic matrix. The mineral was first described in 1932 by J. Thoreau and J.F. Vaes, named for A. Salée, and the spelling was corrected in 1939 by A. Schoep.

This mineral has been known as the "Apollo Stone", bringing rays of sunshine to all who experience the energy, and further assisting one in altering beliefs, structures, and systems.

It is said that Saléeite has the capacity to assist in both the refinement and the recovery of the environment and to ethereally absorb toxic products, and in the secondary manner, to provide for decomposition of negativity and for transmutation of the negative energies to positive force-fields; the positive fields, containing more total energy than the totality of the energy contained in the negativity.

It provides an excellent energy for Reiki, to further ones actions and to stimulate the proper response to the energies applied.

Dowsing with Saléeite can assist in determination of whether a labeled "organic" food is truly "organic" in nature. It can also provide for an indication of pesticide residues on fruits and vegetables.

It is also a "stone of transition", assisting one to see the brilliant tunnel, revealing the path which was forgotten the moment of birth, and summoning one to regain the lost origin of the soul. It further promotes the acceptance that denial, in any form, only works through the guise of self-righteous nobility, bringing nothing in gain. Placing this mineral within an environment will provide for the transformation of any present "Golgotha" to the compassionate space of transition; the idea of smallness of "ones craft and the vastness of ones ocean" will be revolutionized to allow one to realize the whole universe within, the laughter and comradeship, the sentimental moments, and the preciousness of oneself within "All That Is".

It is also said to be used by the Aboriginal Tribes to assist in physical journeys - leading the way from one location to the next, and providing protection during the travels.

Saléeite has been used to enhance new business endeavors and to bring fruition to new and innovative business ideas. It can further promote conservation and economy of ones funds, bringing insight to economical methodologies and assisting in the implementation of same.

It has been used to strengthen the arms and the grasping properties of the hands. It has been used to help one to go "beneath" the physical symptoms of dis-ease and to allow for recognition of the underlying root cause; the cause becoming apparent for all planes of existence. In addition, Saléeite has been used to eliminate alcohol and drug addictions, and to release toxins from the body.

The content of Uranium in this mineral precludes its use in the normal method of preparation of an elixir.

Vibrates to the number 4.

## SANBORNITE

[Astrological Sign of Aquarius]

***SANBORNITE*** **-** $BaSi_2O_5$ with Gillespite; Hardness 5; Locality: Baja CA, Mexico; Photography by Jim Hughes, Assisted by ♪ Melody ♫; Collection of ♪ Melody ♫, Applewood, CO, USA.

Sanbornite crystallizes in the form of pearly white crystalline masses. The mineral was first described by A.F. Rogers in 1932 and named for F. Sanborn.

This mineral elevates insight to the "concealed". It provides for an elimination of blockages on the path to any ventures and acts to enhance ones inborn awareness. It stimulates intent and self-possession. It also dispels harsh and irritating attitudes, subdues ones emotional nature (when required), and helps one to release resentment in a constructive manner.

Sanbornite expedites mobilization on all levels, for all bodies, and automatically. It inspires the loving temperament of ones essence, bringing advancement and promotion of ones natural endowments. It is conducive to bringing expanded experiences in terrestrial affairs; it channels energy in the direction of that which is consciously desired and assists in bringing the conscious desire to the state of comprehension and acknowledgement. It can be used to cleanse the chakras, to clear the aura, and to purify ones mind by eliminating thought-patterns which are not conducive to growth.

It can promote the removal of ethereal "cords" which are sent by others to ones chakras and to assist one in retrieving those "cords" which are personally transmitted. This can be accomplished by carrying the stone and without conscious focus on the removal.

It can also stimulate the Beta state of brain waves and can promote creativity and achievement of ones dreams.

Sanbornite has also been used to elevate ones skills in telekinesis and levitation. It strengthens the "silver cord" during astral travel and assists one in "reading" auras. It can further balance ones volatility and can stimulate astral travel.

It is further the "stone of the good Samaritan", bringing compassion and assistance the user. It can act to further stimulate the physical vitality and to mellow it with clarity. It can be used to help one with both the translation and the understanding of languages unknown; it is also helpful to stimulate automatic writing and ESP. It is an excellent stone for communication with animals, both as spiritual totems and as physical life forms.

It can be used in the treatment of disorders of the eyes, to soothe and smooth the skin, and to bring peace to the body. This mineral has been used in the treatment of leukemia, CFS, bone loss, menopausal complaints, and for intestinal cleansing (as an elixir). It has been used to provide a healthy glow to the skin, to allay wrinkles, and to stimulate elasticity in the skin and muscular system. It can also be used in the treatment of disorders of the arteries and to enhance the response to scent by allowing one to actually experience the electrical waves sent to the brain, and to synthesize the response with the stimulus.

The Sanbornite with Gillespite configuration merges the energies of both to provide a very powerful energy.

Sanbornite vibrates to the number 9.

## SCAPOLITE - PURPLE

[Astrological Sign of Virgo]

***SCAPOLITE - PURPLE*** - $(Na,Ca)_4(Si,Al)_{12}O_{24}(Cl,CO_3,SO_4)$; Hardness 5-6.5; Locality: Morogorro, Tanzania; Photography by Jim Hughes, Assisted by ♪ Melody ♫; Collection of ♪ Melody ♫, Applewood, CO, USA.

Purple Scapolite crystallizes in the form of prismatic crystals. The mineral, Scapolite, was first described by B.J. d'Andrada in 1800 and named from the Greek word meaning "a shaft", referring to the prismatic shape of the crystals. This purple crystalline configuration is included herein due to the additional qualities researched which were due to the structure and colour. The following properties are in addition to those listed in the SCAPOLITE section of "Love Is In The Earth - A Kaleidoscope Of Crystals Update".

Purple Scapolite has been known as the "stone of atonement", bringing clemency and mercy for all feelings of transgressions. It is the ultimate "judge", forgiving with divine blessings and with the knowledge that one completes the cycles of this Earthly realm with reliance upon faith.

It is an excellent stone for the crown chakra, assisting in the higher spiritual pursuits and actualizations. The mineral further helps with the development of worldly friendships on the spiritual level, activates and stimulates and clears the crown chakra, and emanates love. It assists one in understanding the basis for, the consequence of, and the karmic lessons which one has experienced or is experiencing, while prompting understanding of the procedures which can be employed to surmount unwanted circumstances.

Purple Scapolite also encourages positivity, dispels dissention, charges the auric bodies, and facilitates an intense and balanced alliance and connection with the spirit world. It can be used to act as an advisor for accessing past-lives and to access the mature and mellow wisdom involving the precepts of human-potential.

It delivers the force of an energy vortex center, magnifying all mystical proficiencies and originating [when directed] experiences which include the direct contact with those of "Valhalla", revelations, restorations, and unique manifestations.

It can expedite ones projection of the mind, to permit visitation to other domains on this plane and in other dimensions. It can be used to empower one to attain an modified state of awareness and to prompt the Higher Self to perform as a mentor during access of the ancient wisdom of the universe. At this level of cognizance, one can act to disclose the mysteries via automatic writing and/or mystic communication.

Purple Scapolite has been used to stimulate the balancing of the yin-yang energies and to support the balance of the physical body with the ethereal perfection.

It can be used in the treatment of those conditions which are considered age-related mobility-related disorders, assisting one to understand and to resolve the issues behind the dis-ease. It can be used to inhibit the degeneration of cellular structures and to balance the RNA/DNA structures to facilitate healthy cellular development and maintenance. It has further provided for allergy protection (carried or used as an elixir), and has been used in the treatment of carpal tunnel syndrome and shoulder and neck complaints related to the "whiplash" condition.

Vibrates to the number 8.

## SCHORLOMITE [Astrological Signs of Cancer & Sagittarius]

***SCHORLOMITE*** - $Ca_3(Ti,Fe)_2[(Si,Fe)O_4]_3$; Hardness 7-7.5; Locality: Kovdor, Kola Peninsula, Russia; Photography by Jim Hughes, Assisted by ♪ Melody ♫; Collection of ♪ Melody ♫, Applewood, CO, USA.

Schorlomite is a titanium garnet which occurs in the formation of black masses, sometimes with a vitreous lustre. The mineral was first described by C.U. Shephard in 1846 and named for its resemblance to schorl tourmaline.

This mineral works primarily to balance and to heighten the male qualities; hence, providing strength, fortitude, bravery, etc.

The energy of Schorlomite is generated at an atomically high-powered rate of oscillation, and has been used to increase the brain wave frequency, to activate expanded rational capacity and endurance, and to elevate the quantity of brain cells which are readily and effortlessly used.

It can also be used to assist to maintain the courage to voice ones ideas, feelings, and convictions, and to identify and to take action with respect to those who seek to capitalize on ones individual good will. The energy serves to enhance the strength to confront these dissenting situations and to rid one of the cause. It is an excellent energy conductor and can be used to assist in the alignment of the magnetic fields of the body.

Schorlomite also enhances the attractive aspects in relationships, attracting to one not that which is necessarily wanted, but bringing into ones life that which is essential for ones development.

It can be used to assist in clearing the aura, to expand the vision etherically, and to enhance encounters with others such that sharing and giving are accentuated. It further dispels detachment and dis-connectedness and abates unwarranted fears. It also has been used to activate mysticism, bringing total experiences of the body, mind, and spirit, while allowing one to become a part of the known and the unknown.

This mineral also manifests a fusion of physical power and endurance - a forceful blend for assailing difficulties, for legislating resolutions, and for achieving the "target". It provides for valour and steadfast actions in demanding-situations, and promotes timely corrective action to these situations. It assists one in deferring all estimations of oneself and of others, furthering ones ability to embrace human-ness with strength of character.

It is quite helpful in the home to provide equilibrium in structure, to protect against and to help to eliminate infestations, and to produce a sheltered and protected environment.

The ancient cultures of African tribal natives are said to have used the energies of this structure in shamanic ceremonies to provide grounding while providing removal of the cause of dis-ease.

It can be used to facilitate calcium, magnesium, and iron assimilation within the body and to treat associated disorders of the body. It has been used in the treatment of carbon monoxide poisoning, to alleviate tension, to reduce water content of the cellular structure, and to induce sleep for the alleviation of insomnia.

Vibrates to the number 2.

## ,LENITE - WITH COPPER

[Astrological Signs of Taurus, Sagittarius, & Aries]

***SELENITE - WITH COPPER*** - $CaSO_4 \bullet 2H_2O$ (Selenite) and Cu (Copper); Hardness 1.5-2; Locality: Mission Mine, AZ, USA; Photography by Jim Hughes, Assisted by ♪ Melody ♫; Collection of ♪ Melody ♫, Applewood, CO, USA.

Selenite is a transparent colourless to white, somewhat flexible form of crystallized gypsum. The copper inclusions are a metallic copper-red to light rose colour and are, usually, native copper. Selenite was first described by J.G. Wallerius in 1747 and named from the Greek word meaning "the moon", due to the pale reflections inherent within the structure. Copper was first described in The Aes Cyprium of Pliny in A.D. 77 and named from the Greek word meaning "Cyprus", where early deposits of the metal were found. This collective composition of Selenite and Copper is included herein due to the additional qualities researched which were due to the combination. The following properties are in addition to those listed in the SELENITE and COPPER sections of "Love Is In The Earth - A Kaleidoscope Of Crystals Update".

This mineral has been known as the "Venus of alchemists", bringing the powers of transmutation and the promulgation of an elixir of the breath, the steadfast and never-changing bringer of life to ones body. The native

Copper inclusions within the Selenite tend to bring the system of alchemy to life, assisting one in transformation and transmigration.

It has also been used as a window to other dimensions, to access intelligence from the astral plane and the akashic records, and to view the Inner Self. The operation of looking within the self through the utilization of this mineral has allowed one to identify chaotic states and to rationally rearrange and to reorganize the disorder of dis-ease.

It has also been used for "gazing" and for sending and receiving messages.

It can stimulate the sacral chakra, the crown chakra, and the third-eye, being a matchless instrument for communication between the self and other worlds. It can also be used to prompt conceptions and visionary experiences and to actuate the higher psychic abilities.

It can be used to stimulate contact with the Inner Self, to attain resolution for issues of concern. In the meditative or non-meditative state, answers to problems of all magnitudes seem to manifest very quickly to the user.

In addition, this mineral is used to activate other crystals and minerals; one way to accomplish this is to hold the Selenite with Copper in the "hand of preference" and to rub the ones fingers across the clear face [in a spiral motion], while holding the other stone in the other hand.

Selenite with Copper is a powerful guide. The energy allows one to see beyond misconceived identities and into the essence of the self. It often assists one to develop an awareness of the uncertainties which inhibit the expression of the perfect self, allowing for the reflection of ones self-image and the associated perfections or imperfections of the user.

It has been used in the treatment of disorders of, and for pain in, the areas of the intestines, pancreas, and bronchial tubes. It can be used in amelioration of disorders related to the branches of the body, the veins, and the flow of blood. Selenite with Copper has been quite useful in determining the cause of dis-ease.

Vibrates to the number 9.

## SMITHSONITE - GREEN

[Astrological Sign of Sagittarius]

***SMITHSONITE - GREEN*** - $ZnCO_3$; Hardness 4-4.5; Locality: Gila, AZ, USA; Photography by Jim Hughes, Assisted by ♪ Melody ♫; Collection of ♪ Melody ♫, Applewood, CO, USA.

Green Smithsonite crystallizes in the form of crusts, grains, masses, stalactites, botryoidal structures, scalenohedral crystals, and rhombohedral crystals with curved faces. Smithsonite was first described by F.S. Beaudant in 1832 and named for J. Smithson, the founder of the Smithsonian Institute, who had shown that calamine included three distinct minerals, one of which is Smithsonite. The Green Smithsonite is included herein as a separate entry due to the additional qualities researched which were due to the green colour. The following properties are in addition to those listed in the SMITHSONITE section of "Love Is In The Earth - A Kaleidoscope Of Crystals Update".

This mineral inspires innovation and exploration with respect to the nature of the macrocosm and the nature of the time. It allows for liberation from personal and emotional inhibitions, bringing forth verbalization of feelings in a loving and "allowing" manner.

It induces communication with both the plant and animal kingdoms, providing information with respect to herbal remedies and freedom of spirit coupled with the comprehension which is required to suspend and to eliminate exploitation. The communication aspects are endless, and have led many through the path of healing ones spirit and ones life.

Green Smithsonite can be used to decrease "self-centeredness" and to encourage the state of egoless-ness while facilitating the staying power of the self. It insists that one take liability for happiness or unhappiness, for originating ones personal reality, and for acknowledging and employing the authority of self-concept.

It is an excellent stone for the heart chakra, activating, energizing, and cleansing the area while providing for the self-operating opening of same.

It can further heighten ones self-esteem when one maintains the honesty of ones alliance to reality. It is an excellent stone to assist one in growing toward self-confidence and self-respect free of vanity, further assisting one to recognize methods which will enable one to fully "know thyself" and to, subsequently, reach ones highest human potential while acknowledging same.

This mineral is said to bring one "luck", a discriminating mind, and a engaging manner; allowing one to realize the advantageous personality traits. It provides a harmony between the physical plane and the other planes of existence [including emotional, intellectual, astral, etc.], allowing one to grow simultaneously on all planes. It assists one in personal development, in maintaining and/or regaining health, and in understanding and utilizing the powerful intuitive ancient techniques of healing.

It can be used in the treatment of the Hantavirus, for disorders of the blood and cellular composition, to soothe ulcers, to reduce pain, and to act as an emetic. It has been used to treat muscular rigidity, hair loss, skin cancer, blood and lung disorders, to assist in the assimilation of minerals, and to provide support for dieting, body maintenance and shaping, and agility.

Vibrates to the number 2.

## SMOKEY QUARTZ - ENGRAVED [Astrological Sign of Scorpio]

***SMOKEY QUARTZ - ENGRAVED*** - $SiO_2$ with organic impurities or due to natural exposure to radioactivity; Hardness 7; Locality: Arizona, USA; Photography by Jim Hughes, Assisted by ♪ Melody ♫; Collection of ♪ Melody ♫, Applewood, CO, USA.

Engraved Smokey Quartz is a form of quartz occurring in the crystalline formation with the unique attribute of the presence of engravings which are in the manner of intaglio, usually with white borders. The colour range includes light smokey grey to dark smokey grey, and black. Smokey Quartz was first described by J.S. Dana in 1837 and named for its colour which has been likened to smoke. The word "Engraved" is used to convey the presence of geometric engravings. The following properties are in addition to those listed in the SMOKEY QUARTZ section of "Love Is In The Earth - A Kaleidoscope Of Crystals Update".

This mineral can assist one to achieve whatever effect one intends, bringing the attainment in whatever form is resolved.

It is reminiscent of the method of information transfer from the Celtic civilization. The interpretation of the engravings can be accessed through personal meditation, through placing the engraving upon the third-eye after centering and while implementing circular breathing (allowing the knowledge to enter), and by activating the engraving by rubbing. The transliteration of the symbols bring information germane to ones life at the time of transcription.

The Engraved Smokey Quartz crystals were once used in the healing centers (often only shelters of stone) of the Celtic civilization; the engravings also containing details of experiences in which these Celtic healers have participated. They also have contained information with respect to the remedies applied and the cures facilitated.

This mineral can also be used to cleanse and to energize both the base chakra and the crown chakra, allowing for the light of the Sun to shine from both directions, and instilling the omnipresent energy of positivity.

In addition, this configuration can act to authenticate transcendent deductive capabilities, to enhance ones skills, and to promote the increase of ones discoveries and conceptions with inventive ingenuity and proficiency. It actually produces the memory of an undaunted pristine universe, such that one perceives that the conception and the development of that world is within the self.

It can be used to both repel and to protect against negativity. It acts to shield one from being exploited by the dissenting energy of another. It has also been used as an energy deflector, being an excellent stone for those with potential for exposure to excessive amounts of toxic waste or irradiation. It provides for an escalation in ones tangible stamina, emotional balance, and rational acuity, and can maintain ones faith and trust even in circumstances which appear to issue the messages of darkness and obscurity.

It can be used to activate the reflex points adjunct with the lower back. It can be used in the treatment of arthritis, dyslexia, trauma, disorders of the thyroid and spleen, atrophication of the thymus, and disorientation. It can also provide for both the stimulation and the balancing of the adrenal glands and for stimulation of the immune system.

Vibrates to the number 6.

## SMOKEY QUARTZ - "HOT" SPOTS

[Astrological Sign of Scorpio]

***SMOKEY QUARTZ - "HOT" SPOTS*** - $SiO_2$ with organic impurities or due to natural exposure to radioactivity; Hardness 7; Locality: Minas Gerais, Brasil; Photography by Jim Hughes, Assisted by ♪ Melody ♫; Collection of ♪ Melody ♫, Applewood, CO, USA.

Smokey Quartz with "Hot" Spots is a form of quartz occurring in the crystalline formation with the unique attribute of the interior presence of spots of a deeper and richer colour. The colour range includes light smokey grey to dark smokey grey, and black. There is a theory that the "Hot" Spots occurred due to highly radioactive intense fission product fragments which were scattered within the quartz solution during formation, being incorporated in portions of the crystalline quartz as it formed, with the intensely radioactive (now dissipated) fragments producing the darker spots. Smokey Quartz was first described by J.S. Dana in 1837 and named for its colour which has been likened to smoke. The words "Hot Spots" are used to convey the presence of maculation (spotting). The following properties are in addition to those listed in the SMOKEY QUARTZ section of "Love Is In The Earth - A Kaleidoscope Of Crystals Update".

It is said that the "Hot" Spot Smokey Quartz came from an ancient nuclear reactor, theorized to be Lemurian due to the location in which they have been found. Although this is speculative, the mineral has been accessed and has provided Lemurian ceremonial information. It has been used to contact a "committee of authority" in order to gain information concerning a specific question, dilemma, or situation; the diverse range of committee members being available for the entire range of information.

In addition, it is an energy for circumspection, bringing careful deliberation and prudent vigilance to any "work", Earth plane or otherwise, which one deems necessary for progression. The energy of this mineral can actually alter ones perspective such that the "eye", physical or third, which is necessary for that particular piece of "sight", will then be focussed upon the information that is both necessary and evident.

The crystal is impressive in its forcefulness; worn or carried, it cannot and will not be forgotten or neglected. When this mineral comes to ones dominion, it appears to be time to seek both the truth and the actualization of the self, allowing analytical intuition and intuitive analysis to find their places in balance.

Great strength is given to the user, allowing for discordance to be eliminated and for determination of the nature of any conflict to be explored.

It has been used to facilitate continuity in circular breathing during healing and/or meditative states. It unites the qualities of initiative and independence with the furthering of human-kind, producing a circular energy which penetrates from the crown to the base chakra.

It can also be used to affect nutritional stabilization within the body, to improve the digestive processes and related organs, and to assist in the elimination of toxins leading to the decrease in dis-ease. It further assists in the treatment of inflammations and microbic infections and has been quite useful in the treatment of imbalances in RNA/DNA and in cellular metabolism and in alterations of tissue formation within the body.

Vibrates to the number 8.

# SMOKEY QUARTZ - SKELETAL, WITH LEPIDOCROCITE & HEMATITE

[Astrological Signs of Sagittarius & Scorpio]

***SMOKEY QUARTZ - Skeletal, with Lepidocrocite & Hematite;*** $SiO_2$ with organic impurities or due to natural exposure to radioactivity (Smokey Quartz), $Fe_2O_3$♥$H_2O$ (Lepidocrocite), and alpha-$Fe_2O_3$ (Hematite); Hardness 7; Locality: Minas Gerais, Brasil; Photography by Jim Hughes, Assisted by ♪ Melody ♫; Collection of ♪ Melody ♫, Applewood, CO, USA. Gift of Bob Jackson, Applewood, CO, USA.

Skeletal Smokey Quartz with Lepidocrocite and Hematite is a double-terminated form of smokey quartz occurring in the skeletal crystalline formation with the unique addition of both Lepidocrocite and Hematite. The colour range includes semi-translucent smokey black (Smokey Quartz), with silvery to silvery-red (Hematite), and rose-red (Lepidocrocite). The Hematite provides for a sparkle; the Lepidocrocite is recognized in the areas of red non-sparkle and when a light is shined throughout the specimen. Smokey Quartz was first described by J.S. Dana in 1837 and named for its colour which has been likened to smoke. Lepidocrocite was first described as "Rubinglimmer" by J.F.L. Hausmann in 1813; J.C. Ullmann, in 1814, described Goethite as "Lepidokrokit" and derived the name from the Greek words for "scale" and "fibre"; <u>and</u> in 1901, A. Lacroix transferred the name, "Lepidokrokit" (inadvertently, but correctly) to the actual and correct Lepidocrocite composition. Hematite was first described by Pliny in 77 A.D. and was named "Haematite" for the likeness to haemoglobin, etc.; In 1773, Romé de I'Isle changed the spelling to "Hematite". The word "Skeletal" is used to convey the structural formation. The following properties are in addition to those listed in the SMOKEY QUARTZ, LEPIDOCROCITE, and HEMATITE sections of "Love Is In The Earth - A Kaleidoscope Of Crystals Update".

This mineral facilitates the "Science of Luck", bringing one good fortune, advantage, and success in a rather serendipitous fashion, with no deliberation with respect to the action one would pursue to promote the gain. The gain or success actually happens when one is obliged or compelled to take a specific path; the consequences of this path being the "path of luck". It is said to have been used by the three princes of Ceylon (originally known as Serendip), who exhibited this faculty.

It further acts to release the bonds of servitude and to assist one in decision-making and in furthering ones assertiveness, allowing one to know the direction is "right" and serving to assist in the fortitude to continue in the direction chosen.

Skeletal Smokey Quartz with Lepidocrocite and Hematite expedites pursuits in architecture, construction, business and personal organization, manufacturing, and in establishment of any business. It tends to augment the ability (intellectual, emotional, or physical) which is necessary for attainment. It further assists one in determining the basis for any intellectual, emotional, or spiritual pursuit.

It is a tool for the transfer of information in all realms - without absolute out-of-body travel (i.e., with "intellectual" travel). This configuration has also been used to stimulate the recognition of details related to Earth-changes, astrological significance, and weather patterns.

The mineral has been used to remove unwanted extraterrestrial "implants", to assist in child-birth and procreation, and to assist in healing the bone structures and disorders of the bone.

Vibrates to the number 4.

## STELLERITE

[Astrological Signs of Cancer & Aries]

***STELLERITE*** - $CaAl_2Si_7O_{18}$♥$7H_2O$; Hardness 3.5-4; Locality: Ritter Hot Springs, Grant Co., OR, USA; Photography by Jim Hughes, Assisted by ♪ Melody ♫; Collection of ♪ Melody ♫, Applewood, CO, USA.

Stellerite occurs in the formation of white tabular parallel crystals, many times joined to provide the appearance of a rather thick plate. This mineral was first described by J.A. Morozewicz in 1909 and was named for G.S. Steller.

This mineral brings the energy for metamorphosis and abiding change, bringing with it the power to create, to unify with this power, and to release contention. It further promotes the mental act of knowing that any negative condition need not "be" within ones existence and removes the obstacles preventing the realization of truth; it provides for a clearing of the mental channels preceding the building of positive constructive endorsement to actual perception.

It further assists one in understanding that metamorphosis is "effect" and that all metamorphosis is subject to its causative factors, allowing one to recognize and to act upon the causative factors.

It introduces the exoteric teachings given to the multitudes, but have not yet been recognized in substance and in practice.

The mineral can be used to prompt and to assist one in "stepping-back" when one is undergoing negative emotions (e.g., regret, anger, etc.), such that one can recognize what is being experienced and can see the event as ineffectual; hence, releasing the emotion and releasing the associated negativity. It assists one in learning from the occurrence which prompted the emotion without engrossing oneself in the negativity.

Stellerite facilitates knowledge and practice of the "Eminent Innovation", the discovery of the creative power of thought and the ability to affirm, bringing progress toward the compatible relationship with the macrocosm and within the self. Dispelling "Maya", the illusion of the mind in the subjective universe and the illusion of the material universe, it promotes the recognition of the true and the false and allows one to realize that all illusion is never in the "thing", but in the way one perceives it to be.

It has also been used during the meditative state to manifest stellar contact with the preeminent order of angels, with knowledge disclosed which is inordinately germane and of vast import to the users.

Application at the crown chakra has aligned the chakras and has accorded a centering effect. At the base chakra, it acts to order the region and to elevate preservation and centering simultaneously. It assists one in cognizance of the phases of ones life and acts to provide insight to changes required to promote peace and happiness within ones life.

It also can be used to align the chakras and to affect an orderly arrangement between the ethereal and physical nervous systems.

It can be used in the treatment of disorders relating to the blood plasma, glaucoma, and muscular structure, to conditions of osteoporosis, bruxism, and Alzheimer's Dis-ease, and to lessen leg cramps. It has been used to assist in the amelioration of autism. It can also be used to improve conditions causing extreme cases of suffering and/or distress, assisting in the release of negative feelings.

Vibrates to the master number 44.

## STURMANITE [Astrological Sign of Leo]

***STURMANITE*** - $Ca_6Fe_2(SO_4)_2[B(OH)_4](OH)_{12}$♥$25H_2O$ or $Ca_6(Fe^{3+},Al,MN^{2+})_2$ $(SO_4)_2[B(OH)_4(OH)_{12}$♥$25H_2O$; Hardness 2.5; Locality: N'Chwaning Mine, Kalahari Manganese Field, Cape Province, Republic of South Africa; Photography by Jim Hughes, Assisted by ♪ Melody ♫; Collection of ♪ Melody ♫, Applewood, CO, USA.

Sturmanite crystallizes in the formation of vitreous bright yellow crystals and as druse. This mineral was first described by D.R. Peacor, P.J. Dunn, and M. Duggan, in 1983, and named for B.D. Sturman.

This mineral activates, aligns, and clears the solar plexus chakra, stimulating personal power, intent, reasoning, astral force, and aspirations and sentiments based upon intellect. It furthers the ability of "touch" and is an excellent stone for application during all "hands-on" healing techniques.

It further provides for a protective energy, protecting against any intellectual negativity which is from outside the self, while assisting in the cleansing of the chakras of mentally-generated negativity arising from within the self.

Sturmanite mobilizes more of the yin attributes, but also provides for balancing of the yang emotions and corporeal qualities while dispensing strength and vitality to the physical body. It can be used to allow one to be able to distinguish between openness and hidden agendas, frankness and evasion, caring attitudes and disdainful attitudes, etc. It actually provides for a mechanism to elucidate conditions of duality. A message of Sturmanite is that if one discharges trust in another, one will find trust in oneself.

It helps one to experience the diversions in life with openness, to be receptive and understanding of fluctuating emotional states, and to augment ones knowledge with the pieces of each anomaly.

It is an excellent mineral for intellectual pursuits and to advance higher education, to expedite studying and comprehension of details, to increase knowledge associated with aesthetics, epistemology, ethics, ideology, teaching, and religion, to enhance mental exploration, theoretical analysis, and cognitive understanding, and to further the study of languages.

It can also be useful in the rectification of affairs of possession, proprietorship, and lawsuits.

The mineral has been helpful to educators and lecturers, providing for an expansion of the proficiency required to summon understanding, and imparting the capacity to maintain audiences in a state of composed, stable rationality.

It also enhances ones self-esteem, providing for growth with modesty, and progress through humility.

Sturmanite has been used to assist in the assimilation of iron and Vitamin C, in the treatment of disorders of body tissue, the tendons, throat, stomach, liver, gall bladder, sympathetic nervous system [activating involuntary muscles which enhance the mobilization of the physical body], pancreas, and adrenal glands. It has acted to support cycles of toxic elimination and to control emotional disorders.

Vibrates to the number 5.

## SUNSTONE - BI-COLOUR [Astrological Signs of Leo & Gemini]

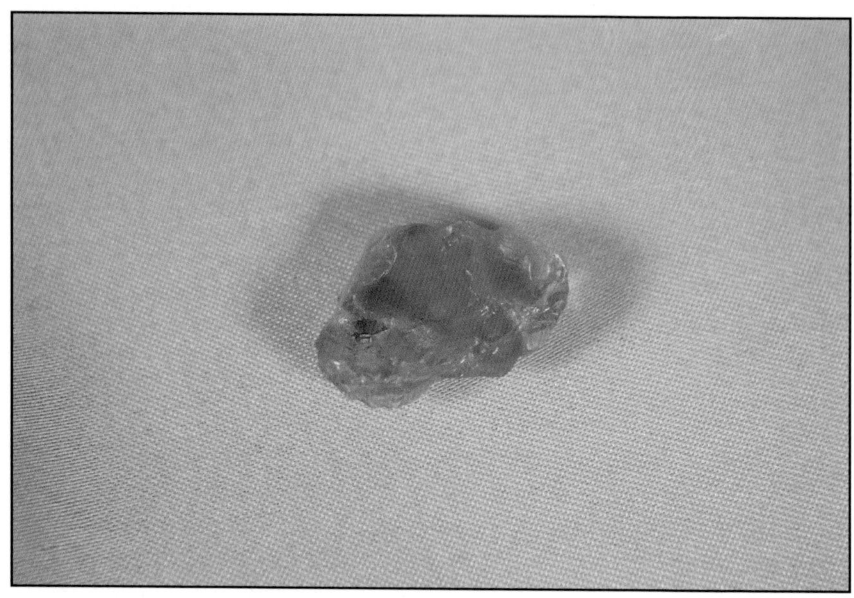

***SUNSTONE - BI-COLOUR*** - $(Na,Ca)AlSi_3O_8$ with inclusions of sub-microscopic lamellae; Hardness 5-6; Locality: Pink Lady Claim, Plush, Oregon, USA; Photography by Jim Hughes, Assisted by ♪ Melody ♬; Collection of ♪ Melody ♬, Applewood, CO, USA. Gift of Bill Horning, San Diego, CA, USA.

Bi-Coloured Sunstone is a two-colour transparent to sub-translucent vitreous, and possibly reflective, form of oligoclase [a type of feldspar]; it crystallizes in the form of masses and, rarely, tabular crystals. Sunstone was originally described by J.D. Dana in 1837 and was named for the brilliant reflections within the stone. Bi-Coloured Sunstone is included herein as a separate entry due to the additional qualities researched which are attributable to the exhibition of more than one colour. The following properties are in addition to those listed in the SUNSTONE section of "Love Is In The Earth - A Kaleidoscope Of Crystals Update".

This mineral has been used to strengthen knowledge and right action in the field of law enforcement and holistic medicine. When used in channeling activities, it can convey information involving herbal remedies and holistic remediation. It is one of the stones which also facilitates the transfer of energy from other minerals; hence, using this mineral in conjunction with other minerals during healing sessions promotes an increase in energy transfer.

Bi-Coloured Sunstone has been used in Native American rituals and ceremonies for providing clarity of thought during the vision quest. It acts to bring both elucidation and illumination of that which is experienced during the journey, assisting one also in the maintenance of cognizance while experiencing an altered state.

This mineral exhibits alternating currents which are joined via the ethers to the forces of revelation through which attraction and preference are promulgated. When a request is directed through the Bi-Coloured Sunstone to the objective or to the application which is desired, the mineral functions as a conductor for the message - sending the communiqué to the ethers via a stream which infiltrates the energy course related to revelation and subsequent manifestation. The communiqué is then transferred to the infinite mind which, in turn, perfects the transmittal and assures that the purpose is for the good of all, before sending the transmission directly toward actualization on the physical plane. The energies of the mineral prevail over both time and space, inducing harmonious interaction and tributes which grow from the idea/ideal which one desires to manifest.

It can also be used to provide for unification for groups which hold a "separate-ness" concept; acting on the intuitive, intellectual, and communication levels, it brings forth a melding of the three, and the concept of group-effort, to recognition and actualization.

Bi-Coloured Sunstone also activates and energizes the sacral, solar plexus, heart, crown, and throat chakras, providing for clarity of path for the movement of the Kundalini.

It has been used in the treatment of dysfunction due to trauma, throat disorders, intestinal blockage, stomach ulcers, gall bladder disorders, and cataracts. It can assist in the regulation of the proper flow of insulin to the blood stream.

Vibrates to the number 6.

# "SUPER SEVEN"

[Astrological Sign of All]

***"SUPER SEVEN"*** - Amethyst-$SiO_2$ w/Fe, Cacoxenite-$Fe_{24}AlO_6(PO_4)_{17}(OH)_{12}$♥$75H_2O$, Goethite-alpha-FeO(OH), Quartz-alpha-$SiO_2$, Lepidocrocite $Fe_2O_3$♥$H_2O$, Rutile-$TiO_2$ or $FeTiO_3$, and Smokey Quartz-$SiO_2$ with impurities/natural irradiation; Hardness 7; Locality: Espirito do Santo, Brasil, South America; Photography by Jim Hughes, Assisted by ♪ Melody ♫; Collection of Bob Jackson & ♪ Melody ♫, Applewood, CO, USA.

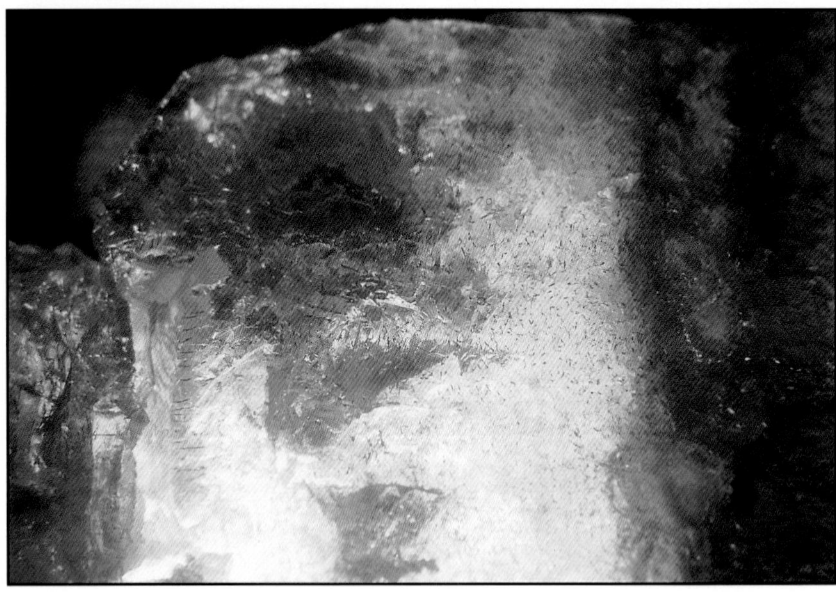

"Super Seven", also known as the "Sacred Seven", and coined in California as the "Melody Stone", is a combination of seven minerals - Amethyst, Cacoxenite, Goethite, Lepidocrocite, Clear Quartz, Rutile, and Smokey Quartz. At this time, there is no defined/accepted mineralogical name for this combination of minerals. In addition to the properties of these minerals listed in "Love Is In The Earth - A Kaleidoscope Of Crystals", the following attributes apply. It should be noted that the two photographs shown provide an indication of the "zoned" quality of the mineral. It has been found that smaller segments of the mineral (e.g., tumbled stones), contain all of the energies of the total configuration, although each mineral is not exhibited separately.

The "Super Seven" is a "flambeau" mineral which is known to exhibit, the phenomenon of St. Elmo's Fire, an ethereal auric light reminiscent of the "holy light" which has been seen due to atmospheric electricity on church towers and treetops. It produces electromagnetic waves providing the self-luminous quality and assists one in "seeing" auras and in maintaining the connection between the physical and ethereal planes.

Analogous to Sirius, the "brightest" star in the heavens, it can assist one in all endeavors, promoting conscious awareness of that which has remained hidden for aeons. It provides for mental impressions denoting spiritual/intellectual truths, allegories to assist in advancement, and images of ones position, appointment, and progress in the "Cosmic Plane".

The "Super Seven" is being used as the nucleus of the universal "brotherhood" of humanity, embracing karma, causation, and the potential for reincarnation, all based upon the science of theosophy. It presents information for both individuals and for the collective, assisting one to understand and to facilitate the changing of ones "thinking" in order to set in motion the new "laws" allowing peace, harmony, and love to guide and govern ones being. It never needs cleansing or energizing.

It has also been used to promote telekinetic pursuits, telepathy, clairaudience, clairvoyance, awareness-channeling, universal creativity, to further healing and well-ness on all levels, and for Earth-healing.

"Super Seven" vibrates to the numbers 5 and 9; "Sacred Seven" vibrates to the number 7; and the "Melody Stone" vibrates to the number 3.

## SYLVITE

[Astrological Sign of Leo]

***SYLVITE*** - KCl; Hardness 2; Locality: Carlsbad Potash District, Eddy Co., NM, USA; Photography by Jim Hughes, Assisted by ♪ Melody ♫; Collection of ♪ Melody ♫, Applewood, CO, USA.

Sylvite crystallizes in the formation of cubes, often with octahedral truncations, granular crystalline masses, and compact masses. The colour ranges from vitreous colourless to white, grey, yellow, and red. The name is sometimes spelled with a "n" replacing the "t". This mineral was first described by F.S. Beaudant in 1832 and was named Sylvine from the alchemical name Sylvii; in 1868, J.D. Dana modified the name to Sylvite.

This mineral can be used to free the mind of inconsequential content. It provides for the equilibration of both feelings and passions, for the stimulation of both instinct and creativity, and for a lucrative channel for ambition. It helps one during periods of change and provides a multitude of insights with respect to the available options.

It also enhances ones abilities in the pursuit of mathematics, stimulating analytical thinking and inducing the mental state required for problem-solving.

It further brings the energy to affect talent in acting and in participating in the theatrical aspects of circumstances; providing, in addition, the essential action of laughter during the aimless considerations of any adventure.

Sylvite provides for faithfulness and uniformity to the truth of ones nature. It sustains the facility of "exactitude" when one is uniting in ritualistic activities and when one communes with the world of spirits.

It advances articulation in self-expression and in narrating the components of divination, spontaneous encounters, and psychic experiences. It further grants understanding of the interpretations intrinsic to these ventures.

It has been used to open and to stimulate the base, sacral and crown chakras. It tends to further the opening of the crown chakra to a violet flash, bringing spirituality on all levels.

It brings the energy to enhance cooperation and stimulates ones personal affinity with "All". It is a purifier and is quite useful for cleansing the aura, the chakras, and the energy meridians.

It is a stone for deflecting the lower energies into socially constructive and creative channels, for refinement and purification of the environment and the body, and for the development and growth of ingenious ideas.

It has been used in agricultural pursuits to stimulate growth.

Sylvite can be very helpful in the actualization of weight loss, in the treatment of intestinal absorption problems, disorders of the reproductive glands, and bacterial infections. It can enhance stability in ambulatory disorders, and can assist with the assimilation of potassium and in the elimination of toxicity from the system. It is an excellent healing mineral, acting as an anesthetic during times of pain.

The solubility of this mineral precludes its use in the normal method of preparation of an elixir.

Vibrates to the number 4.

**"DON'T JUST "DO" SOMETHING, "SIT" THERE"**

Osho

## TEKTITE - GUANGDONG [Astrological Sign of All]

***TEKTITE - GUANGDONG*** - Meteoritic glass from outer space; Hardness 5-5,5; Locality: Guangdong, China; Photography by Jim Hughes, Assisted by ♪ Melody ♫; Collection of ♪ Melody ♫, Applewood, CO, USA.

The Guangdong Tektite from China is a natural glass of meteoritic origin. The name Tektite was first described by F.E. Suess in 1900. This mineral has been found in the same location as the newly discovered glyphs (said to be Mayan) unearthed in China. It has been known as "the Ambassador of Highest Order", sent to save the Earth and her children, and acting as a heaven-sent reminder that all things are one - it has come to the Earth, becoming a part of the Earth and a part of all we share.

It is the stone for ushering-out the Kali Yuga, the exhibition of the deficiency of Dharma in our world today, and ushering-in the freshness of the Krita Yuga, the age of perfection and total gain, possessing divinity and ascendancy for all. Carrying the Guangdong Tektite provides for ones preparation for the new world and acts as a constant reminder and an <u>attunement with</u> the Krita Yuga and the Mayan glyphs which provide information about the reformation of our world. It is for the "emperor" within each of us, promoting the acceptance of responsibility and the release of subjectivity to the "beliefs" or constraints of others. It allows for the creation of power, harmful to none, on all levels through accountability and guardianship of the self and the Earth.

It is a catalyst to the expedition of progress and to the re-awakening and recognition of those with whom one has been closely connected in "previous" lives. It helps one to surmount the third dimension, and assists one in uniting with those of this dimension, of the spiritual and astral spaces, and from the stars; during these activities, the supreme energies are synthesized to exact the shared essence of the life force. Holding a Guangdong Tektite with another person provides for information with respect to times and places where the inner essence of each person related in form - on other planes, in other times.

It has been used to remove unwanted "implants", concurrently healing breaches within the chakra system and filling the voids which remain after the removal of the implant, with the healing light of love.

It is an excellent third-eye stone, stimulating visionary experiences and providing for the activation and energizing of the third-eye chakra. It assists one in traveling deeply within the inner being and in maintaining the intensity while integrating the myriad of available visual images. It assists the energy from the third-eye to be transported throughout the body, producing an intuitive understanding of the complete cellular, emotional, spiritual, and intellectual structures.

The Guangdong Tektite stimulates intuition, enhances awareness, provides for freedom in accessing pre-determined sites during astral travel, and assists one in both lucid dreaming and dream recall. It has also been applied to the amplification of the auric field, and, via testing with Kirlian photography, has been shown to increase the range and to both intensify and brighten the energies.

It brings forth a polarizing energy, which engenders a spectrum of energy to clear and to activate all of the chakras. It acts in the healing realm to activate minerals and to assist in the restructuring of the body to promote perfection. It never needs cleansing or energizing.

Vibrates to the number 9.

## TYROLITE

[Astrological Sign of Aries]

***TYROLITE*** - $CaCu_5(AsO_4)_2CO_3(OH)_4$♥$6H_2O$; Hardness 2; Locality: Majuba Hill, Pershing Co., NV, USA; Photography by Jim Hughes, Assisted by ♪ Melody ♫; Collection of ♪ Melody ♫, Applewood, CO, USA.

Tyrolite crystallizes in the formation of masses, coatings, foliated aggregates, and fan-shapes. The colour is a lovely light turquoise blue-green. This mineral was first described as "Tirolit" by W. Haidinger in 1845, with modification of spelling in 1850 by J.D. Dana, and named for the localities in the Tyrol, Austria, where it was first discovered.

This mineral represents the initiation of learning and is conducive to all intellectual, emotional, and spiritual educational pursuits. It assists in providing for clarity in material and in lessons.

It can induce the energies of enterprise, helping one to find that which is lost - physical objects, awareness, memory, etc. It can also assist one in discernment of the reasons behind the actions of another, allowing one to honour the effects of the physical plane upon the spirituality of humanity, and motivating one toward personal improvement.

Tyrolite assists in explicit analysis of problems and circumstances. It stimulates a powerful intellect and provides for balancing between the caring features of ones character and the obdurance of rationality.

It provides for a harmonic connection between the physical and astral bodies and aligns the subtle bodies. It has been used successfully to amplify and to transmit thought. It is said to be a "bestower" of "good", bringing benefit to the user. It is also reported to bring "luck" to persons in the recovery of property.

It further assists one in examining ones strategies, designs, and tactics, and provides for the reminder that although a strategy is beautiful, one must occasionally examine the results, the consequences, and the conclusions, to assure that the beauty remains.

The mineral also acts, without conscious direction, to bring frugality to ones actions, assisting in economy and conservation, and discouraging activities which impart wastefulness.

It further brings strength to ones lifework, providing a foundation and perspicacity to assist one toward a pre-defined goal. It can assist when one is inquiring for employment or during the decision-making process of selection of a new or different career. In the pursuit for employment, the energy of Tyrolite acts to bring both instinct and providence, and assists one in selecting which gateway to enter; upon establishment of the gateway, it tends to empower one to acquire the situation which will foster ones progress and development.

It has also been used to diminish the proportion of addiction and to both reassure and steady the addictive personality. It tends to guide the focus of the user toward recovery and toward rejuvenation. Tyrolite has been used in the treatment of arthritis, leukemia, birthing, to discourage disorders of the body at the onset, to allay bone calcification, and to ameliorate disorders of the thyroid and the muscular structure.

The arsenide content of this mineral precludes its use in the normal method of preparation of an elixir.

Vibrates to the number 7.

**♪ THERE IS NO EVIDENCE TO SUPPORT**
**THE PRECEPT**
**THAT LIFE IS SERIOUS ♬**

## URALITE

[Astrological Sign of Pisces]

***URALITE*** - $Ca_2(Mg,Fe)_5OH_2,(Si_4O_{11})_2$; Hardness 5-6; Locality: Calumet Mine, Salida, CO, USA; Photography by Jim Hughes, Assisted by ♪ Melody ♫; and in the Collection of ♪ Melody ♫, Applewood, CO, USA.

Uralite crystallizes as a green, generally fibrous or acicular, formation. It was first described by G. Rose in 1831 and named for the Ural Mountains in Russia, where it was first discovered.

This mineral activates the increase of advantageous change to ones life, bringing the energy of action without reaction and a lucid mission for progress.

It is a unique shielding device and augments the energy bodies providing for a synthesis with the absolute while facilitating both fellowship and "esprit de corps".

It accounts for an intimacy and informality with all of those who one encounters, promoting the energies bringing the affable and intimate acknowledgement, action, or reality.

Uralite can be useful for providing guidance during spiritual growth and for help in clearing the self of negative emotional, physical, or spiritual concerns.

It acts to provide remediation to painful transformations while allowing one to remain grounded and centered in this reality, and can be used to enhance the understanding of metamorphosis in ones life. With the experience of the state of constant change of form, structure, and substance, Uralite can be used to ameliorate the more trying transformations.

The mineral has been used to promote exterior transformation - ones look, ones reflection, ones glow.

Allowed to rest within ones environment, the energies tend to bring protection and to banish sorrow. It promotes the flow of extroverted nature (when consciously directed), bringing security from outside influences, exactness in speech, and intuitive precautionary measures.

It has further provided protection against "discovery" of clandestine and secret activities and meetings. The energy acts to provide insight to methods of eliminating discovery and methods for securing all sights from intrusion.

It has been used in neuro-linguistic programming to facilitate exacting communication, such that a programmer could not instill that which was unwanted or unnecessary.

By focusing the mineral on an unwanted condition, lessening is both facilitated and enhanced. It can be used to help one with strengthening basic conditions and/or decreasing unwanted conditions, further acting to ameliorate deficiencies within the body. Uralite has provided assistance in examination of the depths of the self to facilitate insight into the conditions underlying dis-ease and dysfunctional behavior patterns. It has also been used in the treatment of numbness and is an excellent environmental presence during both acupressure/acupuncture.

Vibrates to the number 5.

## UVITE

[Astrological Sign of Sagittarius]

***UVITE*** - $(Ca,Na)(Mg,Fe^{+2})_3Al_5Mg(BO_3)_3Si_6O_{18}(OH,F)_4$ or $Ca(Mg,Fe)_3Al_5Mg(BO_3)_3Si_6O_{18}(OH)_4$; Hardness 7.5; Locality: Brumado, Bahia, Brasil; Photography by Jim Hughes, Assisted by ♪ Melody ♫; Collection of ♪ Melody ♫, Applewood, CO, USA.

Uvite crystallizes in the form of vertically striated prismatic crystals, sometimes slender, sometimes needle-like, sometimes in small clusters. The colour range includes deep red, vitreous black, brown, colourless, and light green. This mineral was first described by W. Kunitz in 1929 and was named for the locality of Uva, Sri Lanka where it was first discovered.

This mineral has been used to stimulate, to activate, and to open the base, heart, and crown chakras, while producing a grounding effect on the total being.

It assists one to concentrate upon ones breathing and to live in ones own actions, ever present, ever mindful of ones actions. It provides for a connection with the ethereal energy, with attachment via the intellect; hence, promoting intellectual attentiveness on all planes. Assisting with the concept of time, it facilitates the knowledge that time is relative to ones being and the enjoyment of all time is essential to ones progression and ultimate transcendence of the physical realm.

Uvite can be used to eliminate negativity from ones environment, by simply being a part of that environment. Worn, carried, or used as an elixir, it removes forces opposing positive energy from ones energy field and provides a barrier against further entry of same.

It can balance the male/female energies, bringing forth the qualities of clarity, and clear spirit, and equilibrating the many facets of ones temperament.

It has been used to stimulate balance between the left and right sides of the brain and to enhance cooperative efforts in the areas of creativity and healing.

It further provides for examination of the depths of ones being with as much belief in the reality of the inner world as one maintains for the outer world. It helps one to release the concept of being the victim <u>and</u> to maintain fortitude and calm while retaining awareness.

It has been used by shamen among the African and Aboriginal tribes. It is thought to bring healing powers to the user and to provide protection from all dangers occurring on the physical plane. The African shamen have used the mineral to promote the awakening from fantasy and to promote the conscious experience of the self.

It is the "super activator" of the protective instincts of ones nature and encourages one to examine the seriousness of any condition.

It has been used in the treatment of disorders of the intestinal tract, to reduce spots on the skin, in the treatment of nervousness, disorders of the heart and lungs, and in dysfunctions of the emotional system. It has assisted in providing stimulus to the immune system.

It has also been used to stimulate the growth of plants.

Vibrates to the number 5.

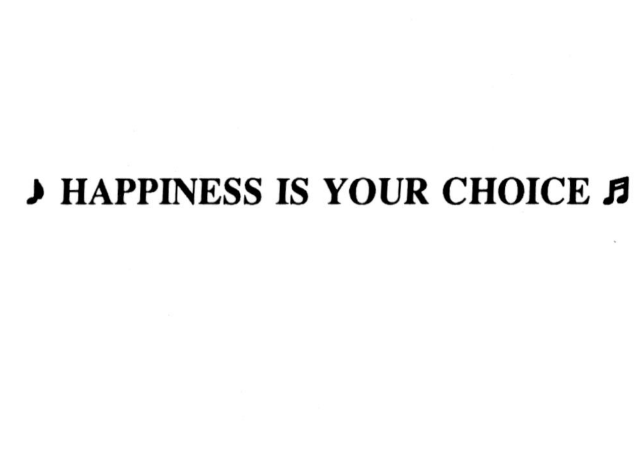

♪ HAPPINESS IS YOUR CHOICE ♫

XV

## WOLLASTONITE

[Astrological Sign of Aquarius]

***WOLLASTONITE*** - $CaSiO_3$; Hardness 4.5-5; Locality: Lake Bonaparte, Lewis County, NY, USA; Photography by Jim Hughes, Assisted by ♪ Melody ♫; Collection of ♪ Melody ♫, Applewood, CO, USA.

Wollastonite occurs as translucent to subtransparent fibrous crystalline configurations, tabular and short prismatic crystals, and perfectly cleavable and compact masses. It sometimes exhibits a silky luster. The colour range includes white, grey, yellow, red, and brown. This mineral was first described as "Tafelspath" by A. Stűtz in 1793 and subsequently described in 1818 by J. Léman when he renamed "Tafelspath" to Wollastonite for W.H. Wollaston.

This mineral is a filter for the universal energies, purifying and refining the energies from outside the self, with which one can be bombarded.

It furthers interest in many fields, encouraging one to experience the diversification and to apply the laws of similarities in order to integrate the whole. It can help to reduce the "plastic" fragile facade that one may sanction or adopt, allowing for the introduction of both surety and confidence.

Wollastonite helps one to exercise dignity objectively, providing both modesty and respect for the superior exhibition of intelligence. It allows one to recognize that the strength of the opposition is less than that which is within oneself. This mineral strengthens the energy of success in principle and challenges. It reconstructs the inferior forms of response and reaction to caring forms of acknowledgment.

It also inspires the ideal of service, providing for cooperative endeavors and ingenuity in maintaining the effort.

It allows one to understand the duality within the self, and further stimulates retrieval of the feminine side of nature, being a good stone for healing those who will not allow themselves to cry.

It activates clairaudience while providing grounding; this enables one to contact the other worlds while remaining totally conscious of the self. It can enable one to predict future events and can be used to enhance the abilities of a divining rod. It is an excellent mineral for inclusion within any type of wand.

In addition, Wollastonite may be used to grid an area to enhance the energy for welcoming spaceship landings. It has also been used to grid "crop circles", bringing the implementation of safety for both the other-worldly beings and for the self.

It can be used to balance the energy fields, to align the meridians of the body, and to connect the physical body to the perfection of the higher orders of the universe.

It has been used to facilitate the state of correct alkalinity within body, to assist in repairing the structure of the body and in refurbishing the skin, and has been used in the treatment of chills, the arteries (for strength), bronchitis, and pneumonia. It can be used in the treatment of physical weakness and psychological disorders.

It is an excellent stone for runners, helping to eliminate the muscular spasms and "stitches" and encouraging flexibility.

Vibrates to the number 3.

**"WHEN YOU CREATE YOUR OWN REALITY,
IT IS MUCH EASIER
IF YOU LEAVE-OUT THE DETAILS"**

Rob Dubois
Colorado, USA

## YODERITE

[Astrological Signs of Libra & Scorpio]

***YODERITE*** - $(Mg,Al)_8O_2(SiO_4)_4(OH)_2$ or $(Al,Mg,Fe)_6Al_2(Si,Al)_4O_{18}(OH)_2$; Hardness 6; Locality: Mautia Hills, Tanzania; Photography by Jim Hughes, Assisted by ♪ Melody ♫; Collection of ♪ Melody ♫, Applewood, CO, USA.

Yoderite crystallizes in the monoclinic system in the form of translucent purple twisted fibrous structures, masses, coatings, and long-bladed crystals which are either plated, twisted, or straight. The mineral was first described in 1959 by D. McKie and was named for the subsequently modified formula determined by H. S. Yoder.

This is one of the minerals in the mineral kingdom which never needs cleaning or clearing. It will not accumulate or retain negative energy or vibrations.

It brings composure and a composed effect to the whole being, with particular focus on the crown chakra and the third-eye. It stimulates discourse and psychic awareness on all levels. It dispels hostility and disillusionment and helps to advance precision with respect to cognitive perception and linear reasoning. It influences one to persist in activities and in circumstances which would, generally, diminish ones vitality; it provides a inspiring energy and strengthens one in the continuation of projects. It progresses the sentient connection between the higher levels of instinct and altruistic and unconditional love, producing grace in both communication and decision-making.

It also assists in dissipating disorientation arising from emotional, spiritual, and intellectual concerns.

Yoderite aligns all chakras automatically and immediately, with no conscious direction. If directed with the consciousness of the user, it can also open the chakras. Conscious direction of the energy can also align the emotional, intellectual, physical, spiritual, ethereal, astral,.... bodies.

It facilitates the meditative state by producing a calm, clearing effect which is functional and practical. It allows for the energy to be attainable, gentle, and balanced. It is also quite useful when accessing the astral plane and when connecting with ones guides.

It further helps to provoke the memory for recounting dreams and to promote dream-solving, providing for access to the solution plane during the dream state and/or during meditation.

It provides for balancing of the yin-yang energies, bringing an orderly growth to the intellect, emotions, and physical body. It dispels energy blockages, moving energy from the ethereal plane, in a gentle, yet, forceful way through the physical body.

It can be used during radionic analysis; holding a sample and placing a sample on the witness <u>or</u> using a pendulum of this stone, the energy of the stone interferes with the energy of the user and points to the problem(s) involved.

It can be used in the treatment of disorders of the brain, the adrenal glands, the throat, the muscular and urogenital system, and the parathyroid glands. It is a beneficial stone to place at the crown chakra during the healing activities associated with the "laying-on-of-stones".

Vibrates to the number 2.

♪ WITH A DREAM
OF PARADISE IN OUR HEARTS,
OUR PLANET
WILL FLOURISH ♫

# LABORATORY-PRODUCED STONES (I.E., MAN-MADE)

This section provides information for two Laboratory-Produced minerals. Normally, the author does not report on man-made stones; however, the two stones within this section have been highly recommended and, hence, the researched properties are given.

The positive aspects are that there is no question that these minerals are not from the Earth, no one represents them as being naturally occurring, and they do not have the appearance of any other natural mineral; this is quite refreshing since there **is** absolute confirmation that <u>emerald without silk, ruby, amethyst, citrine, quartz, sapphires in normal and non-existent colours, spinel single crystals and spinel crystals on matrix, tanzanite crystals and tanzanite on matrix in the 1-1 1/2" size, alexandrite crystals and alexandrite crystals on matrix, and malachite</u> are currently being manufactured and being sold as natural minerals from the Earth. Please beware! Research has indicated that, although these laboratory-grown minerals do have the same chemical composition as the naturally occurring minerals, the vibratory energies tend to be discordant (this could be from the intent or due to the actual process).

## SILICON

[Astrological Sign of Capricorn]

***SILICON*** - Laboratory Produced Silicon as $SiO_2$; Hardness 7; Photography by Jim Hughes, Assisted by ♪ Melody ♫; Collection of ♪ Melody ♫, Applewood, CO, USA; Gift of Bob Lewis, California, USA.

Laboratory-Produced Silicon appears to have the properties of quartz, but on a higher vibratory level, providing for a cleaner and higher silicon energy level to be experienced by the user. It has been used for mental attunement, for memory enhancement, and to improve manual dexterity. Even with the high energy, it helps one to attain a "soft" meditative state, providing for smooth grounding concurrently.

It, however, does not have the crystalline structure, and, hence, does not bring in the properties relative to specific configurations.

This element has been used to balance the energy fields and to assist one in the elimination of ego conflicts and feelings of futility, helping to mitigate the overburden of personal liability and opposing feelings of despondency and unimportance. It further promotes one to both understand and to dispense with self-rebuke.

It has also been used to calm excitation and states of anger and to open and to activate the throat chakra.

It has been used in the advancement, refinement, and equilibration of the crown chakra (interesting, because it would have been the last place I would have thought) and for the expansion of thought-forms. The purity of silicon has assisted in the preservation of significant thought forms for later recovery.

In a controlled situation, it has been attributed as bringing honors; wealth has increased in situations of placing a small tumbled piece in cash drawers and on top of the cash registers. It has also been attributed as a mineral which will amplify positive feelings.

It appears also to be a "master healer". It has been shown to be an excellent mineral for purification of the physical body, clearing negativity from the chakras and the energy fields of the physical, emotional, intellectual, and spiritual bodies, while transferring the vitality of any companion mineral to the affected area.

It produces an energy which appears to be both cooperative and receptive, allowing for extensive use with other gem stones, and appears capable of attracting and maintaining those qualities which are inherent within the additional stone. Also, when in proximity to another mineral, it grants a stabilizing influence to the energies of that mineral.

Laboratory-Produced Silicon has been used to diminish fever and to eliminate chills. It has been an excellent "remedy" for flu and cold symptoms, providing for the dissipation of the symptoms.

It is currently being used in the treatment of Alzheimer's dis-ease, to alleviate symptoms. It has also been used to assist in the enhancement of the muscular structure and in the relief of atrophied muscles.

It should be noted that in the author's research, there was no apparent difference relative to the shape of the silicon.

Vibrates to the number 9.

# VICTORIA STONE

***VICTORIA STONE*** - Laboratory Produced fibrous amphibole-like aggregate comprised of natural minerals; Hardness 6; Photography by Jim Hughes, Assisted by ♪ Melody ♫; Collection of ♪ Melody ♫, Applewood, CO, USA.

The Victoria Stone is a beautiful laboratory-produced mineral containing natural minerals from their naturally occurring states, such as quartz, calcite, fluorite, magnesite, feldspar, etc., which are fused together at a sufficiently high temperature to produce a molten magma and then mineralized via the influence of specific crystalizers and crystal-habit regulators to produce the lovely fibrous aggregate structure.

It is a stone to assist one in acknowledging that "If you stop demanding the answer, the answer will come in its own time". It has also assisted in "blowing" ones troubles away, such that they are never to return.

It has been carved for use as a talisman of protection, by Native Canadians, to provide an invisible barrier against attack and illness.

The Victoria Stone has been considered to be a sacred mineral in the countryside of Japan, being used as the material for fashioning sacred implements and articles. It is said to bless that which it touches and to facilitate the transfer of energy from object to user.

It has also been used to produce a wearing-away of that which is unwanted.

It furthers the forming of attachments and the continuity of love affairs, bringing the actualization of "love as the victor over all". It has been used to promote recognition of the love connection between the physical manifestation of, and the spiritual being of, each person in a relationship. It opens, energizes, and cleanses the heart chakra and the solar plexus chakra.

The Victoria Stone represents a symbol of life and social and emotional interaction. It provides for the activation of both receptivity and dynamic and charismatic attraction, assisting one in recognizing that which is being attracted via emotional actions and guiding one toward the furtherance of attracting that which is desired.

It can be used to help one to attract people, experiences, or objects which have been defined as necessary to ones growth, stimulating ones creative emanations and bringing them to the world of elemental actualization.

Gridding of pets, gardens, or agricultural areas [or a photograph of same] can promote healthy pets and plants. It has been placed upon a photograph of a home and has been used in gridding a home to assist in the maintenance of the security of ones possessions. It can also be used to grid the photograph of a person to protect against contagious disorders.

Carrying the Victoria Stone has facilitated "one fitting-in" anywhere, and stimulates the knowledge of comportment for all situations.

It has been used to promote cooling of the body (for fevers and for extremely high environmental temperatures), in the treatment of the central nervous system and in the re-establishment of the freedom of movement in the body, assisting the body in self-healing abilities. It is an excellent energizer for salves, elixirs, and tinctures.

Vibrates to the number 8.

**"IRRESPECTIVE OF WHAT YOU DO,**
**OPINIONS WILL DIFFER;**
**EVEN YOUR OWN OPINION,**
**FROM TIME TO TIME"**

Mulla Nasruddin

# MINERALS AND CONFIGURATIONS AND UPDATES OF MINERALS AND CONFIGURATIONS

This section provides information for the following:

1- Minerals and Configurations which were in "Love Is In The Earth - A Kaleidoscope Of Crystals Update", but for which information from further research has become available.

2- Minerals and Configurations which were not in "Love Is In The Earth - A Kaleidoscope Of Crystals Update", but were shown in "Love Is In The Earth - Mineralogical Pictorial".

**"And the foundations of the wall of the city *were* garnished with all manner of precious stones. The first foundation *was* jasper; the second, sapphire; the third, a chalcedony; the fourth, an emerald; the fifth, sardonyx; the sixth, sardius; the seventh, chrysolyte; the eighth, beryl; the ninth, a topaz; the tenth, a chrysoprasus; the eleventh, a jacinth; the twelfth, an amethyst."**

Revelation, 21, 1611 King James Version

Note: The geological references translate sardius to be a translucent brown to deep orange-red variety of chalcedony similar to carnelian, but of less intense colour than the typical carnelian. The geological references translate jacinth to be a yellow, brown, red or orange Zircon or as an orange-red to orange type of grossular garnet which contains iron (also known as Hessonite).

## ALBITE - SHEET [Astrological Signs of Aquarius & Libra]

Sheet Albite is a form of feldspar which crystallizes in flattened patterns. The colour is usually white. Albite was first described by J.G. Gahn and J.J. Berzelius in 1815 and was named for the colour, from "albus" which is defined as "white". In addition to the properties listed for ALBITE in "Love Is In The Earth - A Kaleidoscope Of Crystals Update", the following further information is provided.

Sheet Albite provides for a flow in relationships, cooperative activities, and a "coming together".

It assists one in understanding the reasons behind situations of non-responsiveness; e.g., when one cares fiercely and all-consumingly for another, and the other does not feel the same. It promotes looking toward the karmic connection and researching the "whys" and "why nots".

It further assists one in perceiving the aspects of karma, inducing the appreciation that one does not **need** to experience other than "good times", and promoting the learning of lessons without personal participation in negative episodes.

The mineral does, however, tend to inspire an overwhelming passion in others, bringing moral strength and a single-minded dedication to ones purpose, and promoting a "caring" attitude with no equivocation or hypocrisy.

It has been used in the treatment of disorders of the joints and to relieve headaches.

Vibrates to the number 7.

## ALTAITE [Astrological Sign of Leo]

Altaite crystallizes in the form of masses and, rarely, in cubic or octahedral crystals. The colour ranges from yellow (sometimes tarnishing to bronze-yellow) through tin-white. Altaite often occurs with silvery Petzite (♪ "some are silver and the others gold" ♫). Altaite was first described by W. Haidinger in 1845 and was named for Altai, Russia, where it has been found. When the occurrence is with Petzite, please combine the properties of Petzite from "Love Is In The Earth - A Kaleidoscope Of Crystals Update".

This mineral has been used to promote the actualization of an abundance of physical energy during hostile situations; it provides protection via energy stimulation and encourages the protective mechanisms of the self. It can also act to balance ones volatility and to purify the emotions, allowing for release of anger.

Altaite has been used in the treatment of pneumonia and to facilitate the tightening of muscles and epidermic connective tissue.

Due to the lead content of this mineral, an elixir preparation via the normal method is not recommended. However, an elixir (non-normal method) is recommended, due to the ability of the energy to stimulate the energies of the physical form.

Vibrates to the number 5.

## AMETHYST

### Amethyst From Other Countries:

Amethyst is a variety of quartz which occurs [throughout the world] either in crystalline or massive form. The associated colour ranges from deep purple to pale lavender. The presence of manganese in clear quartz produces amethyst, while additional amounts of iron content alter the purple colouration.

The information concerning the properties of Amethyst can be found in "Love Is In The Earth - A Kaleidoscope Of Crystals Update".

It is interesting to note the varying distinctions that each Amethyst exhibits with respect to the country, and the location within the country, in which it is found. The reader is encouraged to experience the subtleties as well as the conspicuous diversities of the varying country-specific forms.

Oregon Amethyst: [Astrological Sign of Virgo]

Oregon Amethyst crystallizes in a very light purple colour in the configuration of crystals with three large and three small sides. Some of the crystals are skeletal.

This mineral may be utilized to assist one in both transcending pre-programmed patterns and in understanding the mechanisms of biofeedback. It induces a "triangular balancing" which is applied to the biofeedback exercise, assisting one in determining personal patterns of response to stress and negativity. It provides for verification of the extent of self-control and self-awareness one maintains and arouses insight regarding methods which can improve ones response to stress [i.e., such that the response is "action" and not re-action].

It further assists one in recognizing and acting upon the inhibitions caused by a multitude of programs, some of which have been ingrained during this lifetime and others which are deep-seated remnants from former lives. It promotes the transcendence of contradictory ideas, promoting both the forces of manifestation and spiritual illumination. It furthers "witnessing" to emotions such that one does not initiate reaction and such that one may act as a mirror to all, reflecting the feelings of others without experiencing the sensations; with this energy, there are no events which can "push your buttons" to initiate negative emotional re-actions.

Oregon Amethyst can assist one in transcending physical discomforts and pain, negative emotions, trauma, and dis-ease. It assists one in witnessing the situation and in understanding the process of disengaging the intellect from the condition. It further reinforces ones perception and promotes the resolution of emotional situations which induce over-indulgence [in food, alcohol, drugs, relationships, etc.], providing for the recognition of the issues involved and stimulating positive action toward the amelioration of the problem.

It is an excellent energy for the practice of self-regulation, assisting one to recognize when there is "something amiss" in the body, where the condition is located, and what manifestation the condition has assumed; at this point, diaphragmatic breathing is initiated and one breathes "into" the area of concern, releasing the associated tension and stimulating renewal. It is fascinating to monitor the self, via this mineral, during changes in lifestyle.

Vibrates to the number 5.

## AMETRINE - ELESTIAL [Astrological Signs of Gemini & Libra]

The Ametrine Elestial is an elestiated mixing of citrine and amethyst. The following properties are in addition to the properties listed in the AMETRINE, AMETHYST, and CITRINE sections of"Love Is In The Earth - A Kaleidoscope Of Crystals Update".

This mineral is excellent for those encountering resistance to change and transition, helping one to anticipate change. It soothes the spirit, quiets the emotions and the intellect, and furthers ones inner knowledge of ones personal reality.

It provides a multi-faceted energy and can be used in the transference of healing energies during both present and absent-healing situations, in the transference of protection, love, etc., and for thought transmission. For healing energy transference to a distant location, the mineral is placed upon a photograph of the subject in conjunction with a description of the condition one is addressing. Protection of a person, animal, or object may also be facilitated via the photographic method.

The Ametrine Elestial, used at the third-eye, can assist in the transmission of ones thoughts to another. Thoughts of well-being, healthfulness, etc., the mental body is sufficiently uncluttered - at the time of clarity, it will discharge to the mental body; this delayed action is dependent upon the sufficiency of the strength of the thought-form. The thought is strengthened via repetitious contemplation of the precise thought, and by repeated sending of the thought via the channel of the third-eye.

If, however, the auric field/energy field of the potential recipient does not possess the capability of reception, the thought-form will be repelled and returned; for example, a thought form, which requires an action which is adverse to the potential recipient, will not be accepted. In addition, if one is protected from thought-entry via one of the various personal metaphysical protective mechanisms which are available, the thought will be returned to the source (similar to the "Caller I.D. which blocks anonymous calls). With all of the loving protection which is being transmitted throughout the world today [e.g., during meditation, healing gatherings, retreats, etc.], any negative thought forms will, in all likelihood, be declined and reversed. Conversely, a consciously directed thought-form of love and protection will operate as a shielding and protective instrument, seeking all opportunities to benefit and to defend the recipient; it will also strengthen the positive forces and weaken the negative forces which attempt to infringe upon the auric field. Hence, the positive thoughts tend to maintain a "guardian angel", ever near the recipient. This is an excellent exercise for instilling protective force fields around lifeforms, objects, and the totality of our Earth.

Vibrates to the number 6.

## AMETRINE - CRYSTAL [Astrological Sign of Libra & Pisces]

Ametrine Crystals are crystal structures exhibiting a mixture of citrine and amethyst. In addition to the properties listed in the AMETRINE, AMETHYST, and CITRINE sections of "Love Is In The Earth - A Kaleidoscope Of Crystals Update", this mineral has been used to facilitate placement of the concentrated thoughts of the self in another location; when this is successful, ones form can be seen for those who possess advanced intuitive and clairvoyant faculties and/or ones presence can be felt by those who are intuitively sensitive or clairsentient. The metaphysical-scientific hypothesis explains the phenomenon as form created from ethereal/astral matter. This action has been accomplished via one placing the self within the crystal and, subsequently, sending ones form through the termination to the location determined.

It has also been used to assist in dancing; promoting ease, grace, and stability in career dancing and in meditative dancing.

The Ametrine crystal brings divine order to ones personal life, and further promotes the implementation of both societal organization and systematic resolutions.

Vibrates to the master number 66.

## AZEZTULITE

The form of Azeztulite described in "Love Is In The Earth - A Kaleidoscope Of Crystals Update" and which was discovered in the beryllium mine, is no longer available.

## BOLIVIANITE [Astrological Sign of Aquarius]

Bolivianite crystallizes in the form of masses, grains, and pseudo-isometric tetrahedral crystals. The colour ranges from white-blue to black. It sometimes occurs with Dolomite. Bolivianite is a "Dana" mineral said to be Stannite with impurities; further research has also indicated that it may be a mixture of Sphalerite and Covellite. One is encouraged to read the applicable sections in "Love Is In The Earth - A Kaleidoscope Of Crystals Update" and to combine the appropriate properties based on the inclusion of same within the mineral.

A "stone of energy transfer", this mineral has been utilized to stimulate well-ness of body, mind, spirit, and emotions; it can assist in balancing polarities, in dissipating energy blockages, and in creating harmony within the energy flow patterns of each of the participants. It stimulates breath currents within in the body to facilitate cellular balance and coordination.

It has also been used during group re-birthing activities and during group meditation, and for the promotion of correct results during divination.

During group activities, the energy tends to move through the mineral and from ones body to the contact point of the next person; a piece of Bolivianite is required for each participant. After several minutes, one will feel the energy entering and flowing through his/her body, to exit via the pre-determined contact point. During this time period, energy blockages and polarity imbalances will be felt. After a predetermined time period, the participants [by verbal agreement] reverse the direction of the energy flow, and continue the reversal process until the energy flow through the Bolivianite dissolves the energy blockages, instilling polarity balancing.

Vibrates to the master number 55.

## CAVANSITE

[Astrological Sign of Aquarius]

In addition to the properties listed in "Love Is In The Earth - A Kaleidoscope Of Crystals Update", this mineral can bring the physical, mental, and emotional bodies to convergence, such that all are working together to create the reality which is desired. It has also been used to stimulate the clearing and melding of the physical, etheric, and astral bodies in order to promote healing on all levels and to assist one in the conscious recognition of the locations of disorderly energies and dis-ease.

Cavansite distributes electrical stimulus when under pressure, tending to amplify energy. It is said to assist both the mind and body to remember: the mind, to remember information which has been brought to bear during astral travel and channeling experiences; the body, to remember the state of perfection during dis-ease in order to return to the natural state of flawless-ness.

It is an excellent mineral for stimulating the intuitive faculties during metaphysical pursuits. It is useful in multi-directional energy dissemination; it appears that the energy, which is directed inward toward the central forces of the mineral, separates and returns at double the intensity. It brings forth a polarizing prismatic energy, which engenders a spectrum of energy to clear and to activate all of the chakras.

It is a useful mineral for the stimulation of the third-eye and for bringing the art of visioning and clairvoyance to the heart space.

Cavansite has been used as a protective mineral in the areas of the home and the automobile.

It has been used in the treatment of disorders associated with joints, muscular tissue connectiveness, calcium deficiencies, body building and flexibility, and blood flow. It has also been used to assist in the treatment of AIDS and Crones Disease.

Do not prepare an elixir of this mineral via the normal method.

Vibrates to the number 4.

## CERITE [Astrological Sign of Pisces]

Cerite crystallizes in the form of masses, grains, and rarely, tetragonal or orthorhombic crystals. The colour ranges between clove-brown and cherry-red to grey. In Sweden, the mineral usually occurs with Lanthanite. Cerite was first described by W. Hisinger and J.J. Berzelius in 1804 and was named for its content of the newly discovered Cerium element and for Ceres, an asteroid, which had recently been discovered.

This mineral has been used for future-telling for another [when the other is present]; the tarot, Neo-tarot, I Ching, Runes, astrological readings, and corresponding activities are all promoted. During this time, the subject is attuning with the practitioner by holding the Cerite with the practitioner.

It has been used to provide comfort during times of sadness, to stimulate the intellect to look beyond a situation and to recognize the cause behind conflict [hence, to understand and "let it go"], and to enhance ones solitary moments [to increase both ones awareness and appreciation of these moments].

It further promotes contact with the energy of those of asteroidal origin and can promote the correction of disorders of the body and the mind which are said to be related to malfunctions of the organs. It has also been used to stimulate optical improvement and to relieve intense pain.

Vibrates to the number 7.

## CITRINE - With HEMATITE

[Astrological Signs of Gemini, Leo, & Aries]

Citrine with Hematite is a variety of quartz, the colour of Citrine being in the range from yellow to golden brown to burnt amber, and the colour of Hematite ranging from red to brown to black. Citrine was first described by E.E. Dana in 1892 and was named for the Greek word "citron", referring to its colour. Hematite was first described by Pliny in 77 A.D. and was named "Haematite" for the likeness to haemoglobin, etc.; In 1773, Romé de l'Isle changed the spelling to "Hematite". The following properties are in addition to those listed in the CITRINE and HEMATITE sections of "Love Is In The Earth - A Kaleidoscope Of Crystals Update".

This mineral has been used to dispel negativity from intellectual thought. It is quite easy for the intellect to recognize and to vocalize thoughts of incompetence; however, this energy boosts the spiritual level of the intellect to assist one in gaining the facility for non-judgmental-ness and to promote the recognition that "we are doing the best we can (for now)".

It further helps one to be pleasantly captivated by the spirit of practical observation, allowing one to look at otherwise tedious routines with an excitement that helps all activities to be interesting.

Citrine with Hematite is also said to increase fidelity and loyalty, and to magnify ones sensitivity toward others. It also enhances perception and discernment, enabling one to make decisions which painlessly further ones development.

It has been used in the treatment of disorders associated with fatty tissues and to promote the stability of the mind.

Vibrates to the number 6.

## DRUSY MINERALS

Drusy Minerals are defined to be minerals which are encrusted with small to microscopic projecting crystals, usually of the same mineral. These minerals tend to bring in a higher elevation of energy and to stimulate the exactness of the energy of the specific mineral, enabling acceleration in the process for which it is used.

To determine the vibratory number for specific minerals showing the Drusy configuration, one may add 24 to the sum of the numbers representing each letter of the name of the other mineral.

## EPIDOTE

[Astrological Sign of Gemini]

Epidote crystallizes in the form of plates, needle-like and prismatic crystals [the prismatic crystals being sometimes longitudinally striated and terminated on one end], granular masses, fibers, and deeply striated masses. The colour range includes yellow, yellow-green, pistachio green, brown-green, green-black, grey, and black; it also occurs in transparent reds and yellows. Epidote was first described by R.J. Haüy in 1801 and was named from the Greek word "increase", due to the prismatic base of some forms having one side longer than the other. The following properties are in addition to those listed in the EPIDOTE section of "Love Is In The Earth - A Kaleidoscope Of Crystals Update".

This mineral has been used to assist one in augmenting in the material world. It has also been used via placement in the stalls of horses for treatment of disorders of ligaments.

In addition, Epidote can be used to facilitate weight gain.

Vibrates to the number 2.

## FADEN - QUARTZ CRYSTAL [Astrological Sign of Scorpio]

The Faden crystal has also been used to trace the locations of implants. After locating the implant with the Faden, one may also use, for example, nephrite-quartz to go to the source and to release same.

The combining of the Faden crystal with Jin Shin Jyutsu (Jin Shin Jee-**Yoot**-Soo) is an excellent technique for directing disorders to a receptacle filled with white light in order to transmute any concomitant negativity into positivity. The technique is a body/energy balancing art, based on the precept that energy is a primary life force. The technique is based upon the concept that "normal everyday" tension and stress can both block and disrupt ones energy flow, placing the physical body in an unbalance and eventually being a cause of illness. The technique acts to maintain the natural energy of the body in an open and circulating flow; the process is initiated by first determining which attitude or symptom will be addressed. The following provides a list of associations:

Thumb: Worry perspectives (depression, hate, obsession, anxiety, self-protection; Physical symptoms (stomachache, headache, nervousness, superficial skin problems such as rash or acne).

Index Finger: Fear perspectives (timidity, mental confusion, depression, perfectionism, criticism, frustration; Physical symptoms (digestive problems, muscle-related problems including backache, and arthritis).

Middle Finger: Anger perspectives (cowardice, irritability, indecisiveness, instability; Physical symptoms (eye and vision problems, vascular problems such as blood or circulation disorders, constant fatigue or tiredness).

Ring Finger: Sadness perspectives (grief, negativity, lack of common sense, conniving, rejection complex); Physical symptoms (digestion, breathing, deep skin problems).

Little Finger: Pretense perspectives (pretending to be someone/something other than oneself, insecurity, nervousness, confusion); Physical symptoms (bone or nerve problems, sore throat).

Holding the selected finger, with the Faden crystal on the finger and with the thread of the Faden crystal pointing away from the body, one waits until a pulsing sensation is felt, continuing for no less than five minutes. After the time specified, one releases the finger and the Faden crystal.

In addition the Faden crystal has been used to access the Higher Self in order to promote the retrieval of information concerning "why" an event or condition (considered to be negative) occurred within ones life.

The Faden crystal has also been used to provide a path for lumps to leave the body.

Vibrates to the number 2 and the master number 88.

## HALITE - TRANSLUCENT MASSIVE

[Astrological Signs of Cancer & Pisces]

Translucent massive Halite crystallizes in the form of masses; the colour ranges from peach to peachy-red. Halite was first described by E.F. Glocker in 1847 and was named from the Greek word "salt" due to its composition. The following properties are in addition to those listed in the HALITE section of "Love Is In The Earth - A Kaleidoscope Of Crystals Update". In the exhibition of the following properties the translucent massive Halite was activated by electricity. It has been used to soften trauma and to provide an atmosphere of repose during healing sessions. It has been reported that the air adjacent to the crystal is fresher and more stimulating than "normal" air (this also worked in an environment where there was cigarette smoke and allergies to same; those who are allergic to cigarette smoke tend to forget entirely about the allergy when the Halite is electrified).

It has also worked well among electronic equipment; testing results indicate that computer users feel less tired and actually have more energy when placed in an environment with the electrified Halite.

Placed in an area which is felt to hold danger, it dissipates the cause of danger and releases negativity from the area. The electrification of the mineral also precludes the necessity for cleansing the mineral; it is actually self-cleansing, so that no further exercises need to be performed in order to cleanse the stone.

Used in an environment or situation of anger, it dispels the anger and initiates a remedial action through self-realization that anger is always personal, and cannot be based upon outside influences. It also tends toward self-realization and actualization on the emotional plane and seems to be a true illuminator of the light within.

In addition, it has assisted greatly in meditation and has stimulated the movement of the Kundalini from the lower chakras to the heart chakra.

The electrified translucent massive Halite further supports super negative ion generation.

In astral travel and in channeling, it has facilitated contact with the ancient Polish civilizations; use of the Halite with amber has provided a melding of the qualities of both and assisted the Kundalini movement to the crown chakra.

Due to the solubility and the electrification of this Halite configuration, do not prepare an elixir of this mineral via the normal method.

Vibrates to the number 1.

## GILSONITE

[Astrological Sign of Taurus]
[Also Known as Uintahite]

Gilsonite is a black brilliant lustrous oxygenated hydrocarbonaceous resin. The mineral, as Gilsonite, was first described by E.S. Dana in 1892 and was named for S.H. Gilson. The mineral, as Uintahite, was first described by W.P. Blake in 1885 and is named for a location in the Uinta Valley in Utah, where it is found.

This mineral has been used to provide foundations for ones goals; acting to assist one in building the foundation and in organizing its structure. It has also been used to guard "secrets" in communication, in relationships, and in that which is in the past.

Gilsonite has been used to bring the energy of "faultless action", such that the user acts in accordance with laws of the universe. It stimulates the base and crown chakras, bringing a radiant light to ones physical form.

Gilsonite vibrates to the number 2. Uintahite vibrates to the master number 44.

## OBSIDIAN - SHEEN

[Astrological Sign of Sagittarius]

Sheen Obsidian is a lustrous volcanic glass, exhibiting an internal sheen (caused by various needle-like inclusions) which is reflected in a variety of colours. Obsidian was first described by Pliny in 77 A.D. and named for its resemblance to a stone found in Ethiopia by the Roman, Obsius (aka Obsidius); the name was also reported since Medieval days through the authors of natural history documents. The following properties are in addition to those listed in the SHEEN OBSIDIAN section of "Love Is In The Earth - A Kaleidoscope Of Crystals Update".

This mineral has been used to quicken the removal of non-harmonious energy from patients who are undergoing treatment in the chiropractic and holistic disciplines. It has also been used to promote accuracy in shooting and in focussing directional energy.

To determine the vibratory number, one may add 61 to the sum of the numbers representing each letter of the name of the specific sheen colour or representation.

## OLIVENITE

[Astrological Sign of Capricorn]

Olivenite crystallizes in the form of sub-transparent to opaque fibers, masses, grains, and prismatic crystals. The colour range includes various shades of olive green and brown, yellow, and white. The mineral was first described by R. Jameson in 1820 and was named for the discovery colour of olive green.

This mineral has been used to stimulate ones latent abilities to action; it assists one to recognize and to take appropriate action during the "turning points" in ones life. It furthers spontaneity and pioneering adventures. It promotes motivation, inspiration, creativity, assertiveness, and courage. It has been employed to arouse the pursuit of ones personal spiritual path and the awareness of ones personal potential, helping one to remain aware of individual objectives. It can assist one to identify and to remove obstacles in ones path. It encourages independence/self-direction. It furthers ones access to seclusion when directed.

Olivenite has been used in the treatment of insomnia, migraine headache, inflammation, encephalitis, convulsions, burns, apoplexy, cerebral congestion, and hemorrhages, and can assist in after-surgery recovery.

The arsenide content of this mineral precludes its use in the normal method of preparation of an elixir.

Vibrates to the number 3.

## QUARTZ

Quartz was first described as "Crystallus" (representing the crystalline formation) by Pliny in 77 A.D. and was further described by U.R. vor

Kalbe in 1505 to present history of the name. The name "Quartz" was originally spelled "Quertz" (representing Quartzite, the compact granular massive configuration); it was named for the Saxon word "cross-vein ore". In the late 1700's, the two configurations (crystalline and massive) were found by T. Bergman to have the same chemical composition and, hence, were consolidated and provided with one name (Quartz).

## Quartz From Other Countries:

Quartz, as naturally occurring silicon dioxide, crystallizes in the form of masses, grains, druses, and prismatic hexagonal crystals. It is also known as rock crystal. The information concerning the properties of Quartz can be found in "Love Is In The Earth - A Kaleidoscope Of Crystals Update".

It is interesting to note the varying distinctions that each Quartz crystal exhibits with respect to the country in which it is found. The reader is encouraged to experience the subtleties as well as the diversities.

### Green Phantom [Astrological Sign of Libra]

Green Phantom Quartz is recognized by a "phantom" crystal within the crystal. The phantom is comprised of either Chlorite, Caledonite, Prasiolite, or a varying combination of other minerals. The word "Phantom" was named for the Late Latin word "Phantasma", with usage in mineralogy beginning in the 1800's.

Green Phantom Quartz has also been used in the treatment of Panic Disorder and manic-depressive states. When holding the mineral, the panic has tended to melt away, bringing a comforting and peaceful restful state.

Vibrates to the number 5.

### Pink Phantom [Astrological Signs of Virgo & Aries]

Pink Phantom Quartz is recognized by a "phantom" crystal within the crystal. The phantom is comprised of a combination of Hematite and

Kaolinite may be partial or complete. The colour ranges from pink to red, and has, when containing a greater amount of Hematite, has also been known as "Red Phantom Quartz". The word "Phantom" was named for the Late Latin word "Phantasma", with usage in mineralogy beginning in the 1800's. In addition to the properties listed in the QUARTZ, PINK-PHANTOM, and PHANTOM sections of "Love Is In The Earth - A Kaleidoscope Of Crystals Update", Pink Phantom Quartz is a "stone for restoration", restoring the celestial correlation between the self and "All That Is". It helps to guide one through the voyage of life, promoting a stable connection between the conscious self and the inner "knowing".

It teaches regard and non-violence, providing for sustenance in all facets of progress. It assists in helping one to liberate old "patterns", to deepen wisdom in psychological matters, and to cleanse and to refine the mind and the heart-space. At the heart chakra, it seems to cleanse the area and to promote protection and love simultaneously.

It assists one in regarding and in appreciating the phases of ones life and acts to provide insight to modifications required to promote accord and gratification within ones life.

In addition, it has been used in the treatment of lupis.

Vibrates to the number 8.

## Tibetan Quartz [Astrological Sign of Scorpio]

Tibetan Quartz Crystals have been found in Tibet and occur as both double terminated and singly terminated crystals in the clear quartz and smokey quartz compositions. These crystals exhibit a multitude of the "specialty" formations which are discussed in "Love Is In The Earth - A Kaleidoscope Of Crystals Update". In addition to the properties listed in the same book, the following qualities apply.

It is said by the Tibetan monks (living in the locality where the Tibetan Quartz is found) that the Tibetan Quartz Crystals are found exclusively in the location where a race "from the heavens" landed many milleniums antecedent to our time today. In this location, they are used primarily for meditation and for connecting with the realm of the unknown.

In ones daily life, the mind is the "motor". In Tibetan Pulsing the heart becomes the motor. While heart and the emotions have a type of innocence, the mind tends to associate and attach itself to problems. Because of those attachments and since the mind functions in a polarity environment, one can experience only a portion of the available joy, love, and pleasure. The pattern of the polarity is, for example: right/wrong, yes/no, good/bad, etc. When one is part of a positive experience, one tends to cling to both the experience and the memory; however, the function of the mind, coupled with ones belief system, tends to bring an automatic experience of negativity, following a positive experience. Since the heart only lives in the moment, and desiring unification and melding with other hearts, the positive energy of the heart can neutralize negative energy through relaxation; pain can be transformed into pleasure, suffering into relief, and tears into bliss. The Tibetan Quartz crystal has been used to further enhance, to amplify, and to intensify, the pulsing activities and to facilitate rapidity in the concomitant transformation, releasing self-limitations and dis-ease and disorders. The mineral is placed between the hands of the practitioner and the chakras of the subject, during the process of "laying-on-of-hands-with-laying-on-of-stones". It is an excellent activator and enhancer when also used in conjunction with stones selected for the specific chakras. At each location (and for a period of no less than five minutes), the hands of the practitioner are pulsed (upon the Tibetan Quartz and, if desired, additional "chakra stones") in the rhythm of the heartbeat of the subject; centering is required of the practitioner and is enhanced also by the utilization of the Tibetan Quartz. One can also perform this exercise upon oneself - the timing is the only consideration and awareness of the time can be promoted via "asking" the Inner Self.

Transformation of eating disorders (through the Tibetan crystal and either via Tibetan Pulsing or via placement of these crystals at each chakra) has been facilitated via discharging the tension held in the Vagus Nerve (the nerve is responsible for eating disorders). The energy of the crystal acts to relieve this tension such that one may understand negative dependence upon love from outside - parents, friends, lovers - and can transform to a new sensitivity and love for oneself. This healing can enable one to relate to others with more sympathy and friendship. The process requires between 5-20 sessions to produce the release of the dependence.

Tibetan Quartz vibrates to the number 3.

## ROSE QUARTZ - BUTTON

[Astrological Signs of Libra & Capricorn]

Rose Quartz Buttons occur in the configuration of a flat "tiddly wink" configuration, sometimes with a swirling pattern. The following properties are in addition to those listed in the ROSE QUARTZ section of "Love Is In The Earth - A Kaleidoscope Of Crystals Update".

Rose Quartz Buttons have been used to transform hatred to understanding and/or love, to facilitate secret meetings, to expedite expansion of actualization of ones dreams, to promote release of trapped emotions, to promote removal of toxins from the body, to stimulate the olfactory senses, to soothe the nervous system, and to alleviate addictions.

Vibrates to the number 9.

## STALACTITES/STALAGMITES

[Astrological Sign of Taurus]

Stalactites and Stalagmites are mineral formations which occur in pendent columns, cylinders, or elongated cones. Stalactites are produced by the percolation of water, holding mineral elements in solution, through the rocky summits of caverns, such that the evaporation of the water produces a deposit of the mineral in the elongated configuration. A Stalagmite grows from the floor of the cavern in an upward direction such that the trickling of percolating water from the cavern roof to the cavern floor produces a deposit of the mineral in the elongated configuration. These minerals have been shown to stimulate growth in the physical, emotional, intellectual, and spiritual realms.

The configurations further act to increase the focal emanation of the energy of the appropriate mineral and to enhance same. They have also been used to increase ones conscious connection with the higher realms, to align the subtle bodies with the physical form, and to establish a highly-charged and smooth energy connection between the energy of the mineral and the energy of the physical body (wonderful for healing situations), and to increase mental clarity and perception.

To determine the vibratory number, one may add 29 (for the Stalactite configuration) or 35 (for the Stalagmite configuration) to the sum of the numbers representing each letter of the name of the host mineral.

## TITANITE [Astrological Sign of Taurus]

Titanite crystallizes in the form of transparent to opaque masses and, rarely, crystals. The colour ranges from adamantine to resinous brown, grey, yellow, green rose, red, black. The mineral was first described correctly by M.H. Klaproth and was named for its Titanium content.

It serves to kindle the intellect and to provide stimulus to intelligent articulation and to comprehensive understanding during listening, bringing the cognitive processes toward the maximum proficiency. As Plato said "thoughts rule the world" and the energy of Titanium is the cerebral activator, the explicit delineator, and the teacher of discrimination.

Titanite can be also be used to stimulate "right-brain" creativity and receptivity. It is excellent for reinforcing public communication and interaction; introversion is diminished and the balance in interactive-ness is maintained.

It furthers pursuits in mystical, alchemical, theosophical, and astrological fields, sharpening the senses and perceptions. It can further be used to bring stability/security to ones environment.

It has been used to strengthen the nails, the teeth, and the hair. It has been used in the treatment of dysfunctional speech patterns and pleurisy and can stimulate the health of the vital fluids which control and interact with the nervous system.

Vibrates to the number 8.

## URANINITE

[Astrological Sign of Scorpio]

Uraninite crystallizes in the form of masses, botryoidal configurations, grains, octahedrons and cubes. The colour ranges from green to grey, brown, and black. The mineral was first described by the name "Uranin" by W. Haidinger in 1845, modified by J.D. Dana to "Uraninite" in 1868, and was named for its Uranium content.

This mineral, having a high Uranium content, has usually dissipated most of the harmful radiation prior to leaving the interior of the Earth. It is, however, recommended that either there is little physical interaction with the mineral (allowing it to rest peacefully in a selected location in ones environment) or that the radioactivity is assured (Geiger Counter) to be dissipated prior to handling and placing the mineral upon the body.

The mineral can assist in the decline of claustrophobia and can promote the desire for freedom and independence. It furthers the situations which will be conducive to attaining the freedom to act as one desires.

Uraninite can also assist one in discovering that which is hidden about another; in addition, it promotes flexibility in relationships. It further serves to assist in protection during, and to increase the abilities of those involved with, water travel, sailing, submarines, etc., and can also be used to assist in the activities associated with "cloud-busting". During cloud-busting activities the mineral has been placed within the rod.

It has been used to assist in the amelioration of addictions, lethargy, catalepsy, water retention, somnambulism, mononucleosis, chronic fatigue syndrome, pyorrhea, goiter, tooth decay, excess body fluid, swelling, oxygen deficiencies, internal/superficial poisoning, rickets, and poliomyelitis, and for mending muscular and bone structures. It has provided an exceptional grid for use by vegetarians to stimulate the assimilation of nutrients. It can also stimulate positive interest in those who have lost interest in life; by placement of the stone in ones environment, a change should be evident.

Preparation of an elixir via the normal method is not recommended.

Vibrates to the number 3.

## ZINCITE - POLISH

Several years ago there was a type of semi-natural Zincite which has been named "Polish Zincite"; this formation was said to have been produced in a Zinc mine in Poland, nearly 100 years ago, during a naturally occurring mine fire. Although the fire was naturally-occurring and was not due to the action of man, the mineralogical community did not accept this Zincite as natural.

**UPDATE!!!!!!!!** The "Polish Zincite" which is now available is not from the mine fire. It occurs as a by-product from an industrial zinc-white production kiln in Silesia, Poland. Hence, there is a similarity with the common glass slag, produced in the US and throughout the world, in its formation. This is another case of a change in the vibratory frequencies.

# PHOTOGRAPHS OF MINERALS NOT INCLUDED IN "... MINERALOGICAL PICTORIAL" BUT DESCRIBED IN "...KALEIDOSCOPE UPDATE".

This section provides photographs of the minerals which were described in "Love Is In The Earth - A Kaleidoscope Of Crystals Update" and were not included in "Love Is In The Earth - Mineralogical Pictorial".

**"IF YOU WANT ENTERTAINMENT,
BUY ATTENTION;
IF YOU WANT ENLIGHTENMENT,
BUY A MIRROR"**

Bob Jackson
Earth-Love Gallery
Colorado, USA

***AEGIRINE***
***$NaFeSi_2O_6$; Hardness 6;***
***Locality: Quebec, Canada***

***Photography by Jim Hughes, Assisted by ♪ Melody ♫***
***Collection of ♪ Melody ♫, Applewood, CO, USA***

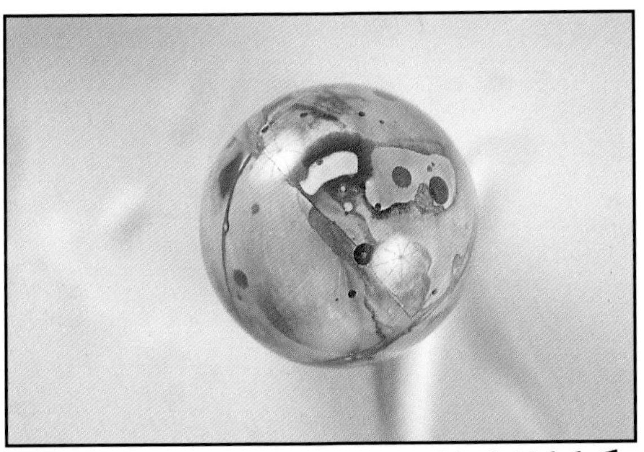

***AGATE - POLKA DOT***
***$SiO_2$ with other polymorphs of silica; Hardness 7;***
***Locality: Oregon, USA***

***Photography by Jim Hughes, Assisted by ♪ Melody ♫***
***Collection of Bob Jackson, Applewood, CO, USA***

***AGATE - PURPLE SAGE***
***$SiO_2$ with other polymorphs of silica; Hardness 7;***
***Locality: Arizona, USA***

***Photography by Jim Hughes, Assisted by ♪ Melody ♫***
***Collection of ♪ Melody ♫, Applewood, CO, USA; Gift of Gil Nelson, AZ, USA***

***ANTIGORITE***
***Composition: $(Mg,Fe)_3Si_2O_5(OH)_4$;***
***Hardness 2.5-3.5;***
***Locality: Africa***

***Photography by Jim Hughes, Assisted by ♪ Melody ♫***
***Collection of ♪ Melody ♫, Applewood, CO, USA***

***ARGENTITE***
***Composition: $Ag_2S2$:***
***Hardness 2-2.5;***
***Locality: Mexico***

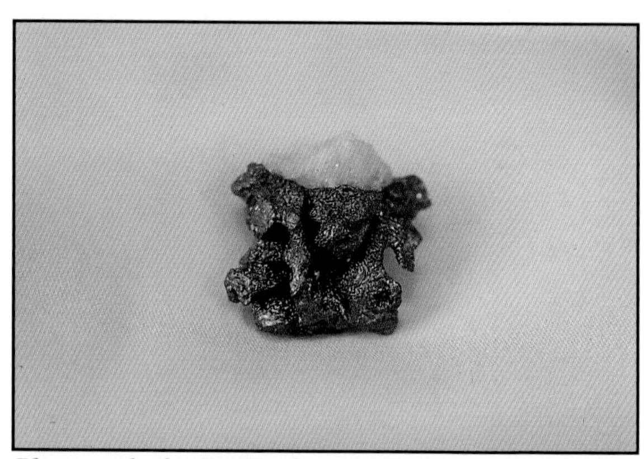

***Photography by Jim Hughes, Assisted by ♪ Melody ♫***
***Collection of Bob Jackson, Applewood, CO, USA***
***Gift of Angel Torecillas, Mexico.***

***BROCHANTITE***
***Composition:***
***$Cu_4SO_4(OH)_6$;***
***Hardness 3.5-4;***
***Locality: Wellington, NV***

***Photography by Jim Hughes, Assisted by ♪ Melody ♫***
***Collection of ♪ Melody ♫, Applewood, CO, USA***

*Photography by Jim Hughes, Assisted by ♪ Melody ♫*
*Collection of ♪ Melody ♫, Applewood, CO, USA*

***CALCITE - PHANTOMS***
***$CaCO_3$;***
***Hardness 3;***
***Locality: Racine, Wisconsin***

*Photography by Jim Hughes, Assisted by ♪ Melody ♫*
*Collection of ♪ Melody ♫, Applewood, CO, USA*

***CAVANSITE (Blue)***
***$Ca(VO)Si_4O_{10}$♥$4H_2O$;***
***Hardness 3-4;***
***Locality: Pune, India***

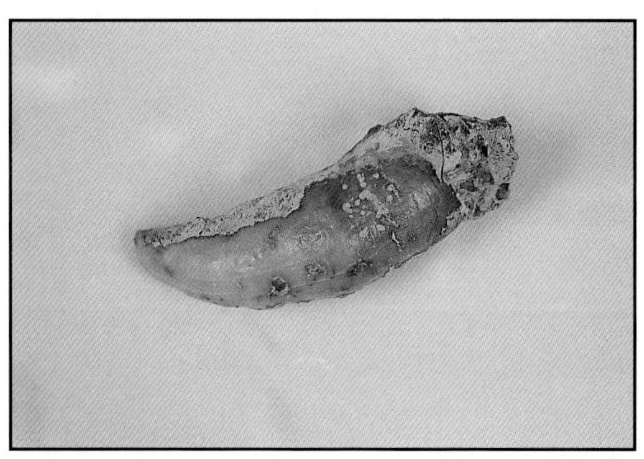

*Photography by Jim Hughes, Assisted by ♪ Melody ♫*
*Collection of ♪ Melody ♫, Applewood, CO, USA; Gift John Crowley, CA, USA*

***CORAL - HORN***
***(Dragon Tooth Coral);***
***(Grewing Kia Rustic)***
***Ordovician Age;***
***Locality: Eaton, Ohio, USA***

***GYROLITE***
***Composition:*** $NaCa_{16}AlSi_{24}O_{60}$
$(OH)_8$♥$14H_2O$;
***Hardness 3-4;***
***Locality: Pune, India***

***Photography by Jim Hughes, Assisted by ♪ Melody ♬***
***Collection of ♪ Melody ♬, Applewood, CO, USA***

***GYROLITE***
***Composition:*** $NaCa_{16}AlSi_{24}O_{60}$
$(OH)_8$♥$14H_2O$;
***Hardness 3-4;***
***Locality: Pune, India***

***Photography by Jim Hughes, Assisted by ♪ Melody ♬***
***Collection of Bob Jackson, Applewood, CO, USA***

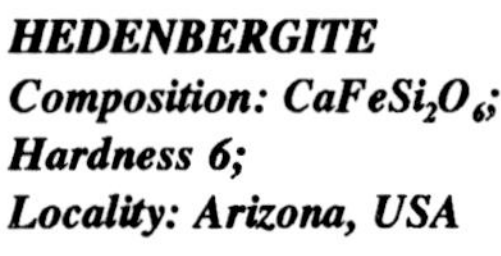

***HEDENBERGITE***
***Composition:*** $CaFeSi_2O_6$;
***Hardness 6;***
***Locality: Arizona, USA***

***Photography by Jim Hughes, Assisted by ♪ Melody ♬***
***Collection of ♪ Melody ♬, Applewood, CO, USA***

*Photography by Jim Hughes, Assisted by ♪ Melody ♫*
*Collection of ♪ Melody ♫, Applewood, CO, USA*

***MOCHI BALLS ©***
***(Iron & Sandstone Concretions)***
***Locality: Utah, USA***

*Photography by Dave Shrum, Colorado Camera*
*Collection of ♪ Melody ♫, Applewood, CO, USA*

***MOCHI BALLS ©***
***(Iron & Sandstone Concretions)***
***Locality: Utah, USA***

*Photography by Dave Shrum, Colorado Camera*
*Collection of ♪ Melody ♫, Applewood, CO, USA; Gift of Clara Utter, NY, USA*

***MOLYBDENUM***
***(Molybdenite)***
***With Quartz;***
***MO and $MOS_2$;***
***Hardness 1-1.5;***
***Locality: Minas Gerais, Brasil***

***"OAXACCAMERS" (AMETHYST HERKIMERS)***
*Composition: $SiO_2$ with ferric iron;*
*Hardness 7;*
*Locality: Mexico*

*Photography by Jim Hughes, Assisted by ♪ Melody ♫*
*Collection of ♪ Melody ♫, Applewood, CO, USA*

***PHENOMENITE***
*Composition: Sandstone and Quartz;*
*Hardness Variable;*
*Locality: India*

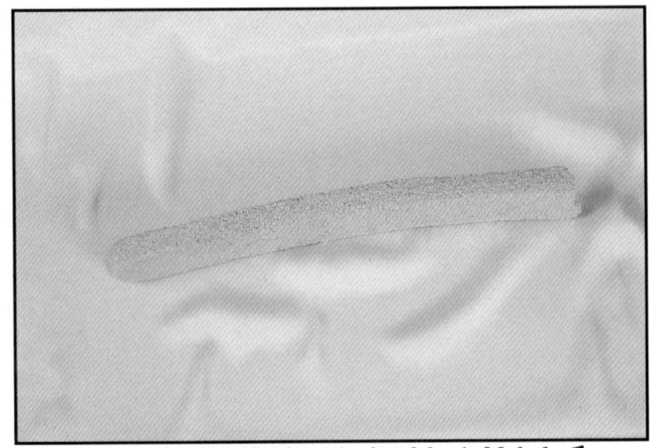

*Photography by Jim Hughes, Assisted by ♪ Melody ♫*
*Collection of Bob Jackson, Applewood, CO, USA*

***QUARTZ - REVERSED SCEPTOR***
*Composition: alpha-$SiO_2$;*
*Hardness 7;*
*Locality: Minas Gerais, Brasil*

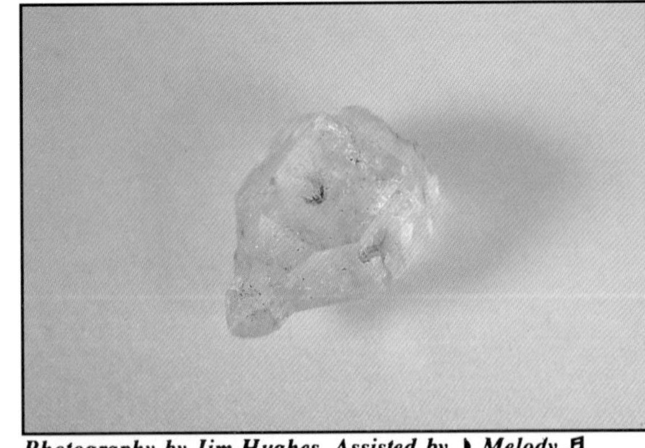

*Photography by Jim Hughes, Assisted by ♪ Melody ♫*
*Collection of ♪ Melody ♫, Applewood, CO, USA*

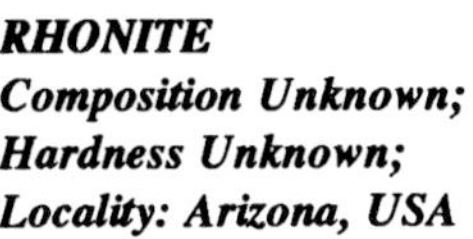

***RHONITE***
***Composition Unknown; Hardness Unknown; Locality: Arizona, USA***

***Photography by Jim Hughes, Assisted by ♪ Melody ♫***
***Collection of ♪ Melody ♫, Applewood, CO, USA***
***Gift of Judy & Ray, Sedona, AZ, USA***

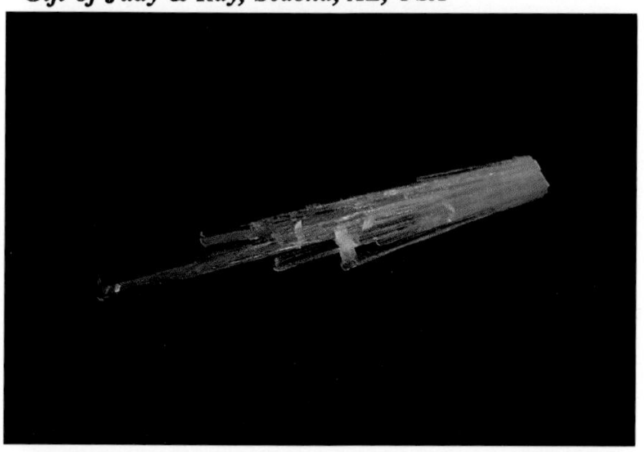

***SCOLECITE***
$Ca(Si_3Al_2)O_{10}$♥$3H_2O$; ***Hardness 5-5.5; Locality: Nasik Dist., India***

***Photography by Jim Hughes, Assisted by ♪ Melody ♫***
***Collection of ♪ Melody ♫, Applewood, CO, USA***

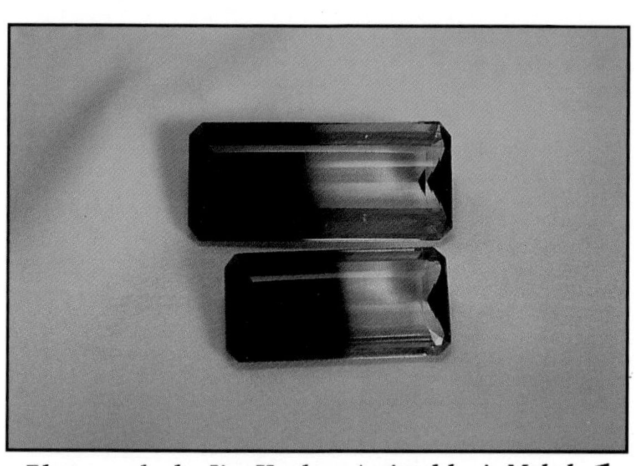

***SMOKEY-CITRINE***
$SiO_2$ ***with (Smokey) organic impurities or due to natural exposure to radioactivity and with (Citrine) colloidal iron hydrates; Hardness 7; Locality: Minas Gerais, Brasil***

***Photography by Jim Hughes, Assisted by ♪ Melody ♫***
***Collection of ♪ Melody ♫, Applewood, CO, USA***

***USSINGITE***
***Composition: $Na_2AlSi_3O_8(OH)$;***
***Hardness 6-7;***
***Locality: Russia***

***Photography by Jim Hughes, Assisted by ♪ Melody ♫***
***Collection of ♪ Melody ♫, Applewood, CO, USA***

***ZEOLITE WITH QUARTZ***
***Composition: From a family of well-defined hydrous silicates (Zeolite) with $SiO_2$ (Quartz); Hardness 2.5-7.5 (Zeolites) with 7 (Quartz); Locality: Pune, India***

***Photography by Jim Hughes, Assisted by ♪ Melody ♫***
***Collection of Bob Jackson, Applewood, CO, USA***

# CROSS-REFERENCE INDEX ZODIACAL DESIGNATIONS - MINERALOGICAL ASSOCIATION

**"WISDOM COMES SO RARELY, ONE SHOULD NOT COMPLAIN OF ITS TARDINESS"**

Felix Frankfuter
(Judge)

## CROSS-REFERENCE INDEX
## ZODIACAL DESIGNATIONS - MINERALOGICAL ASSOCIATION

This cross-reference index has been developed from the astrological sign designations which were described for each mineral discussed within this book. Please note that some minerals are related to more than one astrological sign.

CANCER (cont.)
OZOKERITE
QUARTZ - FLAME AURA
QUARTZ - With Mica Inclusions
QUARTZ - STARBURST
RHODIZITE
SCHORLOMITE
SILVER AURA GARNET
STELLERITE
"SUPER SEVEN"
TEKTITE - GUANGDONG

LEO
ANDERSONITE
ALTAITE
BISMUTHINITE
CITRINE - With HEMATITE
ELECTRUM
GALAXYITE
GOLDEN AURA GARNET
ISIS & OSIRIS © (Pyrite)
JAMESONITE
JASPER - MOOKAITE
KAURI GUM
MINIUM
OPAL - LEMON
OPAL - CAT'S EYE
PETALITE
PYRARGYRITE
QUARTZ - FLAME AURA

LEO (cont.)
QUARTZ - YELLOW PHANTOM
QUARTZ - TANGERINE
RHODIZITE
RHODONITE - GEMMY
STURMANITE
SUNSTONE - BI-COLOUR
"SUPER SEVEN"
SYLVITE
TEKTITE - GUANGDONG

VIRGO
AMETHYST - FLOWER
AMETHYST - OREGON
BINGHAMITE
EUDIALYTE
GASPEITE
GEARKSUTITE
JOHANNSENITE
PRICEITE
QUARTZ - FLAME AURA
QUARTZ - LINEATED
QUARTZ - Pink Phantom
RHODIZITE
ROSASITE - Green Banded
SCAPOLITE - PURPLE
"SUPER SEVEN"
TEKTITE - GUANGDONG

LIBRA
ALBITE - SHEET
AMETHYST - FLOWER
AMETHYST - Pink Snowball
AMETRINE - CRYSTAL
AMETRINE - ELESTIAL
COLUSITE
EUCRYPTITE
"MALACHITE - RED"
PORPHYRY - IMPERIAL
QUARTZ - FLAME AURA
QUARTZ - Green Phantom
QUARTZ - PLATES
QUARTZ - TANGERINE
ROSASITE - Green Banded
ROSE QUARTZ - BUTTON
RHODIZITE
"SUPER SEVEN"
TEKTITE - GUANGDONG
VICTORIA STONE
YODERITE

SCORPIO
AMETHYST - ELESTIAL
CALCITE - ELESTIAL
DELAFOSSITE
FADEN - QUARTZ

SCORPIO (cont.)
FLUORITE - BLUE JOHN
GALAXYITE
GOLDEN AURA GARNET
GILLESPITE
"Green AMETHYST"
HOLMQUISTITE
HUNTITE With DAQINGSHANITE
ISIS & OSIRIS © (Pyrite)
JASPER - SNAKESKIN
KAERSUTITE
ONYX - PERFORATED
OPAL - CAT'S EYE
PORPHYRY - IMPERIAL
PRASIOLITE
QUARTZ - With Feldspar Stratification
QUARTZ - GROWTH INTERFERENCE
QUARTZ - FLAME AURA
QUARTZ - YELLOW PHANTOM
RHODIZITE
SMOKEY QUARTZ - ENGRAVED
SMOKEY QUARTZ - "HOT" SPOTS
SMOKEY QUARTZ - SKELETAL, WITH LEPIDOCROCITE AND HEMATITE

SCORPIO (cont.)
"SUPER SEVEN"
TEKTITE - GUANGDONG
TIBETAN QUARTZ
URANINITE
YODERITE

SAGITTARIUS
ALGODONITE
"AURORA BOREALIS STONE"
BINGHAMITE
JASPER - OWYHEE
LÖLLINGITE
MERWINITE
OBSIDIAN - SHEEN
PYRARGYRITE
QUARTZ - Blue Phantom
QUARTZ - FLAME AURA
RHODIZITE
RHODONITE - GEMMY
SCHORLOMITE
SELENITE - With Copper
SMITHSONITE - GREEN
SMOKEY QUARTZ - SKELETAL, With LEPIDOCROCITE & HEMATITE
"SUPER SEVEN"
TEKTITE - GUANGDONG
UVITE

CAPRICORN
ANKERITE
BINDHEIMITE
DIABOLEITE
FLUORITE - ENHYDRO
FLUORITE - RAINBOW
"GREEN AMETHYST"
HANCOCKITE
HOLMQUISTITE
MACFALLITE
MISERITE
OLIVENITE
ONYX - PERFORATED
OPAL - CAT'S EYE
PRASIOLITE
QUARTZ - FLAME AURA
QUARTZ - GROWTH INTERFERENCE
RHODIZITE
ROSE QUARTZ - BUTTON
SILICON - Man-made
SALÉEITE
"SUPER SEVEN"
TEKTITE - GUANGDONG

AQUARIUS
AGRELLITE
ALBITE - SHEET
AMETHYST - ELESTIAL
BINDHEIMITE
BOLIVIANITE

AQUARIUS (cont.)

CALIFORNITE
CAVANSITE
GARNET - RAINBOW
ISIS & OSIRIS © (Pyrite)
METEORITE - NANTAN
OPAL - LEMON
POLLUCITE
QUARTZ - Blue Phantom
QUARTZ - With Feldspar Stratification
QUARTZ - FLAME AURA
QUARTZ - REVERSED SCEPTOR
QUARTZ - WATERFALL
RHODIZITE
SANBORNITE
"SUPER SEVEN"
TEKTITE - GUANGDONG
WOLLASTONITE

PISCES

AMETRINE - CRYSTAL
"AURORA BOREALIS STONE"
BAUXITE
CALLAGHANITE
CERITE
CORAL - Agatized
EASTONITE
FLUORITE - ENHYDRO
HALITE - Translucent Massive
NEWBERYITE
QUARTZ - CANDLE
QUARTZ - Consummation
QUARTZ - FLAME AURA
RHODIZITE
"SUPER SEVEN"
TEKTITE - GUANGDONG
URALITE

# CROSS-REFERENCE INDEX NUMERICAL VIBRATIONS - MINERALOGICAL ASSOCIATION

**"AN INORDINATE FONDNESS FOR CONSISTENCY IS THE INDICATION OF A SMALL MIND"**

Bob Jackson
Earth-Love Gallery
Colorado, USA

## CROSS-REFERENCE INDEX
## NUMERICAL VIBRATIONS - MINERALOGICAL ASSOCIATION

This cross-reference index has been developed from the numerical vibration designations which were described for each mineral discussed within this book. Please note that some minerals are assigned more than one numerical vibration due to variation in spelling and/or name designation.

NUMBER 7 (cont.)
Andersonite
Binghamite
Cerite
Delafossite
Electrum
Eucryptite
Huntite
Lőllingite
Minium
Ozokerite
Petalite
Prasiolite
Quartz - Candle
Quartz - Reversed
Sceptor
Quartz - Starburst
Quartz - Tangerine
"Sacred Seven"
Tyrolite

NUMBER 8
Allura
Apatite - Blue/Green
Bindheimite
Fluorite - Rainbow
"Green Amethyst"
Johannsenite
Merwinite
Ozokerite
Porphyry - Imperial
Quartz - Consummation
Quartz - Pink Phantom
Quartz - Reversed
Sceptor
Quartz-Yellow Phantom
Scapolite - Purple
Smokey Quartz -
"Hot" Spots
Stalagmite
Titanite
Victoria Stone

NUMBER 9
Eastonite
"Malachite - Red"
Newberyite
Onyx - Perforated
Pyrargyrite

NUMBER 9 (cont.)
Rhodonite - Gemmy
Rost Quartz - Button
Sanbornite
Selenite - With Copper
Silicon - Man-Made
"Super Seven"
Tektite - Guangdong

MASTER # 44
Agrellite
Hancockite
Kauri Copal
Miserite
Rhonite
Stellerite
Uintahite

MASTER # 55
Bolivianite
Calcite - Elestial
Isis & Osiris © (Pyrite)
Jasper - Snakeskin

MASTER # 66
Ametrine - Crystal
Quartz - Waterfall

MASTER # 77
Moonstone - Rainbow
Pyrolucite - Velvet
Quartz - Blue Phantom

MASTER # 88
Faden Quartz Crystal

MASTER # 99
Huntite With
Daqingshanite

# ILLUSTRATIONS OF QUARTZ STRUCTURES AND CONFIGURATIONS

Due to "popular demand", the following illustrations were prepared to show the structures and configurations of the many and varied forrmations of the Quartz Crystal.

# "ERLICHDA" (LIGHTEN-UP)"

Antar Pushkara
Oregon, USA

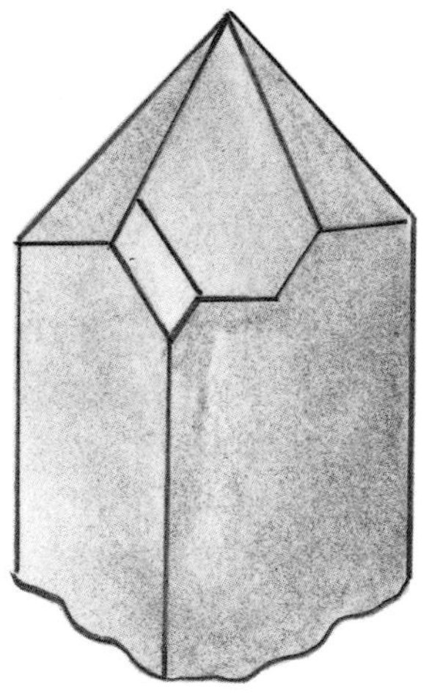

ACTIVATION (LEFT) QUARTZ CRYSTAL

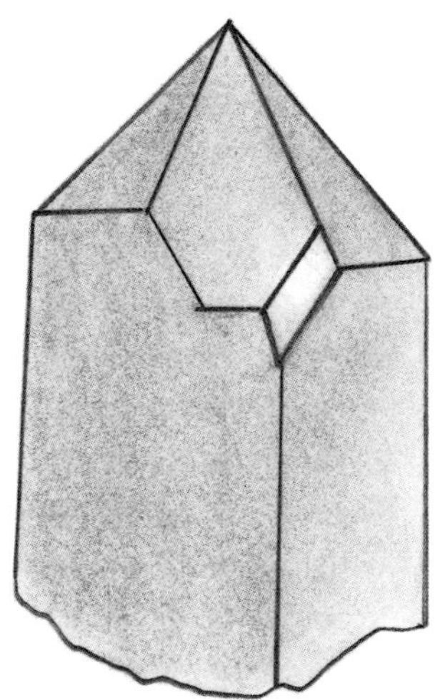

ACTIVATION (RIGHT) QUARTZ CRYSTAL

BARNICLE QUARTZ CRYSTAL

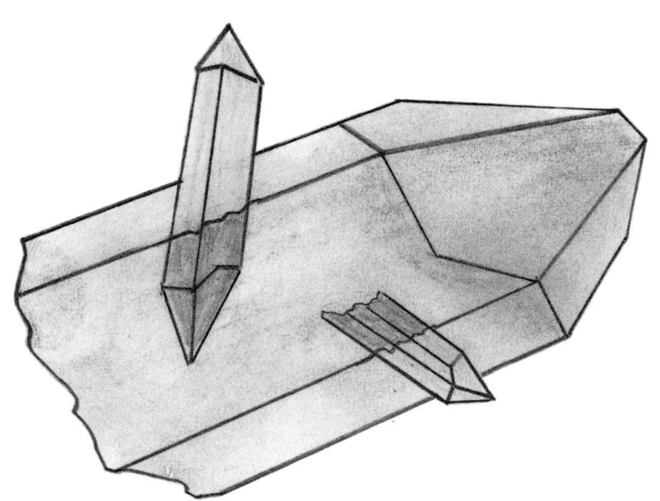

BRIDGE QUARTZ CRYSTAL

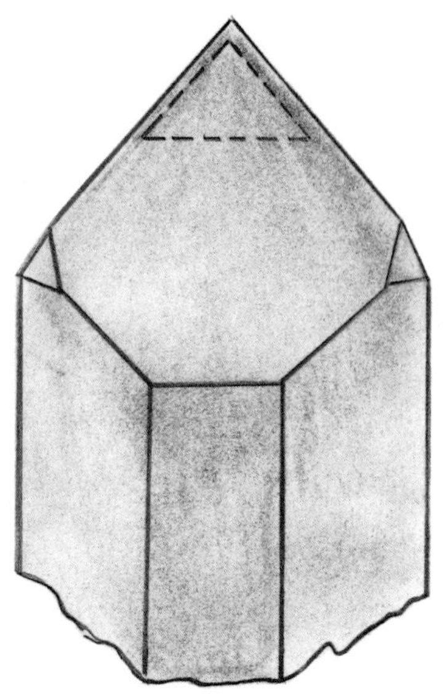

CHANNELER QUARTZ CRYSTAL

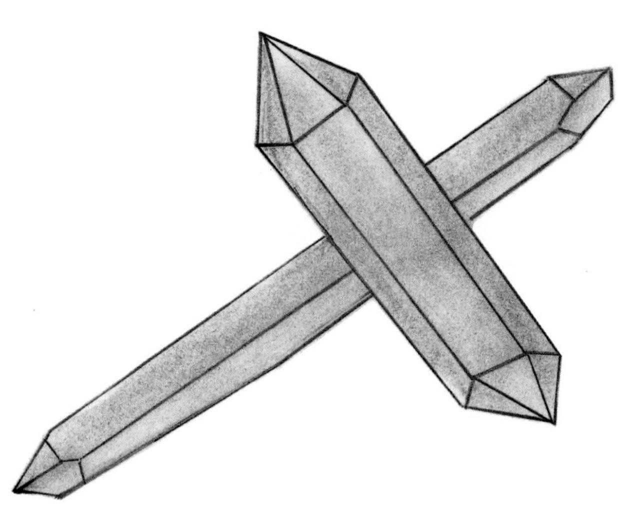

CROSS QUARTZ CRYSTAL

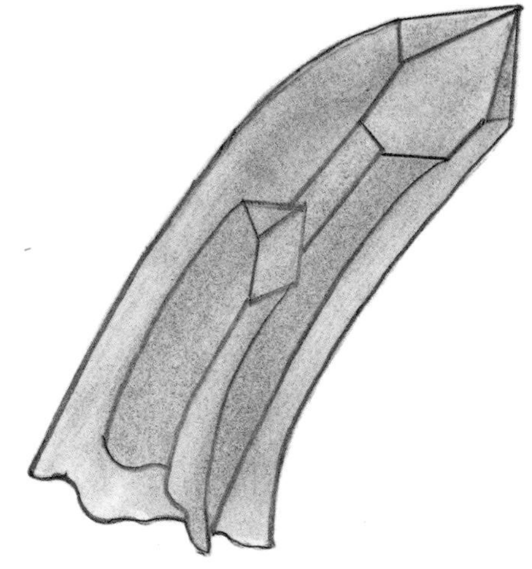

CURVED QUARTZ CRYSTAL

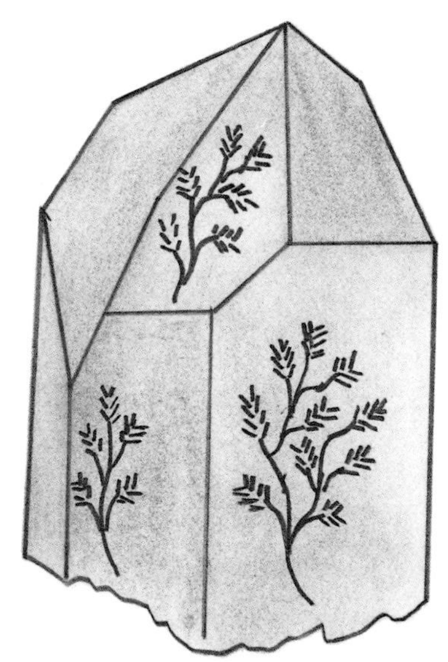

DENDRITIC QUARTZ CRYSTAL

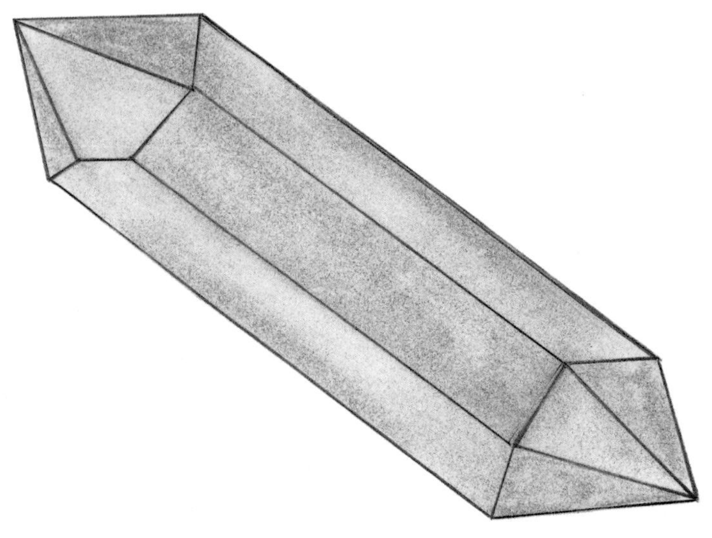

DOUBLE TERMINATED QUARTZ CRYSTAL

ELESTIAL QUARTZ CRYSTAL

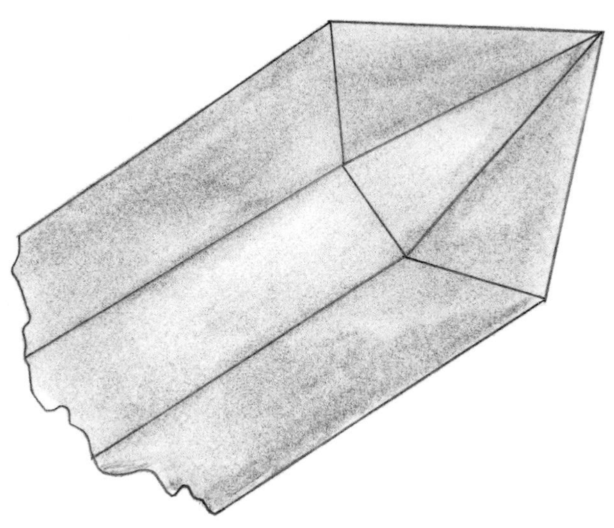

GENERATOR QUARTZ CRYSTAL

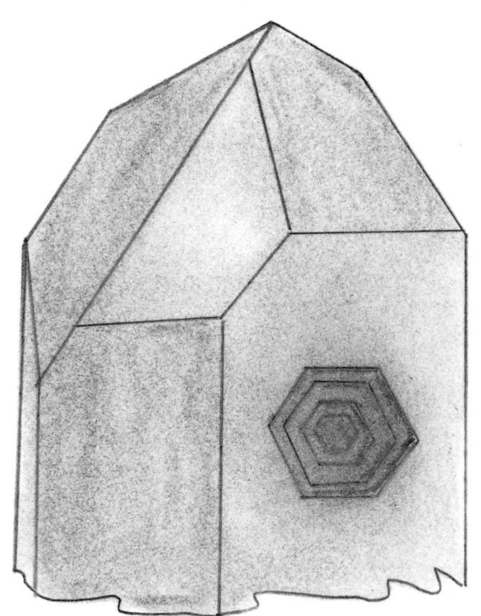

KEY QUARTZ CRYSTAL

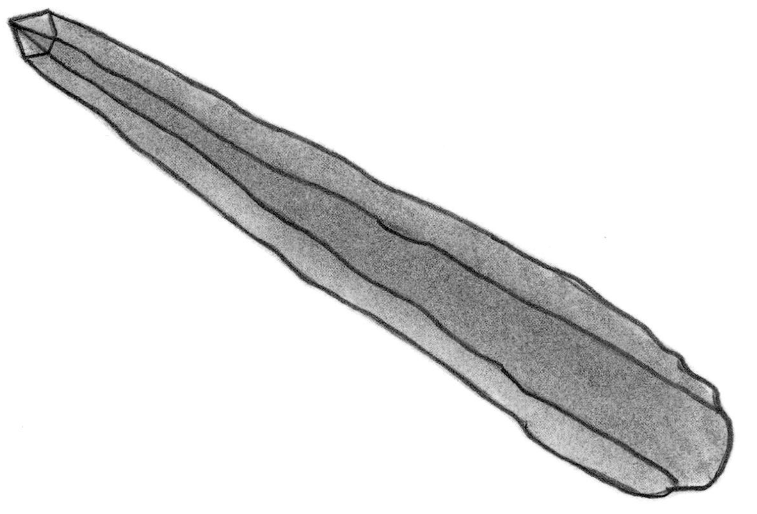

LASER WAND QUARTZ CRYSTAL

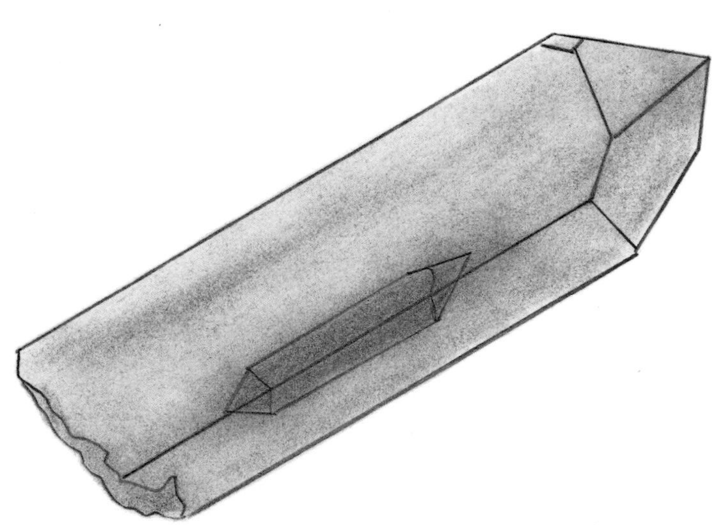

MANIFESTATION QUARTZ CRYSTAL

**PHANTOM QUARTZ CRYSTAL**

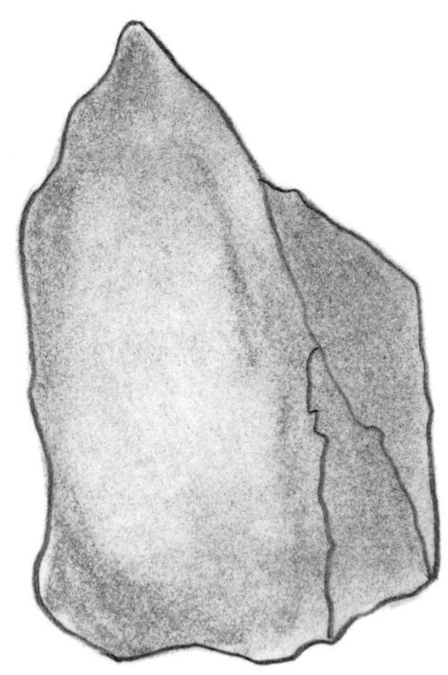

**PINNACLE QUARTZ CRYSTAL**

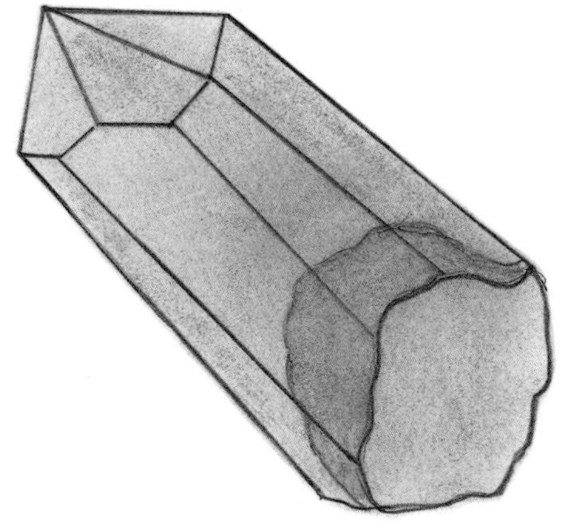

**POCKET QUARTZ CRYSTAL**

**RECORD KEEPER QUARTZ CRYSTAL**

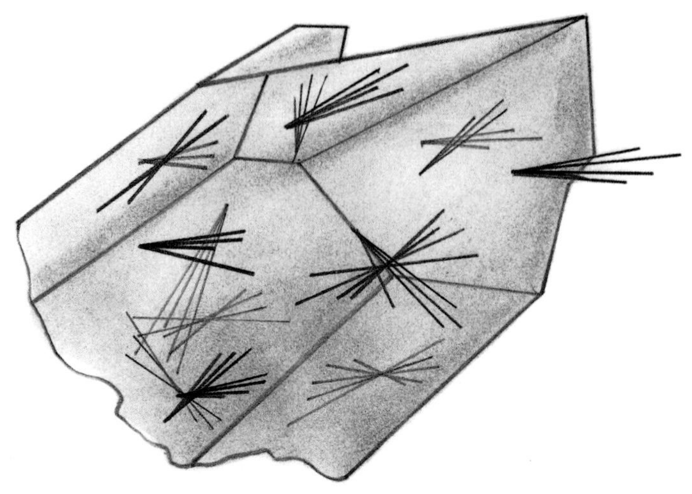

RUTILATED QUARTZ CRYSTAL

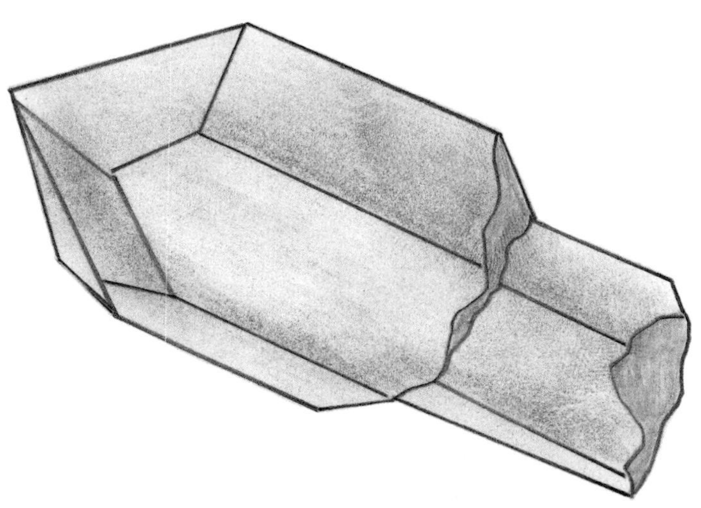

SCEPTOR QUARTZ CRYSTAL

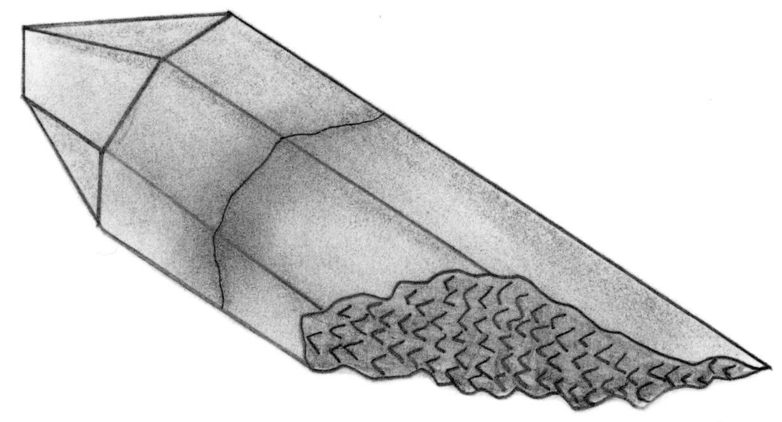

SELF-HEALED QUARTZ CRYSTAL

SHEET QUARTZ CRYSTAL

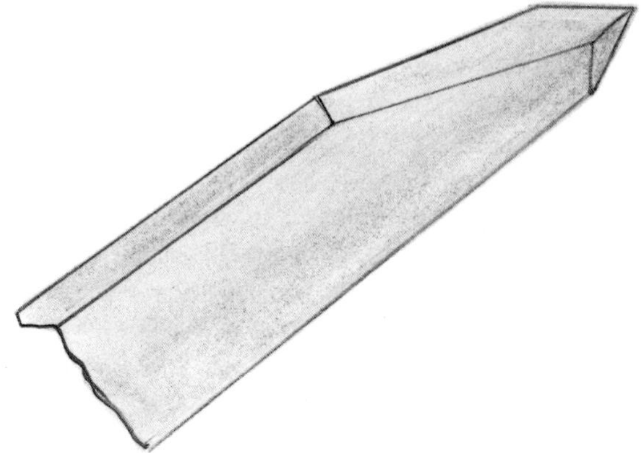

SHOVEL QUARTZ CRYSTAL

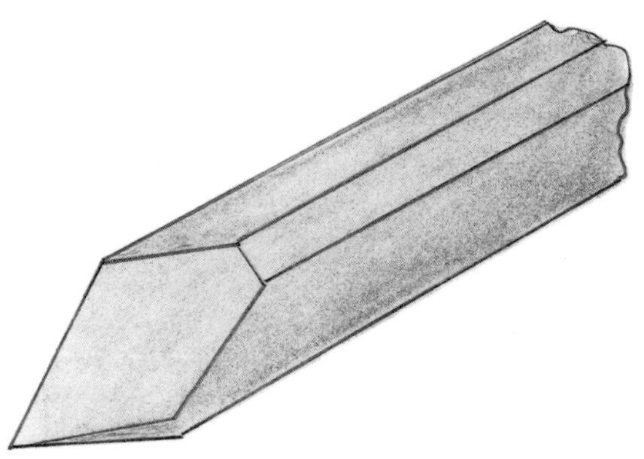

SPADE QUARTZ CRYSTAL

SPIRAL QUARTZ CRYSTAL

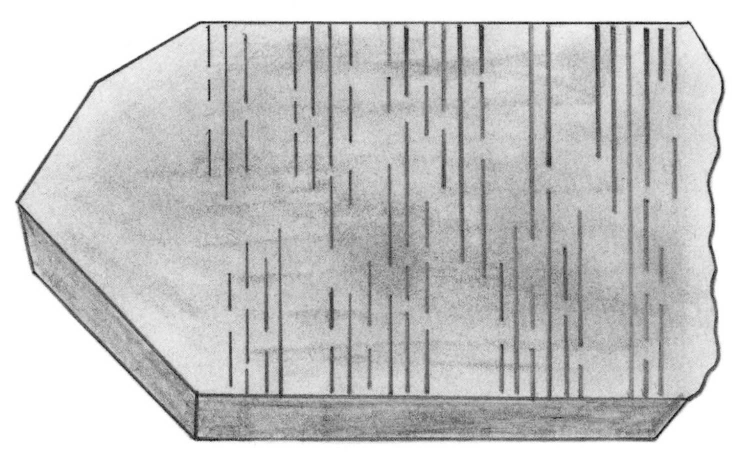

TABBY QUARTZ CRYSTAL

**TRANSMITTER QUARTZ CRYSTAL**

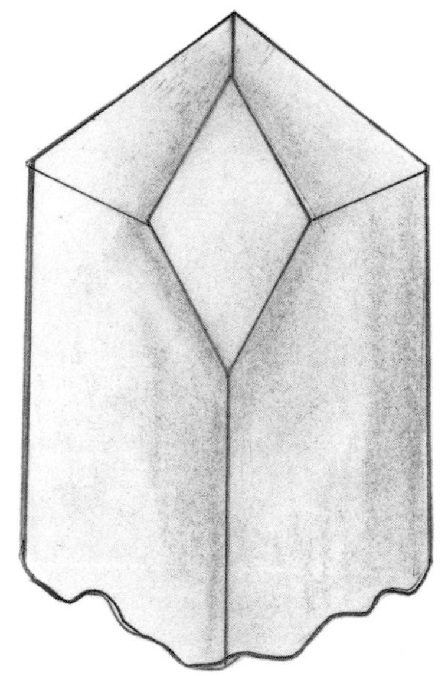

**WINDOW QUARTZ CRYSTAL**

**"IF YOU CAN'T SEE THE BEST IN SOMEONE, DON'T LOOK!"**

Julianne Guilbault
Colorado, USA

♪ THE FUTURE IS NOW ♫

INDEX

**♪ ONE MAY HEAR THE WORDS SO NICE,**
**"ONE CANNOT STEP IN THE SAME RIVER TWICE"**
**BUT HAVE YOU EVER HAD THE HUNCH,**
**ONE CANNOT STEP IN THE SAME RIVER ONCE? ♫**

# INDEX

EARTH NOTES

EARTH NOTES